Quentin

NOT ALL
SUPERHEROES
WEAR
CAPES

Quentin

NOT ALL
SUPERHEROES
WEAR
CAPES

QUENTIN KENIHAN

hachette
AUSTRALIA

Published in Australia and New Zealand in 2016
by Hachette Australia
(an imprint of Hachette Australia Pty Limited)
Level 17, 207 Kent Street, Sydney NSW 2000
www.hachette.com.au

10 9 8 7 6 5 4 3 2 1

Copyright © Quentin Kenihan 2016

National Library of Australia
Cataloguing-in-Publication data

Kenihan, Quentin, 1975– author.
Not all superheroes wear capes / Quentin Kenihan.

978 0 7336 3535 9 (paperback)

Kenihan, Quentin, 1975–
Osteogenesis imperfecta – Patients – Biography.
Celebrities – Australia – Biography.
Heroes – Australia – Biography.

362.196710092

Cover design by Christabella Designs
Cover photographs courtesy of Quentin Kenihan
Text design by Bookhouse, Sydney
Typeset in 12/19 pt Minion Pro
Printed and bound in Australia by McPherson's Printing Group

This book is dedicated to all the experienced and caring doctors, nurses and carers who continually put Humpty Dumpty back together again.

Contents

Foreword
by Ray Martin

'So c'mon, Q,' I asked Quentin. 'Who's YOUR character in *Mad Max*?'

'I'm Corpus Colossus, son of the bad dude,' he laughed. 'My body's covered in scars, because . . . things happened to me. My job is to sit on high and watch everyone.'

Typecast again. Life's a bitch.

Quentin Kenihan has been watching us and taking life head-on since he was born with eight broken bones four decades ago, refusing to lie down and do what he's told.

Of course he's cast as the son of the bad dude. Dr George Miller has impeccable taste.

Q's right. Things DID happen to him. And they keep on happening. He's like The Black Knight in Monty Python. Bring it on.

At birth they gave Quentin 'twenty-four hours' to live, then it was 'a few years', then 'maximum thirty' and here he is now – having racked up more than forty years – still refusing to bow to his disability. (He straightened Dicko out on that li'l matter years ago, as I'm sure he'll tell you in this book. Pow!)

He's been to the Oscars, featured in a couple of films, produced documentaries and television shows, sung on *Young Talent Time*, done regular movie reviews on radio and last season starred in his own live stage show.

Despite the wheelchair and the travelling oxygen bottle, he's a proven, inspirational stayer. He can make you laugh, make you cry and make you angry about the way he sometimes gets treated. Mind you, he likes stirring and shoots quickly from the lip. A diplomat he is not.

I remember meeting Quentin in the make-up chair at Channel 9 in Sydney, when he did his first interview with Mike Willesee, back in about 1982. 'The most fragile boy in the world,' was the way Willo first introduced him to Australia – 'with bones that snap like chalk.' Propped up with a shock of blond hair, big Elton John–style glasses, a cute-kid's laugh and a cheeky, inquisitive voice, he didn't muck around. 'You're on *60 Minutes*,' he announced. 'You and George Negus, right?'

When I smiled and nodded in agreement, he proffered, 'You want to interview me? Well, you're too late. Mike got in first.'

Pow!

Three decades later Quentin still reminds the world that, due to his magnetic appeal, 'Quentin' was 'the highest rating doco in Australian history'. Still, in his more thoughtful – even poignant – moments he'll contemplate what life might have been like without the fame and notoriety that that initial TV doco gave him, at the tender age of seven years.

He's still not sure. He won Australians' hearts and became a household name overnight. Everybody thought they knew Quentin.

But they weren't there when he cried in pain. Or when he almost died of pneumonia. When Mike Willesee came to Adelaide recently to interview him for the *Sunday Night* program, Q wasted no time in reminding Willo that he hadn't bothered to contact him for more than a decade.

'It was like I got money on the dresser drawer and no phone call at the end of it,' he told the TV legend.

Pow!

It's a tough metaphor. I regret to say, television shows do that too often.

Willesee dipped his head and apologised. Quentin Kenihan says quite bluntly what he thinks. When you're living on borrowed time anyway, life is too short for beating around the bush. Bring it on.

Still, Q's longstanding appeal with the Australian people won out again with that Willesee follow-up story. 'Highest rating for the night,' Q tweeted the next morning. 'Boom! Still got it.'

And he has.

The truth is, I did get to interview Quentin a couple of times on *Midday*. In fact, it was on one occasion in 1993 – during his bout with pills and booze – that Q appeared on the show, a little under the weather. He was still funny, even witty, but clearly out of it. That spurred him into a rehab program that ended the substance abuse and kick-started his life once again.

I'm proud to have been indirectly part of that change, because he's a mate. I speak to Quentin regularly and get together when I'm in Adelaide – for a meal, a catch-up or on one occasion recently a lively chat with the visiting Sir David Attenborough. Q is always up for something new, especially if there's a celebrity involved. He loves dishing it with the A-List – photos with beautiful women, autographs for rock stars and texting his friend Russell Crowe.

He networks well.

His stage show was co-written by Tim Ferguson of the Doug Anthony All-Stars fame, with feature music by Darren Hayes, the former lead singer of Savage Garden.

Like an old-fashioned broken record, Quentin's quizzical mantra is, 'I'm here for a good time, not a long time.'

There's no doubt about that. No doubt that he's always willing to have a go, either, and push the envelope. It can't be easy for him, but punctures in the wheelchair have never stopped Quentin motoring through life.

I can't wait for everyone to read this book. Warts 'n' all.

Pow! Pow!!

Ray Martin
24 April 2016

Preface

When I was a kid I loved Superman. I guess there is some irony in that he was a perfectly formed man of steel who could leap tall buildings in a single bound while I was a not-so-perfectly formed young boy, more chalk than steel, who would injure myself should I attempt to bound anywhere. I didn't need kryptonite to reveal my weakness – my bones were able to crumble without any help.

But what I've learnt is that we all have our kryptonite but we also all have our strengths. The key to a good life is learning to cope with the bad and celebrate the good. It's taken me a long while to work that one out. I have battled illness, addiction, dysfunction and my own demons along the way. I've had my share of anger and resentment and I've wasted a lot of energy dwelling on what might have been. I recently turned forty-one, which is a big deal for someone with the health issues I have, and I had an epiphany of sorts. I have always been obsessed with movies – they've been my escape at the worst of times – and one of my favourites is *Star Wars*. I've listened to Yoda say 'Always pass on what you have learned' more than 150 times and it's finally sunk in. The time is right to share my story. Everything I've faced in my life has shaped who I am and what I've done. And I've done a lot! (Wait till you hear what I did to Jennifer Lopez!) My life is pretty unique – from one of Australia's first reality stars to a stand-up comedian, film-maker, actor, part-time celebrity, full-time man negotiating a body that doesn't always do what it should in an environment not built for people like me. I have some great stories to tell and, I hope, an inspiring message to deliver. I'm not going to pull my punches or sugar-coat what has happened or my reactions to things. To share my hard-won wisdoms I have to tell the truth. So I thought I'd share my life and let you know that the kid Mike Willesee called Australia's 'little Aussie battler' has grown up. And boy, have I had some battles . . .

CHAPTER 1
The boy who lived

A long time ago in a galaxy, far, far away . . . Damn it! Copyright laws can suck! I might have to play it straight for this one. Here goes . . .

I was born at Melbourne's suburban Box Hill Hospital in Victoria on 27 February 1975. It was the same day as Elizabeth Taylor (though obviously different years), which means nothing but sounds impressive. My parents had been married for seven years and had already welcomed one perfectly formed boy, Myles, twenty-one months before, so they weren't expecting any problems with their second-born. They had the optimism of ignorance, a lovely state to exist in.

Mum and Dad were both successful journalists. Mum was thirty, working for the national women's magazine *New Idea* at the time. My father was forty-five and a former TV news presenter then director, freelance public relations consultant and writer, who'd worked for Pepsi, Shell and the Victorian Wool Board. Dad stayed at home caring for Myles, while Mum worked. Even though feminism was on the rise, it hadn't really made its presence felt in many other homes in the area so Mum and Dad's arrangement was very cutting edge for the mid-seventies. They'd already proved they had no problem going against the norm when they'd spent months as foreign residents on the Greek island of Kythera with Myles. Apparently I was conceived on the island of Rhodes but the less we all know about that the better.

I also have two half-brothers, Shawn and Christopher. Dad was first married to their mother, Gloria, but she died when Shawn and Chris were young. They were well and truly almost grown by the time I came along. At the time of my birth, Shawn was twenty-two and at university and Chris was seventeen and in secondary boarding school so it wasn't like they were around a lot when I was a kid.

Mum's pregnancy with me was relatively problem-free, although she was very big at an early stage. (I've been told that isn't uncommon with a second child.) From four months on, she suffered from Braxton Hicks contractions, which meant she'd have contractions frequently. Our family doctor explained that these contractions were nature's way of practising labour, which was ridiculous because she'd delivered Myles and surely that was practice enough!

The contractions mightn't have been as much of a problem if she'd been at home but they often occurred while Mum was sitting at her desk in the crowded *New Idea* office. Her male editor was worried it was embarrassing (though I'm not sure if that concern was for Mum or her male colleagues). She'd retreat to the women's rest room until the contractions ceased but getting there was apparently a bit of a spectacle.

Finally, after one too many false labour scares, the editor suggested that Mum work from home and the doctor suggested an ultrasound to make sure she wasn't having twins. She was *that* big! The test showed that I was one apparently normal baby, if somewhat small, which was odd considering how large Mum was looking. Mum was concerned about that and the fact that I didn't move around much. The doctor reassured her that her huge tummy was due to a large amount of amniotic fluid surrounding me in her womb. This would turn out to be one of nature's mysterious ways of protecting me – because, unbeknown to anyone, I was a foetus fracturing inside her.

The predicted date of my arrival was February 17th but it came and went. Days passed by. The Braxton Hicks contractions had stopped and so, in relief, and to distract herself from waiting, Mum went shopping for food to cook and freeze meals for the family while she and I were in hospital. On her way home from the shops, her contractions began strongly so she rushed to the emergency section of the hospital and left her much-loved car, a second-hand Jaguar, with the motor still running, at the hospital entrance. An employee saw and shouted to her that she couldn't leave the car there.

Between contractions, which took her breath away, she managed to say, 'I'm having a baby! Can you park the car, please?'

That's my mum, always polite even when in excruciating pain.

The doctor arrived quickly, followed by Dad. It turned out it was a false alarm but the doctor discovered that something was wrong. I was a breech baby, meaning I was facing the wrong way around. My feet would be born first. He told my parents that many infants didn't survive a breech birth and those who did could be oxygen-deprived when the head arrived last, resulting in mental retardation. No parent wants to hear that. With difficulty, the doctor turned me, using his hands, unaware that this action was breaking my bones. After some hours of observation, the contractions stopped and Mum was sent home. I'm not sure who drove the Jaguar.

The next week Mum's contractions started again. This time they didn't stop. Mum's doctor was away and his junior partner couldn't be located so the senior midwife asked if a student nurse could deliver me. Mum agreed.

After an eleven-hour labour, the labour ward staff were astonished that I was screaming the moment my head emerged. They said I had the lustiest set of lungs of any newborn at the hospital. It was probably the pain! When I was born I had eight broken bones – both arms and legs, plus several ribs – in addition to the many which had been broken in utero. So many other broken bones, some healed, some not, were discovered by X-rays after a young doctor examined me and made an immediate diagnosis, even though he'd only read about my condition. He'd never seen a case before but he knew – osteogenesis imperfecta (OI). (No, it is not a spell from Harry Potter!)

There are two forms of OI: the congenita type (meaning 'born with') or tarda (meaning 'later') when a patient's bones can fracture weeks, months or even years after birth. Tarda OI patients' bones tend to harden as they grow older. The congenital OIs fracture more and continue to fracture into later age, if the patient survives for so long.

With both types of OI, the severity can vary. Some patients can have just a few fractures in a lifetime and lead normal lives. That wasn't my lot. My parents were told it would be extremely unlikely I would ever walk as my fragile legs would break under the stress of bearing my weight. Mum believes that I am the longest-living severe OI congenita in the world, considering the number of fractures I have had. Despite what I said earlier in the preface, my bones are not chalky nor do I have a calcium deficiency. My bones are brittle. They just break, like eggshells.

I was not meant to live beyond my first day. I had so many rib fractures, which the doctor told my parents couldn't be treated or immobilised, and one or several could pierce a vital organ – lung, liver or heart. That was hard enough for Mum and Dad to hear but the list of problems didn't stop there. Many OI patients also have lung problems, and an inability to easily inhale oxygen (as I often experience now), along with asthma. Fluids also build up around my heart and, at times, leak into my lungs. Most OI deaths occur after fatal pneumonia. Only diuretics prescribed by my family doctor in conjunction with a cardiologist and monitored hospital care mean I remain alive.

I was less than a day old, at six pounds one ounce and seventeen inches (forty-three centimetres) long, twisted and deformed. I was transferred to the intensive care unit of Melbourne's Children's Hospital because I was having trouble breathing, but not before I was named Quentin Alexandros Charles Kenihan. My mother baptised me herself as she was a Catholic and didn't want me to die a heathen. A bikie priest was summoned by staff and, still wearing his motorcycle helmet, he repeated the rite in great haste, urged by nurses and ambulance men that my condition was critical.

I was expected to be a children's hospital DOA case (dead on arrival) the day after I was born. But I was a tough little bugger, even back then. I was going to be full of surprises and living through that day was the first of many.

CHAPTER 2
A little less than perfect

Being told your child probably wouldn't live through their first day is hard enough. Learning that if your child did live he or she would be profoundly disabled is an absolute nightmare. In the early days, my mum and dad dealt with that nightmare in very different ways. Dad made every effort to gain as much information as possible about my condition and, as soon as he could, he contacted some doctor friends to seek out counsel and knowledge. He wanted to be informed and do whatever he could from the very beginning.

Mum was the total opposite. Once she'd baptised me, she went into a deep depression and refused to acknowledge me at all. Every mother wants her child to be born healthy. When I wasn't, she wrestled with alternating feelings of anger and guilt. Why her baby? Was it something she did? Ate? Drank? Mum's main worry was that I would be intellectually disabled, although there was no evidence of that at the time. She retreated into herself and refused to breastfeed. I was in hospital on a life-support system in a humidicrib, splayed out because of my fractures. (I wasn't put in plaster because that could have caused more breaks.) It would have been tough to physically breastfeed me but the Box Hill Hospital staff offered to send Mum's expressed milk to the Children's Hospital ICU to give me that benefit. Mum couldn't do it. Within two days her milk dried up naturally so the pressure was off in that regard. She couldn't cope with any of it and, in what I can only see as complete denial, she returned to work and visited me only once during the six weeks I was in the ICU, even though the *New Idea* office was only a short walk from the hospital. My father visited nightly and, after I had a drip feed removed, he attempted to give me my first bottle of milk. I didn't drink much.

I was oblivious to all this drama playing out but Dad waited patiently for Mum to come around and learn to cope with her new son. After my bones had healed and I was discharged from hospital, my parents took me home and Mum was forced to step up. And she did.

I had to be handled with great care but even that wasn't enough to protect me. My parents broke my legs when changing nappies or my arms when putting me into clean clothes. I fractured when being bathed. Often Mum would have to cut me out of my clothing because I'd broken an arm or leg. My parents had to learn to push their guilt aside because it didn't matter how cautious they were, my bones still broke. Not surprisingly, Mum and Dad were always exhausted. I slept in my crib in Mum's study. Mum slept two hours a night. She was working for the magazine from home so she'd tap on her typewriter with one hand and bottle-feed me in my crib every few hours with the other. Dad would take over after a feed and, because I couldn't be patted or rubbed on the back like most babies lest I break more ribs, he'd rock me in his hands to burp me.

Myles had been told he could not touch his little brother. He obeyed but didn't understand why. He stood by helplessly, dissatisfied with the only interaction he had on offer: sprinkling me with talcum powder. His sparkly personality began to disintegrate because of it.

Most people, even my grandparents, rejected me because my body was so twisted and ugly. People also struggled to deal with a disabled baby. (I hadn't developed my charming disposition and cheeky grin back then.)

According to my parents, I never smiled as a baby. Not surprising really. Most people would find it tough to be happy if their bones were constantly breaking. It wasn't like I was on painkillers the whole time so I could goofily drift through babyhood in a drug-induced haze. I wasn't even on kiddie Panadol. I couldn't roll over but Mum and Dad had been told to carefully turn my head frequently so it wouldn't develop a flat spot at the back. It would be many months before I had the strength to move or lift my head. Over more months and with the assistance of physiotherapists, I was finally able to sit without being propped up by pillows.

Since Mum and Dad were professional journalists, they researched OI as much as possible, and together they worked out how to bring me up, one day (and one fracture) at a time. They weren't afraid to disagree with a doctor or get another opinion. Once they got over the guilt and the worry, my parents decided fairly early on not to wrap me up in cottonwool and hide me away from the world. And they weren't going to modify their lives for me. They wanted to return to normal and I would come along for the ride. Literally!

Mum's first novel, *Cirigo*, which was set on the Greek island of Kythera, was published and launched when I was in hospital for the surgical removal of two hernias. A movie producer wanted to make a movie of it and, when I was six months old, the producer asked Mum to work on the production in Greece. My parents hesitated for a moment but then started talking about going. Almost everyone criticised Mum and Dad for talking about taking me to Greece, but it didn't stop them. It was agreed my father would look after me while Mum concentrated on working with the film producer in Athens. Myles wasn't so lucky. He went to stay with Mum's brother, Uncle Paul, and his wife, Auntie Sue.

Apparently Olympic Airways bent all the rules to let me fly on the top of a pram on the floor as I couldn't be held during take-off and landing. But just before the plane landed in Athens, Mum lost it. She couldn't remember her name, let alone the movie task ahead. All she could recall was how to care for me.

She says now that it was a nervous breakdown due to sleep deprivation. Dad took us to Kythera, and the lovely people my parents knew there allowed us to live with them for a while. Mum slowly recovered but the situation quickly became impossible. There was no medical treatment for me on the island. Mum had been taught by our GP how to splint my fractures with foam-lined, light steel splints and surgical tape, or even icy pole sticks and sticky tape, but there was no way she could manage my health in the state she was in and with no medical back-up.

While we were staying on Kythera, Mum, who was recognised as a working travel writer in Greece, had some other work come her way. We sailed on a cruise ship to Egypt and I was carried in a pram some distance up the Great Pyramid of Cheops and saw the Sphinx. I don't remember any of it, which isn't surprising considering I was only about seven months old. As soon as my parents could organise it, we were heading back home to Melbourne.

On return, we stopped at Sydney airport. When Mum looked down into the pram at me, her sunglasses dropped from her head. I jerked and broke an arm. Dad had to ask for some ice from a food outlet to freeze my arm while Mum splinted it. People stared, muttering. An abused child? Out of pain, I slept during the flight home to Melbourne. This always happened. A fracture meant severe pain but once the fractures were immobilised, I'd sink into a deep sleep.

My parents were starting to see a pattern. My sclerae, the whites of my eyes, turned blue just before I was about to fracture. They also discovered a phenomenon, which would add to a diagnostic breakthrough in international research some years later. During what they came to refer to as a 'fracture cycle', I'd sweat profusely and emit a peculiar smell from my skin. My temperature would rise and I would bruise easily at the slightest bump.

In those early years, if we were away from home and something happened and we had to rush to an unfamiliar hospital, some doctors, inexperienced with the disorder and not knowing us, thought my parents were physically abusing me. Mum and Dad would have to explain everything over and over and educate the doctors on my condition.

They became experts at reading X-rays and challenging radiologists and radiographers and both Mum and Dad learned the medical language. Dad grew tired of waiting in queues for hours in casualty departments so he'd call the hospital beforehand and say: 'Kenihan here. I'm with a severe osteogenesis imperfecta patient, Quentin. Please have his records ready as I am bringing him in myself. I suspect fractured ulna and radius and a possible skull fracture. Please alert X-ray.' He'd don his three-piece suit so he arrived looking the part.

The first time he did this he was desperate to have me seen quickly. Mum had left me on a couch to grab a clean nappy, believing I'd never move. But I rolled for the first time and hit the wooden floor. It was late at night and my parents knew my legs and arms had broken but they were worried I'd fractured my skull.

When Dad and I arrived at the hospital and the admitting staff registered surprise that my doctor had brought me in for treatment, Dad confessed: 'I am his father.' They didn't hold it against Dad, and luckily my skull wasn't fractured – but other limbs were.

Worried about Dad's subterfuge, Mum made an appointment with the medical director of the hospital to explain the frustration of being kept waiting behind obviously non-urgent cases in casualty while I was in great pain. She explained that she and Dad had learned to recognise when my needs were urgent and stated they wouldn't seek treatment unless it was an emergency. The director agreed to instruct staff to make me top priority, provided no other life-threatening emergency demanded their immediate action. Little things like this made a big difference.

From their own experiences, my parents realised there was little information or support for families affected by OI and, because they were professional communicators, they wanted to do something about that. With the generous help of Victoria's Vermont Lions Club, of which previously they'd been members, they helped raise money to create the OI Foundation. The foundation aimed to assist research funding, and support me and other OI-affected families if they could be found.

Mum and Dad had been told the incidence of OI was about one in 50,000 but they didn't believe it. Mum had been in contact with the president of the American OI Foundation, Gemma Geisman. Given the USA's much larger population, the comparative statistics suggested that Australia and New Zealand had more OI patients than my parents had been informed.

My mother and father began a publicity campaign and, at six months old, I was introduced to television viewers on the high-rating daytime *Mike Walsh Show*. I was quiet on the program, but just seeing me was enough. The response was tremendous. Other parents of OI children contacted Mum. She and Dad had accumulated so much knowledge about my condition that she felt confident giving practical advice to parents who needed it. I lay on the floor in Mum's study while she counselled parents by phone or letter and worked late into the night.

After Myles was born, Mum had made a rule that there was to be no television except the ABC's *Play School* and occasionally *Sesame Street*. That worked fine when you had a kid who could run around, play outside and be distracted with other things. It didn't work with me.

As I grew older, all Mum's preconceived ideas went out the window. I didn't have the strength to hold any toys, so my parents bought a colour television and settled me on a couch in front of it, my floppy head sandwiched between thick cushions to support it. Television and movies became my imaginative escape. The older I got, the more obsessed I became. The soundtrack to the Kenihan household echoed out of that television's speakers.

So many of my family's decisions were made because of me. My parents sold their small house, bought land on an impossibly steep block and Mum designed a house suitable for me. It was tiled throughout, except for carpeted bedrooms. The doors were wide to allow for wheelchair access as my parents believed I'd be able to manage a manual wheelchair at some stage. A deep

Japanese bath was installed so I could have water therapy. An alarm system ensured that if I cried while my parents were asleep, they'd hear me. I shared a bedroom with Myles. Dad built a double bunk with rails for me at the lower level.

After learning that some OI patients benefited from swimming, they put in a pool. It turned out I wasn't one of them. The water was too cold and deep so Mum abandoned her plans to teach me to swim.

When I was younger and I fractured bones, my parents didn't panic. They knew that if they overreacted, I would as well, which would make the pain more unbearable. Instead, they sat quietly next to me to calm me down. Mum's technique was to ask me to close my eyes and picture being a leaf floating gently down a stream. 'Let the pain be the water and you become the leaf floating on top of it,' Mum would say.

The leaf routine usually worked. I was rarely given painkillers, as our doctor had warned that too many analgesics could harm my kidneys. I learned to cope with pain without medication back then, though that would change as I got older.

At twelve months, I had not uttered a word, unlike Myles who, while living in Greece with our parents, had spoken Greek at seven months. Mum and Dad still worried that I had sustained brain damage at birth and even our family doctor believed that this could be the case as I could do none of the usual physical things preceding the ability to speak, like grasping his thumb.

Life went on. Mum dragged me in the crib all around our house as she worked, always talking to me. She was forever on the phone, reporting for her magazine, speaking to other parents of OI patients or supportive Lions. Then suddenly one day, at thirteen months, my first words spilled out.

No 'goo goos' or 'ga gaas' for me. I practically started speaking in full sentences, asking for milk, the dog, Dad and Myles. (His name was the only word I couldn't pronounce. I called him Mao, which is still my nickname for him.) I guess at the time I must have thought, Why say anything unless you really want something?

After that, no one could shut me up.

Myles now had a friend with whom he could communicate. As I got older and learned to speak more, and it was obvious that I wasn't mentally handicapped, people's attention focused on me. When visitors arrived, Myles would wait patiently for people to greet him or play with him but this didn't happen often any more. He gradually became more independent, learning that he needed to find his own fun, invent his own childhood games and look after himself.

If I have one regret, it is that I caused my brother's life to be shaped so differently to other kids'. I was lucky though. He was very protective of me and I became his little mate. We were inseparable. Myles used to sit with me for hours, drawing and demonstrating Lego. He was very creative, careful not to hurt me, and he never, despite all the attention that came my way, exhibited any jealousy.

But it wasn't going to be the two of us for much longer.

CHAPTER 3

Then there were . . . three

Up until I was two, Mao was everything to me. He was my Batman, Robin and Superman. Every day my parents would place me in my wheelchair so that I could interact with him. We would draw together, play with blocks and I would watch him run around the house or the garden as he tried to keep me entertained. As much as this was great for me, my parents worried for Myles. He avoided interacting with other kids so that he could keep me company. It became painfully obvious to my parents that things had to change and they wondered about having another child. Our GP, Dr John Munro, advised Mum and Dad that another pregnancy came with big risks and possible complications as any future child was at greater risk of being born with osteogenesis imperfecta.

The constant need to take me to hospital with broken bone after broken bone was tough going for my parents and played a big part in their eventual decision not to have another child. They were struggling to look after me at the best of times. But, as is so often the case, life had other plans for my family. Mum and Dad went out one night, had a lovely dinner and then one glass of wine led to another, and . . . soon enough Dr Munro was informing Mum that she was pregnant.

One of my first memories of my mum is her wearing her favourite green leather suit. The green patterned leather pants and jacket were in fashion and she looked very cool. She wasn't going to let her surprise pregnancy get in the way of her fashion sense. Mum has told me stories about how she would struggle to get into those pants as her tummy grew. She's never been what you'd call 'fashion forward' but back in the seventies she had her 'A' game going on and to lose those leather pants was a big disappointment for her. Back then no one looked good in maternity wear. It was all tent dresses with enormous bows attached.

Mum's concern about fitting into the green leather suit was a distraction from the more serious, bigger picture. To be sure that the baby didn't turn out like me, Mum had fortnightly check-ups with the doctor. By the end of the first trimester they had to come to a decision – take the risk to continue the pregnancy and the chance of a baby born with osteogenesis imperfecta or decide to abort the foetus. My parents took advice from doctors and also from genetic experts about what this baby's future would be. Perhaps surprisingly to some, the advice was to go through with it whatever the outcome and treat the pregnancy no differently to any other.

So they did. On 3 February 1977 Mum went into labour and a few hours later my sister, Dionysia Catherine Kenihan, was born. I don't know if everyone held their breath but if they did there would have been a big sigh of relief when it was clear she had no broken bones.

You may wonder how they came up with the name Dionysia. It is the female version of Dionysus, the Greek god of wine and drama, and my parents said that the night she was conceived there was lots of wine and plenty of drama so the name seemed quite fitting. It was also the name of a good friend of Mum's in Greece.

Dionysia was quite a mouthful for everyone to say, so practically straightaway everyone started calling her Sia. This is the only name my sister has ever used in her life.

Myles and I were merciless towards our younger sister. We picked on poor Sia and made her life a living hell. We'd play jokes on her, pick on her and steal her toys, and usually our parents would take our side when she complained. One thing was certain though. From a very young age Sia was protected from the fallout of my disability. That burden was only placed upon my parents and, sadly, my brother. Mum and Dad might have thought they were protecting Sia, but at times excluding her from this part of our lives made her feel unwanted. She felt just as loyal and protective of me as the rest of the family.

As a child Sia was Little Miss Mischief. Mum would sing to her and call her 'Little Madam'. Once she was old enough to hold scissors, Sia would cut her own hair and then Mao's, pretending she was a hairdresser. She wasn't into Barbie but had a teddy bear called Big Ted which she took everywhere and, as far as I am aware, she still sleeps with it to this day. (Yes, that was a big brother dig.)

Around the time Sia was born, other things were happening in the Kenihan family. This was when my parents realised that the small house we were living in was no longer suitable for a growing family, or a child with a disability, and rather than try to buy an existing property they decided to chase the great Aussie dream and build their own home. They bought a block of land in Vermont, Victoria, a few streets over from what everyone now knows as Ramsay Street. The land had a big slope, which needed to be made accessible for a wheelchair.

Mum and Dad built a dream home. Three bedrooms, a dining room, a study, a huge lounge room with a marble-top bar, separate family room and kitchen, a double carport and in-ground swimming pool. By today's standards, it was a mansion. It was all bricks and mortar with double-glazed windows around the sides. Unfortunately, in my opinion, my parents had no taste as far as interior design goes. The family room had wallpaper that looked like Andy Warhol had vomited on it. The dining room had copper wallpaper and a chandelier. The lounge room looked like a Greek villa, painted white with a brick fireplace at the end and surprisingly ugly copper wallpaper on the bar wall. Whilst the judges of *The Block* may have given the exterior a ten out of ten, the interior would have only ever scored a four at best. It did have good storage, which always wins points though.

The wool-covered couches in the lounge area looked like another Andy Warhol experiment, whereas the couch in the family room was like the one you get from your grandmother when she decides to upgrade. It even came with a crocheted rug. I hated that couch. I was three years old and my dad would balance me on it and try to teach me how to steady myself without falling over. I'd be propped up in the corner with pillows surrounding me so I didn't break something.

Life was pretty boring for me at that time. I was either sitting up on the couch, lying on the floor or sitting in the manual wheelchair that didn't go where I wanted it to go without someone taking me there. I was reliant on everyone and had no freedom to explore anything, even my own house.

When I was three that all changed. The Vermont Lions Club of Australia had raised some money so my parents could travel to America to work with others to form an international foundation to support people with OI and research new technology. While they were there, Mum and Dad discovered that I might be able to operate an electric wheelchair. Back then there were very few of these chairs available for disabled kids in Australia and they were very, very expensive. Thanks to the generosity of the Vermont Lions Club, I was going to have access to wheels that would go wherever I wanted them to go. This meant I had freedom.

The day I got my electric wheelchair was a day of complete joy.

As soon as I sat in it, I was off! I raced around the house, hit every wall and smashed into every couch. I also blew up the gearbox and broke my arm. A person in a wheelchair didn't get a lot of exciting 'firsts' back then, but thinking back to that day always makes me smile. It was the beginning of a whole new way of life for me. Finally being mobile under my own steam opened up the world in ways I couldn't have imagined before.

I explored the whole house and the whole garden for the first time alone. As a three-year-old I can remember going outside and discovering bees. I was fascinated; I thought the way they would jump from flower to flower, pollinating, was astonishing. It wasn't until Myles saw me try to capture one that he rushed over and told me that they were dangerous and I should shoo them away. I thought they must be bad because Myles loved bugs; he had twice tried to pet huntsman spiders only to get bitten. If he was shooing away a bee there must be a good reason.

By the time I was three, my mum had become an expert at splinting my bones when they broke. Whilst the pain was always there and breaks were constantly happening, the need to rush off to the children's hospital diminished. A lot of the time things were managed by Dr Munro and Mum and Dad. It was quickly becoming apparent, though, that due to all the broken bones, my body was starting to bow as I grew and I was not going to remain straight. If it went untreated I would never be able to stand or walk and my whole body would look like a bit of a deformed mess. Something had to be done. Soon enough I would embark on the first of two trips that would change my life forever.

CHAPTER 4

Me, my dad and Shirley Temple

You'd think frequent broken bones would be enough to contend with but, as we all know, everything has consequences. Max Rockatansky would never have become that vengeful loner and added the Mad to his name if Toecutter and his gang hadn't dispatched Jessie and Sprog in such a brutal fashion. Consequences.

Early on, my parents had been told that a procedure called 'bone rodding' was available to some children with my condition. This involved the surgical placement of steel rods into the internal cavity of a bone (in my case my leg bones) to strengthen them and reduce fracturing. With their usual tenacity and research skills, my parents explored the options. It turned out that this 'bone rodding' operation was not advised in Australia. The procedure was considered too risky because of the severity of my disorder. However, while my parents were in America purchasing my first wheelchair they met a team of experts working at Stanford University Hospital and nearby Stanford Children's Hospital.

The very good news was that the team leader, orthopaedic surgeon Dr Eugene Bleck, said he would be willing to perform the procedure but the bad news was that I wasn't eligible for American health insurance and Australia's newly formed Medicare wouldn't pay for it either. So the *really* bad news was that it would cost tens of thousands of dollars, money that wasn't readily available to my family.

Ron Bromley, the man behind the Vermont Lions Club's push to support the OI foundation and who helped buy my wheelchair, heard what was going on and encouraged the club to raise the money for the American surgery. It was a big effort and they needed to get people on board. To encourage donations, my family and I were interviewed on TV and in newspapers. This was becoming something I would have to get used to but the commitment by total strangers to help me was amazing. Even today, it blows me away. The Lions Club held a number of functions where all the proceeds went directly into a fund to pay for my surgery. Within a short time, and with help from the media, they had raised enough money for me to travel to San Francisco for the surgery and then have physio to teach me how to stand up.

Mum and Dad must have worried themselves sick about how they were going to manage it all. They decided Dad should be the one to go with me and Mum would stay home with Mao and Sia. I was four years old and my world revolved around my family – Mao, in particular – but spending six months alone with my dad sounded like an adventure. Dad described it as 'two boys on the road again' and he played Willie Nelson's song a lot to get me in the mood to go. He didn't talk about the actual operation much at all, which was smart because that wasn't something to look forward to.

Saying goodbye to everyone wasn't fun but travelling with Dad was. We arrived in San Francisco after a marathon flight and settled into the Palo Alto Ronald McDonald House. California was going to be home for a while.

I met Dr Bleck and he explained as best he could to a four-year-old how the surgery would work. He was going to cut me open, break my legs and insert rods into them. The way he would do this was to drill a hole through my thigh bone to put a rod in the femur and drill through my heel to insert the rod in my tibia. I would be one of the first Australians to receive a skin graft on my heels so that the skin would grow back over.

I am not sure how much I understood of what was to happen but Dad made sure I had some fun moments before the surgery. Every morning he would take me to the big local shopping centre so that we could have pancakes and hash browns at the McDonald's there. And though Mum had always said that none of us was allowed to drink Pepsi Cola (she was a 'no sugar' convert way before the recent trend), Dad relaxed that rule while I was in America.

I made a lot of friends while I was at Ronald McDonald House. The building was pretty clinical, with white walls and handrails all around, but the families were all supportive of one another, and because of the way the place ran, we saw a lot of everyone. Each room was numbered and we were given Room 6, which was basically one room with an ensuite. There was a bed in one corner and a cot for me. There were two large communal lounge rooms in the common areas, one that was used by the parents and a rumpus room with a TV for the kids. There was also an outside patio that was like an enclosed playground, and adjacent to the building was a park that had a slippery dip.

There were kids from all over the world and all over America staying there while I was. It was the first time I spent any time with people from other countries and it was where I learned that skin colour and nationality are irrelevant (I already knew that a wheelchair was only a machine for mobility, not a defining characteristic of anyone). We are all the same. My first six months of schooling were spent in the Stanford Children's Hospital School. Every morning, I entered a classroom full of other sick kids and pledged allegiance to the United States flag. I thought all schools must do that.

There was a lovely guy who worked at the children's hospital. He had an afro so big that whenever I saw him I would scream out, 'Big, big bushy hairdo!' It always made him laugh and he would show me how he could fit pencils inside his hair, which would make me laugh even more.

Just before the surgery, my dad told me that after the operation I would be in plaster for two months, from the middle of my chest to the bottom of my feet. He said it would cover more than 50 per cent of my body and that for a while my independence would be taken away but that I would emerge stronger and faster than ever before, just like Steve Austin from *The Six Million Dollar Man*. I might not have comprehended exactly what that all meant, but becoming like the bionic man sounded pretty cool to me.

Dad and I started a tradition that two nights before any surgery I would be allowed to eat whatever I wanted, and as much as I wanted, because I would have to fast for the next twenty-four hours. Usually this involved a mountain of chicken nuggets, fries and Coke.

All I can remember of the surgical procedure is being wheeled into an operating theatre and having a mask placed on me that dispensed a gas that smelled so horrible it made me want to throw up. I started bucking violently, trying to take the mask off, but I was held down and told to start counting back from ten to one. Anaesthetists always tell you to count down to one but I have never even made it close to that. I've asked other people who have had surgery and they never reach one either, so why don't they just tell you to count down from three? This is a quandary that I have always pondered and no one has ever answered properly for me. If you know, can you tell me?

When I woke up I was, as Dad had warned me, covered in plaster. It was tight and enveloping so I couldn't move much and I couldn't sit up. The heels of my feet were dark red as blood had leaked through the plaster. Dad assured me that I was okay and that I would soon go back to Ronald McDonald House. I remember the pain being unimaginable and the fear intense. Even though I had worn plaster before, and broken legs before, this was something new. I had been torn open and had steel inserted into my body. I still have to warn airport staff that I have rods in my legs before I go through metal detectors.

Due to the way my legs had been set, I had to return to wearing a nappy because placing me on the toilet with plaster on was impossible. I was four and thought my days of wearing nappies were over so it was quite embarrassing. I also had to have cushions made so that I could sit up in my wheelchair and drive it.

I had become good friends with the daughter of the manager of Ronald McDonald House (when you are four you can become besties after an hour). When I got out of hospital and was finally able to get myself around independently, I was excited to see her again. It turned out her father had other plans. I knocked on their door and he opened it and pulled out a single barrel pump-action shotgun and screamed at me to never bother his daughter again. I was a four-year-old in a full-body cast who wanted to play with my friend. *What was he thinking?* I rolled myself away from him as fast as I could, which wasn't very fast when you are terrified and recovering from a major operation.

I immediately told my father. One thing Dad knew was that I didn't make up stories, so he made sure I was safe and then rushed off to have a 'word' with the guy.

The manager ended up with a black eye but I was told I couldn't see his daughter anymore and wasn't to go near their door. I had no idea what I'd done but I lost a friend that day. I also lost my confidence and became too scared to move freely around the house. The manager didn't keep his job and years later I found out that he had been sentenced to life in prison for murder. That didn't surprise me, although I wondered what happened to his daughter.

Life became pretty lonely for a while, until my dad became friends with Wally Motloch.

Wally was a mechanical engineer and designer who built orthotics and repaired wheelchairs for the kids at the children's hospital. My father had this grand idea to build a one-of-a-kind wheelchair which would allow me to stand up so I could be at the same height as four- to five-year-old able-bodied kids. One night, on a giant sheet of butcher's paper, my father drew his brilliant plan. The wheelchair would be fast, functional and look like a racing green Jaguar. (This was the car that my mother sold in order to pay the last bills for the trip.) Dad's idea immediately piqued Wally's interest because it was not only going to be a technological milestone but an engineering nightmare, and Wally loved a challenge.

Dad and Wally gathered parts from everywhere. They created back wheels from one type of wheelchair, front wheels from another. They engineered a drive system which ran on a fanbelt rather than brushes and motors. The wheelchair was high voltage and required two car batteries to run it. It had hydraulics to allow me to sit down and stand up. They even equipped it with headlights from a highway patrol motorcycle and rear lights from a Citroën car. It was a beast, but in my dad's mind it still needed a final touch. My father had seen that actress Shirley Temple, a Stanford Children's Hospital director, owned the same make and model Jaguar that my mother had recently sold, and he assumed it would be intact, with all four hubcaps and Jaguar emblems. In my father's crazed ambition to create the perfect wheelchair, he thought he would hatch the perfect crime and steal Ms Temple's hubcaps and Jaguar emblem off her car.

Who knows how my father knew where Shirley Temple lived (this was *way* before search engines). Maybe it was in the article he'd read or maybe as a journalist and collector of knowledge he'd come across it. It was just one of myriad facts floating around in his brain, but he knew her house wasn't far away. I also don't know how long the statute of limitations is on theft but hopefully it is less than thirty-six years because in the dead of night my father made the journey to Shirley Temple's mansion, snuck over the fence and stole what he needed.

Dad didn't mess around when he got back; he set straight to work. Once assembled, the wheelchair looked absolutely perfect. My father was so proud of himself that he called my mother to gloat about what he had just done. But instead of praising him she was furious. Her words were, 'Our family are not beggars nor thieves so you march yourself back up to Ms Temple's house and return those hubcaps and Jaguar emblem right now.'

Mum was right and, begrudgingly, my father knew it. He was so lost in getting something right for his son that he forgot himself for a moment. The next day Dad did as he was told. He loaded me into the car, a jazzy red Mercury Cougar which had been lent to him by a local American Lions, marched himself to the front door of Shirley Temple's house and confessed to what he had done. Bemused, Ms Temple invited my father in for a coffee and asked him to explain the whole story. I was still in the car, so Dad brought me in and introduced me to Shirley Temple, telling me this was the lady who'd sung 'On the Good Ship Lollipop' when she was not much older than I was then. Dad was tired and remorseful and just wanted to get his punishment and leave, but instead of punishing my father, Shirley Temple gave him the hubcaps and the emblem as a gift. She told Dad she hoped other fathers were as committed to their children as my father was to me. What a kind-hearted woman! This was my first brush with fame . . . but it wouldn't be my last.

•

I wish I could tell you that after I healed from the operation I felt fabulous, but that wasn't the case. The plaster kept me at such an awkward angle that my head was at a half-sitting, half-lying down position and I started getting headaches which rapidly turned into frequent migraines. The doctors couldn't work out what was wrong. They asked my father whether they could use a new type of imaging system on me, which had the ability to not only see your bones but also your vital organs. Dad agreed and I was going to be one of the first people with OI to have his brain and skull scanned.

The machine was like a giant, noisy washing machine. I took one look at it, turned my wheelchair and hightailed out of the room. That was one of the things independence had given me that my parents didn't quite enjoy – a rebellious streak. After my father chased me down he explained the necessity of the test and told me I had to be like the astronauts. Someone had to do it first. I'd like to say that his pep talk worked but in the end he had to bribe me with chocolate and soft drink.

Despite my initial fear, I found the whole experience quite fun. When the diagnosis came back it was discovered that my skull was growing quickly to accommodate my brain. It was another feature of OI. Over time my brain would get bigger and fill up the space but until it did the headaches were just another thing I had to put up with. So when people say I have a big head they are not far wrong. It's a medically based fact, not ego . . . or is it?

Finally the day came when my plaster was to be removed. I'd had to stay in it for an extra month as it had taken a while for the skin to grow over and the bones to heal with the new rods in place. Once I was out, I had complete muscle atrophy. All I wanted to do was get something sharp and scratch every piece of dead skin off my legs. I had never wanted to have a bath so much in my life.

Dad and I had been in San Francisco a total of four months by then and Christmas was coming. Mum, Myles and Sia were given the gift of a flight over and we spent Christmas with Wally and his family in the snow in Nevada.

I wasn't down with this as snow doesn't work well with wheel-chairs, so I spent a lot of time by myself playing 'Pong' on the Motlochs' Atari game system while everyone else roamed outside. But a week later I was rewarded as we all went to Disneyland.

At Disneyland my family discovered one of the benefits of having someone in the family who was disabled. People in wheelchairs don't have to wait in line for rides or attractions. The whole family gets to jump to the front of the queue. How cool is that? For Mao and Sia, who'd missed out on having their dad around because of what was going on with their brother, it was a positive thing which happened because of me. It was one of the first times we all shared a happy vacation moment without the stress of my health or financial issues. Sia looked so happy with her Minnie Mouse ears on, Myles wanted to go on every ride his height allowed him to, and I was happy looking at things I had only seen in story books or on the television.

What astonished me the most was seeing the fireworks over the Disneyland Castle. I had never seen fireworks; I was amazed by their colours and was enthralled to hear from my dad how they were made. That's probably the most memorable part of the Disneyland trip for me – that and my fascination with trying to capture Pluto's tail. I annoyed some poor guy in the suit for half a day trying to catch him. We ate so much junk food, I think we were all sick but we didn't care. It was a family bonding vacation which we needed after so long apart.

The holiday didn't last long as Mum, Sia and Myles had to return home, but Dad, Wally and I had some unfinished business.

In order for me to stand up in the wheelchair, Wally and my father realised that I would need some sort of prosthetic help to give me strength and balance. They designed a full-body exoskeleton brace that went from my armpits to my feet. It had joints at the hips and the knees so that I could move and bend my legs when I wanted. At first I was scared of the braces, as they became known. When Dad placed me in them, they were cold and plastic and rubbed on me. Dad told me to be brave, be strong and keep my eyes forward. Without any warning, he just stood me up and walked away. He was still within arm's reach, but I was standing like a normal boy for the first time in my life.

Everyone else was ecstatic, but I screamed and cried the entire time – petrified that I would fall over on my face. I lasted one minute and three seconds before I did indeed topple over but, when I did, my dad was there to catch me. He was so happy and proud of me. He explained that this was the test so that when I got in the wheelchair I could stand up and sit down of my own free will. Most people don't realise how remarkable it is to do really mundane things independently. Physical restrictions can make even the simplest actions impossible so it was a big moment.

People often talk about the feeling they had when they received their first bike or their first car. Although this wasn't my first wheelchair, this one allowed me to stand up at the height of other four-year-olds and to me that was super. The first time I was placed in the chair and stood up I became dizzy because I had never stood up so high before. I had to sit down and get my bearings but, once I was comfortable with it, I was off. The wheelchair was faster and stronger, and because I now had metal in my legs, I felt I really was the bionic man. Riding around in my mean green machine, I couldn't wait to go back to Australia and show everyone how far I'd come.

CHAPTER 5
Sticks and stones . . . you know the rest!

Excited as I was, coming home to Australia meant big changes. First, I had to learn how to navigate the family home in a wheelchair that was double the size of my original one, so unfortunately walls, skirting boards and furniture were left with giant marks or scratches on them. So much for Mum and Dad's newly built home. I am pretty sure that didn't count as normal wear and tear!

The biggest change for Myles and Sia, besides getting used to dodging me in my new wheelchair, was the very strong Californian accent I had somehow managed to adopt. They hated it and Myles was obsessed with trying to stop it quickly. Mum must have felt the same because she would get me to say the words 'How now brown cow, how now brown cow' repeatedly to try and stop her almost five-year-old Aussie son from sounding like one of the *Brady Bunch* kids.

Now that I was mobile and had become semi-used to a school routine after my time in the Stanford Children's Hospital classroom, Mum and Dad decided I wouldn't go to the Yooralla School for the Disabled, as they'd originally been told was necessary. I would go to the same school as my brother, St James Vermont Primary School.

This meant a whole lot of new challenges. The first was that the school had a uniform that was difficult for me to wear because I still had a full-body brace over me. The uniform was short grey pants, a blue T-shirt or skivvy, and on winter days a maroon jumper and long pants. Because of my braces, I couldn't wear the long pants so I would wear grey stubby football shorts that had a fly made of Velcro to assist me with going to the toilet. Wearing the maroon jumper was also hard as it was difficult to get the whole jumper over the brace, so my mum created a jumper that was like a smock – I could slip my arms through the front and it would Velcro at the back. God bless NASA for inventing Velcro! That stuff has made my life much easier.

But clothing wasn't the only issue. Finding shoes to slip over the orthotics on my feet was another problem. When my father was in a hurry he would slip my socks and shoes on and accidentally break my toes in the process. The silver lining of this means that today I have very prehensile feet and I can still move each toe individually. There's always an upside if you look for it. Well, almost always!

In order to get me to and from school my parents bought a Toyota Land Cruiser and fitted a ramp with a rear, manual winch that could load my huge wheelchair on and off pretty easily. As we got older, my parents started to trust my navigational skills, so during the warmer months all three of us kids would walk (I'd roll) to and from school by ourselves.

I remember my first day at primary school. I was scared. It wasn't like the hospital school, where I was just one of a whole heap of sick kids. And it wasn't like at home, where I was treated like everyone else and was part of a family. I knew I was going to stand out but I had no idea exactly what that would mean. I wasn't sure how to interact with able-bodied kids and I wasn't sure how they would react to me. There were also very practical physical complications. In order to urinate I had to ask one of the teachers to help me during recess or lunch. If I needed to do a poo it was a whole different story. In the past I'd always had someone around me who could take me out of my wheelchair and sit me on the toilet, but now I was expected to stay in my wheelchair for nine whole hours. Let's face it, when you have to go, you have to go, and waiting isn't often an option, especially for a kid.

This was the most difficult and most demanding physical aspect of school for me. For a few years I had a number of accidents that I hid from everyone at school but would have to admit to when I got home. At first my parents were understanding but as the months went by and the frequency of these accidents didn't diminish they started to get quite angry with me. They didn't understand how difficult it was for me to train my bowel to hold on for so long. They thought I should be able to manage better. If I could have, I would have, believe me! No one wants to sit in their own excrement . . . ever! But I could cope with my parents getting cross as long as the kids at school never found out. I had enough problems dealing with them already.

My worst fears were realised as far as my schoolmates went. I was seen by the other kids as something different, something they didn't understand. At first I was ignored, then I was teased and horribly ridiculed. The torment came in a number of ways. When one of the teachers let it be known that my initials spelt QACK (Quentin Alexandros Charles Kenihan), the kids started following me around quacking like a duck. I hated it.

Then someone noticed that my sternum (breast-bone) was growing outwards due to the number of broken ribs I'd had. Basically it looked like I had a giant boob so the kids started calling me 'Quentin the one-tit wonder'. I preferred the quacking.

Everybody knew my whole body was covered from neck to toe in hard plastic so they decided that if something hit me, I wouldn't get hurt. They'd often pelt tennis balls at me in the playground, trying to see who could hit my sternum first. It actually did hurt physically, and emotionally it sucked to have kids throw things at me with such gleeful malice.

At St James I was the odd one out and the kids never let me forget it. When I got home, I would cry and ask my dad why the kids behaved like this to me. He told me they were scared of what they didn't understand, which didn't explain their cruelty at all, really, but helped make me feel better. He taught me a rhyme to say in my head whenever I got upset or frustrated because of the teasing. He would sing, 'Sticks and stones can break my bones but names can never harm me.' My father was always good like that. He'd come up with a song that would help explain things to me a lot better than just words ever could. He had a song about driving us in a truck, and another about when my braces were hurting. None of them was ever destined to become a radio hit but Dad had a special way of helping me understand things about myself and other people that was simple enough for a child to comprehend. And he made me feel less alone. It's one of the things I loved most about him.

I didn't hang out with my brother or sister much at school. I mainly sat around talking with a girl named Samantha Flynn who, like me, was not well liked either. We rapidly became best friends.

So, it's fair to say that school was not great for me but there was one good day I remember – pie day! On pie day you brought money to school and were allowed to buy a meat pie with sauce and a cupcake. On the other hand, rice day, when we were supposed to give thanks to God for the life we had and honour starving Africans by eating nothing but steamed rice for lunch, was not good at all. And it was absolutely no help to starving kids so I thought it was pretty stupid, really.

At least I remained relatively healthy and didn't have too many bad breaks or health issues. Well, except for when Myles was pushing me down a hill in my manual wheelchair. He tripped, and so did the wheelchair. Myles flew over the top of me and I faceplanted headfirst into the road. He suffered a severely scraped knee. I had a shattered skull, concussion, a broken arm and a broken collarbone. If you look at photos of me you will see that I have a flat forehead, and this is the reason why. Myles felt incredibly guilty, as it was the first time he had caused me a major injury. Unfortunately, it wouldn't be the last. My parents never wanted to stop us from being adventurous children like everybody else, so luckily Myles didn't get into trouble, but that didn't stop him feeling responsible.

The best times when I was a kid were the school holidays because I didn't have to worry about any of the hassles and torments of school. We would spend time together as a family. One time we all went up and down the east coast of Australia in a huge caravan, which was good for my parents, my sister and I. It was becoming evident, though, that Mum and Dad were relying on Myles to act as my carer far more than was fair. It was a role he should never have been forced to take on but ultimately it was one that would become a large portion of his emerging years. I couldn't do anything about it because I needed someone to help me.

The trip up the east coast was great – I have wonderful memories of one holiday panning for gold at Sovereign Hill, and travelling on the Puffing Billy train, which was a day trip not far from where we lived – but another holiday we spent together wasn't so full of happy memories. It was on *Fairstar*, the 'Fun Ship'. We boarded the ship in Darwin and it took us to Bali, Singapore, Hong Kong and Manila before returning. The Fun Ship turned out to be very far from it! Bali was scary and I couldn't use my wheelchair because it couldn't be transported by the ship's tender to the island so Mum and Dad pushed me around in a stroller. I'd freak out when people rushed up to sell us stuff and lunged towards my face.

I have a family photo of us from Bali – one of only a few photos ever taken of the five of us. It depicts the family's mood at the time quite perfectly. My father is trying to look capable, my sister is posing like a model, my mother is shielding her eyes, exasperated by the heat. Myles is scowling and I am crying my eyes out, wanting to go home.

Back on the ship we sailed to Hong Kong. Our parents left us in the care of the ship's babysitter so they could have some time together. The babysitter accidentally broke my arm. It wasn't the first or the last time that this would happen but, instead of reporting it straightaway, the babysitter waited until the next morning when my parents picked us up. I still remember my mother screaming and yelling at the babysitter for not telling her immediately. Once she'd finished yelling, Mum decided the ship's doctor was too expensive so she splinted my arm herself. Despite all the broken bones she'd dealt with, Mum was not always expert at splinting bones. I have a very large non-union (a broken bone that hasn't healed) on my upper right arm. Both my left and right arms are slightly deformed from the bones not healing correctly. At the time, I was forced to act like a leaf on the water, grit through the pain and go with the flow. I'd rather have had painkillers.

During the final night of the cruise there was a fancy-dress party. Sia went as a princess, Myles a magician, and the ship's staff turned my wheelchair and me into Batman driving his Batmobile. It was the only happy memory of what was an otherwise difficult trip for all of us.

I turned six in 1981 and late that year I started to outgrow the rods in my legs, which were starting to come through my heels. The braces around my legs became tight and I was developing pressure sores in and around the sides of them. It was obvious that a redesign was needed and that another operation loomed.

More surgery meant another journey to America and more time away from the family. Luckily there were still funds from the Vermont Lions Club. It was decided that I would see the school year out in Australia and head back to America in January 1982. This time Dad would stay home with Sia and Myles, and Mum would come with me. I didn't know it but I was also about to meet a man who would change my world forever.

CHAPTER 6

Where do you go when you die?

I won't bore you with the details of the next operation in San Francisco or our stay at Ronald McDonald House again, been there done that and bought the T-shirt. All I need to tell you is that Dr Bleck sliced and diced, inserted new rods into my legs and I was in plaster for twelve weeks. This time there were no run-ins with deranged caretakers, so that was one good thing.

There was another great thing, though. I was given the opportunity to take part in the Make a Wish program while I was in plaster. After my last trip I had become a mad San Francisco 49ers NFL fan, so I told them my wish was to meet 49ers Quarterback Joe Montana.

The Make a Wish people went one better than that! They organised for the whole 49ers team to visit me at the hospital and I spent the day talking with all the players. It was a dream come true for me back then but I am kicking myself now that I didn't ask to meet Luke Skywalker. That would have been awesome!

Nothing Make a Wish could have done would have been as life-changing as the other significant meeting that happened on this trip.

Back in Australia, I'd been on TV quite a few times to raise money for these trips and raise awareness for children with disabilities. People had started to notice. Mum and Dad had been approached by a number of different media, including a young director named Aviva Ziegler who was producing a set of documentaries for one of Australia's premium journalists, Mike Willesee. Mike had made his name on the ABC's *This Day Tonight* and *Four Corners* and then he'd moved over to commercial television and was one of the stars of both Channel Nine and Channel Seven at different times.

Aviva and Mike knew about my latest trip to America and had discussed with my father the idea of doing a documentary about my life and my journey to try and walk for the first time, which my mother was hoping would happen after this latest operation.

When I was asked whether or not I would like to do the documentary I was unsure, and said so. I had been going through a lot for a six-year-old. By the time I was seven I'd already seen many of my childhood friends die from leukaemia and other types of cancers. Living in a place like Ronald McDonald House means you have support and you make friends but all the kids are sick, some desperately so. Not everyone gets out alive. It was a very sad and dark time and I already grasped that being in a documentary would mean a film crew following me around even when I wasn't feeling good or when something bad had happened. My mother framed the idea by saying that by taking part I would be helping lots of other disabled children because I'd bring awareness to the struggles that people with disabilities go through. I guess that swayed me because, before I knew it, Aviva arrived in San Francisco.

It was about three months into our stay. Mum and I had developed our routines and we were pretty quiet. I watched a lot of TV and movies and we didn't talk a lot. Aviva was like a whirlwind, she was loud, talked all the time, and would ask me a mountain of what I think now are quite adult questions, which I didn't feel very comfortable answering.

A week later Mike Willesee and his camera crew arrived and began filming. The term documentary by definition is to document real life; however, I quickly learned that most of a documentary is set up, rehearsed and acted out. They would get me to talk with Mike up and down hallways, go shopping with him and have 'impromptu' chats. Each time it would be rehearsed and we would do it from two or three different angles. If I said something cute or funny that wasn't recorded, they would ask me to do it again with the same energy and enthusiasm as I had originally.

Initially this was fun. I established a great connection with the cameraman, Brian Doyle, and he would teach me how the camera worked and would motivate me if I was low on energy. But it didn't take long before any fun faded and everything felt repetitive, false and annoying, especially when I was having to film in-between schoolwork and physio, when all I wanted to do was play with my friends or watch TV.

Mike and I had trouble establishing a connection with each other. He was a very serious man and he didn't seem to know how to get to the level of a seven-year-old and ask age-appropriate questions. He was asking me things like what did I want to do, what did I want to be when I grew up, was it important that I was in San Francisco? I had enough trouble thinking about how I'd cope with the next day. After a while, I didn't want to talk to him at all so I'd deliberately make every interview as difficult as possible. I'd give one-word answers, ignore questions and become easily distracted. He probably thought I was a little shit, but I was just a kid and I wanted to be left alone.

I told Mum that I wanted them all to leave, that I didn't want to be part of their documentary, that she should tell them to get on a plane and go home.

Dad called me and asked if I had a problem so I told him what was bothering me. His response was that I had to be a good soldier, to have courage to fix my bayonet, face the front and do what he'd asked, which meant sucking it up, taking part in the documentary and being more accommodating.

The next scene that was filmed was just outside a school room, the second whilst I was having lunch and the third and final one in the garden of the children's hospital. I knew the locations and they told me what was going to happen but no one prepared me for the actual questions.

The first interview was harmless but during the second one Mike asked where my friends went when they died, what I thought would happen if I died and how important it was for me to succeed whilst in America. *What the . . . ?*

If you watch the footage you'll think I answered the questions in a cute, charismatic, childish way but as an adult looking back at his childhood self I think that the questions Mike asked were highly inappropriate. To this day, I think 'How dare he!' Why would you ask a seven-year-old boy, going through the biggest struggle of his life, aware of friends dying around him, about mortality, God, death and what heaven is like? Wouldn't it have been better to let the child be a child and allow him to go through these struggles privately, with parental support and without having to focus on these dark thoughts? I am sure I thought about death and dying at the time but I didn't want to confront these fears on camera. It still makes me angry and I guess I am angry with my parents, too, for allowing me to be in that situation, even though it was with good intentions.

Whilst all this filming was going on, I was back with Wally Motloch getting fitted into a new set of leg braces and a brand new walking frame. I would also go to see the physiotherapist, Barbara, once a day for an hour and a half and she would exercise my legs, core muscles and balance so that my small body was fit enough to take its first steps. To say my time, energy and patience were stretched was an understatement.

It wasn't just the questions or the shadowing that were the problem with being part of the documentary. At one point, Aviva thought it would be a great idea for me to be filmed listening to the motivational tapes that my father recorded and sent over for me whilst I was in the bath. I was not comfortable with this at all. I didn't want strangers like Aviva, Brian and Mike seeing me naked. Not to mention the thought of my penis appearing on camera for all of Australia to see. They assured me and my mum that my penis would not be filmed.

Aviva also thought it would be a great idea to get footage of my mum and me riding on a cable car in San Francisco. During part of the filming, Brian slipped over and his leg went under the cable car. Mum kept a hold of me with one hand and reached out and grabbed Brian with the other so he wasn't crushed to death. He ended up with a large gash to his leg and it was all pretty traumatic.

The final interview between Mike and me will always be the most memorable because instead of treating me as an adult he finally came down to my level and made the interview fun for a kid. He started off by saying, 'I've interviewed about eight prime ministers and you're harder than all of them put together.' He turned it into a game. If I gave a good answer I'd get a point, if I gave a bad answer I would lose a point. If I got five points we would go to the toy store and I could pick whatever I wanted.

Finally, he understood. Mike got the interview he wanted and I got a Hans Solo Star Wars Blaster. Oh yeah!

The last day of filming was long and arduous. I was going through my final fittings with my new braces. This meant constant tweaks, and after about ten hours of me crying and whingeing because I was an overtired seven-year-old, Wally and Mum presented me with the final set of braces. They were designed so that I could bend my knees whenever I wanted to. I could finally sit in a chair the same way as an everyday boy, and I could also bend my knees when I needed to walk.

The new walking frame was ingenious; it had a steering wheel that would propel me forward if I moved it from left to right and walked with it. For safety reasons, the wheels were designed to only ever go forward so there was no chance of me rolling down a hill or somewhere I didn't want to go. They had also shown me how to use my heels and shoes as a brake. I was quite excited about this as it meant that I would finally go through a pair of shoes without growing out of them.

After almost seven months of hard work, surgery, broken bones, training and having an annoying film crew trailing around me, both the goals that Mum had set for this trip had been achieved and the documentary was in the can.

The last moment of filming occurred when I walked out of customs at Melbourne Airport in my new walking frame on my own two feet with no help from anyone and greeted my family. We were all a bit teary. Dad told me how proud he was of me, my sister told me she'd baked cookies for me and Myles just wanted to make sure I didn't have an American accent this time. We were a family unit again and the hope was that I wouldn't need any more surgery for many years to come. The only thing I had to worry about now, besides breaking something, was how the documentary would be received. None of us had any idea how massive it would be.

CHAPTER 7

Hey, aren't you Quentin?

Months passed before we found out the documentary was going to air. For two weeks before it was shown I was pulled out of school so that Mum and I could jump aboard the publicity bandwagon to promote it. Those two weeks are a bit of a blur, going from radio station to radio station around the country. I remember being interviewed by Ita Buttrose, Derryn Hinch and Kerri-Anne Kennerley. Even back then I found radio an interesting medium. It was quick and you got a reaction from people in the studio straightaway and then you were done. No one asked me to redo anything over and over again.

I hadn't been shown any of the documentary during the editing process so all I knew was what I remembered and what I saw during the television commercials. On the night it was to be shown we all gathered around at home as a family to watch it. From the moment it started I hated it. Mike Willesee's first line in the documentary was, 'This may well be the most fragile boy in the world.' To me it meant that there was no one like me, that I was some unique freak of nature, exactly like the kids at school had said. From there it did not progress well. Mike Willesee stated that I was incredibly hard to interview. It was a judgement straightaway. I was seven, recovering from a major operation, and some dude was in my face asking me the same thing over and over again for two weeks at a time. I wasn't an obstructive failed businessman who'd scammed people's money, nor a sportsman dodging questions about bad behaviour. I was a kid!

All that would have been okay, because I didn't really care too much if some old guy thought I was difficult, but it was what came next that freaked me out. The most mortifying thing, and the moment I feared most and had been assured would never happen, happened. In segment four you can see me as naked as the day I was born. My penis in living colour for all to see. Watching with my family, I screamed and then started crying. I knew the kids at school would be watching. Now the kids who bullied me constantly had another weapon. I felt that I had been betrayed by everyone.

Mum and Dad tried to calm me down and told me it wasn't that bad, it was for just a few seconds, blink and you'd miss it. Myles and I knew better. We knew that I'd have to front up to school the next day and suffer the teasing from the kids. My parents said that with any luck not many people would have tuned in. They were wrong again. When the ratings came in they were off the chart – comparable to the ratings for an AFL Grand Final. It was the highest-rating documentary in Australian television history. It's a record which hasn't been broken even thirty-three years after it originally aired. I went from relative anonymity to the most famous seven-year-old in the country in one night. And everyone saw my penis!

The next day at school, people treated me differently. Of course I got teased for 'rocking out with my cock out' on national television but it was more than that. Even the teachers were treating me differently. Suddenly I was no longer just one of the class, I was Quentin, a subject to be discussed as part of the class. Each teacher wanted me to visit their classroom so that they could teach kids about disability, even though I'd been enrolled at the school for years and they'd never asked me about it before. That singling out meant I was even more alienated from everyone else.

It wasn't just at school that I noticed a huge change. On Saturdays I would usually accompany my dad to Forest Hill Shopping Centre in Victoria. The weekend after the documentary was shown, Dad took me to the shops as normal and we were inundated with people wanting to meet me and touch me. Women called me 'a brave little boy', and the men called me 'a little Aussie battler'. I was so overwhelmed by the experience that I was like Justin Bieber on a really bad day. I didn't know what to say or even where to look and Dad had to prompt me to respond. Shopping trips were like that every time for a while and Dad and I learned quickly that he had to watch how people touched me because a couple of times people would shake my hand so hard my fingers fractured.

One time there were so many people coming up to me that Dad and I became separated. I was so scared, I cried and screamed and the centre management suggested that it was perhaps better if Dad did his weekly shopping without me.

The attention didn't stop though. The TV station was inundated with fan mail for me. There were letters and packages from people of all ages. The writers ranged from eighty-year-old pensioners and retirees to whole classrooms of children sending me letters because their teacher had made me part of their lessons. Mum and Dad wanted me to read and reply to each person individually but I just physically couldn't. Mum and the Lions Club's Ron Bromley helped write the letters of thanks.

I didn't understand the emotional responses I was getting. I didn't feel any different than I had before the documentary. I didn't feel extraordinary or brave like so many people were telling me I was. I was just me but now I was trying to get my head around the fact that everyone knew who I was. When you are seven you just want to fit in and now I was even more 'different'.

I don't want to sound like I was ungrateful for people's good wishes. Having people wish you well is a great thing and lots of lovely things happened because of that goodwill.

One of the great things that happened was meeting the McLean family. The McLeans owned a 1600-acre farm called the Susan River Homestead in Maryborough, Queensland, about three and a half hours north of Brisbane. It was a type of 'city slickers' ranch for people who wanted to get out of the city rat-race and learn how to horse ride and muster cattle, as well as waterski and parasail. The McLeans had seen the documentary and Norm McLean and his wife, Faye, got in touch and invited us to visit. My first trip there was pretty eventful. I went out in a speedboat and I loved it. I was urging one of the McLean boys, Scott, to drive faster and faster, and when we hit a break in the wave I went flying into the air and came crashing down with a thud. Oops! I broke my arm that day, but it was probably the most fun I've ever had breaking a bone. While we were there I'd sing and dance as part of the evening entertainment and one of the songs I used to sing was 'The Rainbow Connection' by Kermit the Frog.

Spending time with the McLeans was awesome but when I got back home the intensity of all the media attention was so overwhelming that I started not wanting to go out in public at all. My cousins, Mark, Felicity and Stephanie, visited more regularly so I didn't have to go out and I loved that.

I probably shouldn't say I had a favourite cousin, but I did. As a child, Felicity, whom we called Sissy, was my best friend (apart from Myles). She was a few years older than I was and I loved her to pieces. Felicity was the one person I could really talk to about anything. She knew how to hug me in a way that made me feel loved but didn't break my ribs. One of our favourite games was for me to lie on top of a sleeping bag so she could drag me along the floor all over the house. She would then lie down next to me and hug me while we talked for hours.

At the age of seven I was sure that Felicity and I would grow up and get married. Eventually Mum sat me down and told me why I had to put all thoughts of marriage between Felicity and me aside. I was completely grossed out and I spent a good hour psyching myself up to tell Felicity that we couldn't get married after all. She took it very well but I was devastated.

A few months later, the documentary *Quentin* was nominated for a *TV Week* Logie Award. Mum and Dad were so happy. The media was their world, so it was a big deal for them. Despite the fact that I was still unnerved around heaps of people, I was happy when I heard that we'd get to go to a huge party. But it didn't pan out as we thought. Neither *TV Week* nor Channel Seven invited us to the awards, so we were relegated to watching it on TV like everyone else. Mike Willesee was hosting the ceremony so even if our show won he wouldn't be the person accepting the award. And with no invite, it wasn't going to be us, either.

That year the most popular drama series was *Sons and Daughters*, Daryl Somers won the Gold Logie and Ray Martin won TV Reporter of the Year. When the single documentary category came up we all closed our eyes and crossed our fingers in anticipation. 'And the winner is . . . *Quentin*, Seven Network.' We cheered in delight and watched as Aviva made her way to the stage. She thanked Mike, the crew, Channel Seven, her friends and family and . . . then walked offstage. She didn't mention me or my family. I looked over to Mum. 'Why didn't she thank me?' My mum's reply said it all. She looked back at the screen and then she burst into tears.

Mike Willesee knew how we must have felt and later that night he rang to apologise. Dad was the only one composed enough to take the call. He told Mike that we were all upset and then got off the phone quickly. A few days later we received a package. In it was a note from Mike Willesee along with the first *TV Week* Logie Award he had ever won. In the message he stated that I could hold on to it until I won my own. I knew what it meant for him to give that statuette to me, and I've had it sitting in a prominent spot in either my room or my home as a reminder to constantly strive for excellence ever since.

After that night, we were all a little more jaded than before. We decided that it would be a good thing for the whole family if I no longer had a media profile. We wanted things to go back to normal . . . or as normal as possible. There were offers for me to be the King of Moomba and various other things but we turned them all down. As far as we were concerned I would soon fade into anonymity once again.

CHAPTER 8

Junk food can't cure everything . . .

Facing yet another operation wasn't exactly the normal life I was hoping for, but at the end of 1983 it was obvious that I was going to need more surgery. I was growing up and Mum noticed one rod was beginning to migrate through one foot. I was also developing a sternum that protruded out way more than it should because my ribs were constantly breaking. We couldn't afford another trip to America. Mum and Dad had to find someone in Australia who could perform the required rodding and also see if they could fix my chest.

After doing a lot of research, they found a surgeon who was quite revered in medical circles around the world. Sir Dennis Paterson lived in Adelaide and said that he would be willing to perform the surgery on my legs but only if I was a resident of South Australia.

This was a big quandary for my family. My father was running a printing business called the Quick Brown Fox in Vermont, Victoria, and both my brother and sister were happy at St James primary with me. To pull up the whole family and move to Adelaide was going to be a huge upheaval. Dad flew to Adelaide with me for a couple of weeks to meet the surgeon and to investigate whether working and living in Adelaide was possible. It turned out it was. Dad could get a job as a journalist at the *Adelaide Advertiser,* the place where he'd started his career forty years earlier, so in his mind it was then only a question of finding a place to live.

My mother was against us all moving. She wanted to find a way to pretend that I lived in South Australia so that I could have the operation but come back to Melbourne after the surgery was done. If that meant Dad and me moving over there for a while then that was what would have to happen. But my father didn't want the family to be apart again and that meant making the move. Mum gave in but she insisted Dad find us a place where she could look out from a window and enjoy the view from her study.

That was it. The decision was made that my father would move to Adelaide before the rest of us. He would secure his job and find us a place to live. My mum would pack up the house, sell everything and move us all. I suspect this was the start of a building anger on Mum's part. To her mind, she was being abandoned to look after three kids, pack up an entire life's worth of memories and dreams, and her work, and sell a house that had been built specifically for us when she didn't even want to leave it. Dad was adamant that this was what we had to do: we had to stay together and I needed the operation. For him it was simple. I don't remember Mum and Dad talking it through with me, Myles and Sia but I am sure they did. Though I doubt what any of us wanted held much weight in the decision. We were just kids!

When we arrived in South Australia, we went to the rented house Dad had found for us in Belair, about a twenty-minute drive from the centre of Adelaide in the southern foothills. As soon as my mother saw the house she flipped out, screaming she hated it. The truth was, we all hated it, especially me! It had steps, so none of the rooms were wheelchair accessible, which meant I had to sit on the floor or sit on the couch in whatever room I was in or be in my room or on my bed; there was no way for me to get in or out on my own. I was back to relying on everyone, all the time.

The tension between Mum and Dad was about to get worse. As the house had so many steps, it was going to be difficult for me to come home every night with lots of plaster on my legs and the huge wheelchair that I'd need while I recovered and rehabilitated, so it was decided that I'd do my rehabilitation and respite at the Regency Park Centre for the Young Disabled. This was a residential and rehabilitation place built in the 1970s for children with mild to severe disabilities (both physical and intellectual), whose issues made it difficult for them to live at home with their families. When the subject was first discussed with me, my parents and the doctor pitched it as though it would be one giant holiday – I'd be going off to camp, have surgery and then rehabilitate with all these wonderful new friends I'd get to know and hang out with. I can't say I was happy about it, but it didn't sound too bad so I didn't kick up a fuss. I was oblivious to the fact that it would become the most harrowing ordeal of my entire life and the one thing that has caused me the most angst and psychological damage. If only I'd known . . . but then, what could I have done?

As always before the surgery my parents let me go to my favourite takeaway place, which at the time was Kentucky Fried Chicken, and eat to my heart's content. The next day I went under the knife and had rods placed in both my legs. In the past, Dr Bleck would break my legs and insert the rods into the two halves, but Sir Dennis used an image intensifier and utilised a different procedure. Instead of breaking both my legs first, he drilled through my feet and inserted the rods into the tibia, then broke my legs and inserted and straightened the rods through there. Because of this technique I also needed a skin graft, so I had skin shaved off my left hip and placed on both heels. (Some people have lovingly come to call me butt feet because I literally have skin from my bum growing on my heels.) I stayed in the hospital for three weeks recovering and then it was time to have surgery on my chest.

You know that tension between my parents I mentioned? Well it was about to go nuclear. Again, Mum and Dad had done their research and my father had concluded that this surgery on my chest would kill me and he didn't want it to go ahead. My mother, on the other hand, was of the opinion that no one would accept me with a giant bone sticking out of my chest and so it was a risk that had to be taken. My mother won the battle, and the procedure was performed by another surgeon.

Dr Brown was quite a genius at what he did and I believe I was the first person in the world to have this particular procedure done. Basically it entailed chopping my breast-bone or sternum out, pushing my ribs together and then creating a new sternum from the existing bone that had been removed and grafting it to a new one.

While Mum was right and the actual surgery didn't kill me, the after-effects very nearly did. I developed a blood infection and spiked a dangerously high temperature. In order to get my temperature down, the nurses covered me in ice. I was placed on a life-support system and had to wait until the infection was brought under control. I was in a coma that lasted for three weeks. At the end of the first week, my heart stopped and, just as my dad had feared, I died. I apparently lay dead on the table for six minutes.

People often ask me if I saw something when I was dead. Did I see myself being drawn towards a white light? Well, the answer is yes, I did see something. I saw myself rising out of my body, looking down on my cold lifeless self and then turning to see a bunch of bright coloured lights. I didn't want these lights to appear. To me they were evil and dark and pulling me towards them. At this point the shock of a defibrillator went through my heart for the first time and I was drawn partly back into my body, then a second shock and I was back in my body and my heart started beating.

I don't remember much more but a couple of days later I heard my family talking to me. Sia promised to bake biscuits for me. Myles said he would share all his Lego with me. My mother just cried and apologised, saying she should have never let this happen. Strangely enough, my dad read the newspaper to me; maybe that's the only thing he knew how to do, and it was his way of coping. I suddenly woke up. My ribs were broken, I was incredibly sore, but I was completely and utterly starving and the doctors and nurses thought that was a good sign. They told my parents they should get me exactly what I wanted, which was pizza. Back then junk food was my cure for everything!

As I improved, the doctors encouraged me to do a lot of deep breathing exercises to help my lungs and ribs expand. My parents thought that the best way to do that would be through laughter. Dad sneaked me in a video of Robin Williams performing live. It was full of dirty jokes and some swear words I hadn't heard before. I can say now that this is why I have a dirty mind and a wicked sense of humour. Well, that's my excuse and I'm sticking to it.

When I was well enough I was transferred to the Regency Park Centre for the Young Disabled. I moved into villa six. There were six villas in all. Number six and number five were where the junior kids went, the kids under ten, the ones who needed more care and probably more parenting because their parents weren't around. For the first few days I didn't mind it so much; the nurses were nice to me and I kept to myself pretty well. But it didn't take long for things to change. I was 'Quentin the famous kid' who was famous for nothing other than being disabled, and a lot of the other disabled kids at the centre weren't too happy about me being there. As far as they were concerned, I was the arrogant little shit on TV they'd grown to hate and they weren't shy in letting me know. They started to ram my wheelchair and tell me how much they disliked me. They said if I got out of line they would ram my wheelchair until it no longer worked.

After it kept happening I called my parents to complain, but they told me it was just kids being kids and I should get over it. The house parents and the nurses said the same, so I tried to suck it up and get over it. It didn't make the days very pleasant though.

Bedtime at the centre was 7.30 pm, which to me was ridiculous. I was used to going to bed at 9 pm back home so it took me quite a while to get used to the new bedtime but at least it meant I was safe from people ramming me.

The actual school part wasn't great either. The classes were combined, meaning there was no grade one or six, we were all grouped together in a couple of classrooms. We were given reading books and an age-appropriate curriculum. The teachers had to deal with kids with very different intellects and different abilities, so there was not a lot of learning going on. I didn't find it very challenging at all. I would spend class waiting for recess or lunch so that I could get out into the courtyard first and race around pretending that my wheelchair was some kind of souped-up car. Or I would go out to the basketball court and pretend that I was the American basketballer Kareem Abdul-Jabbar sinking dunks which I could never truly do on my own.

I would have physio twice a day, in the morning and in the afternoon. It would be strength training in the morning and balancing in the afternoon, meaning that the physiotherapists would get me to work on my legs and upper body in the morning, and in the afternoon I would be stood up, with my plaster on, in a frame for thirty minutes so that I could get used to bearing weight on my legs as quickly as possible. That went on for about six to eight weeks until the plaster came off. My heels were still all gummy and nasty from the skin graft and you could clearly see where the drill had gone through. I looked like a burns patient. All my muscles had atrophied, so I wasn't able to walk on them straightaway, let alone lift them up on my own. The only thing I had going for me was that my stomach muscles had strengthened and I was able to sit up pretty well on my own.

After the plaster came off, it was decided that I would stay at Regency Park for another three months full-time so that I could continue my rehabilitation. But this time the staff wanted me to begin hydrotherapy. I don't think I had been in a pool by myself in my entire life, so the idea of having hydrotherapy three times a week scared me.

I was lucky enough to get a swimming teacher named June Jordon, or Jordy for short. She taught me to swim with floaties and flippers first, and then slowly but surely I learned to stand and walk in a shallow pool alone. I would hold onto a walking bar, stand upright and walk up and down the swimming pool on my own. I hated the idea of swimming without floaties, but Jordy would constantly try and get me to lay my head back and backstroke without them on. I would instantly turn into a stone rather than a fish and I usually sank to the bottom of the swimming pool. I'd cough and splutter and get water in my lungs and end up puking straight afterwards. None of that worried Jordy and she continued valiantly trying to get me to swim independently.

By the beginning of 1985 I was ready to go home. The plan was for me to start school with Myles and Sia at Belair Primary. It had been pretty lonely and isolating at Regency Park and I missed my family. I wasn't so sure all of them had missed me, though.

CHAPTER 9

Where's a pair of ruby slippers when you need them?

I hadn't seen my parents very much for months because they didn't visit often, so to say I had lost some rapport with them was an understatement. Things weren't good between them either so it was all a bit strained. My relationship with Myles and Sia picked up where we'd left off and that was a good thing.

Coming home to a house with no ramps and steps in-between levels one and two meant that one of my parents had to pick me up and take me downstairs to the family room every morning, where the television was, and back up to my bedroom every night. This was fine in the morning as my father was the one who would usually carry me downstairs, but the evening was another story.

In the time I'd been away Mum and Dad's bickering had intensified. They were angry with each other and at night they'd both have a wine or three which fed their fights and inevitably led to another few drinks. The atmosphere wasn't good but it wouldn't have mattered so much if I didn't need one of them to carry me to bed. After a few trips and a few bumped heads and broken ribs, thirteen-year-old Myles took it upon himself to relieve them both of that burden and he became the one who would carry me up and down the stairs. It was unfair and a big responsibility for a boy who had just entered his teenage years.

My mother had been asked to write a book about my life. It was really mostly about her and how she'd bravely raised me despite my disability, how she'd discovered the best surgery for me and how I'd survived until the age of ten because of Mum and Dad. I know my parents had done a lot for me, and that my disability put a strain on finances and emotions, but there wasn't anything I could do about that. A huge press tour was arranged around the book's release. But they didn't just want my mum on tour, they needed me to go too. I was sent out to answer questions about living with a disability and how I had enjoyed my life thus far. I was so glad to finally be home, I didn't want to go out and face another media circus, especially after the kids' animosity towards me at the centre.

I was (and still am) angry with my mum and dad because we had decided it was better for me to step out of the spotlight. All that changed when I believed it meant furthering my mother's career.

I quickly became the poster child for disability inspiration, the brave little boy who fought to survive. Inspiring people is not a bad thing (I hope I am doing it with this book) but I was pissed off that I didn't have any choice in whether I participated or not. My parents just expected that I would do what they needed to sell Mum's book.

I did what I was told. I was interviewed on the radio again, there were multiple stories about me in newspapers and I went on *The Midday Show* with Ray Martin. It was our first meeting and immediately I knew Ray was different from other journalists. He didn't speak condescendingly to me. He didn't treat me as just a story. He treated me with a level of warmth and sincerity I hadn't found in anyone else, not even Mike Willesee. I finished the interview and that respect for Ray Martin has stayed with me for many years. I didn't know that he would become one of the most important people I would meet in my life, and that day was the start of a longstanding friendship.

After the media circus was all over it was time to head back to Adelaide and for me to start school at Belair Primary. The school had never had a child with a wheelchair or with a disability before, so the staff were a little unaccustomed to it. I made friends easily and my main memories are about how to play marbles, how to cheat at marbles and how to pelt a marble from the height of my wheelchair at another small one far, far away. Not such a money-spinning talent, but a skill nevertheless.

Unfortunately, because I was the first disabled kid they'd dealt with at Belair, as soon as a problem arose the teachers would freak out and the school principal or secretary would ring my mother to come and pick me up. After the first few times, Mum found these calls infuriating. I get it. She was trying to squeeze her writing career around school hours and having to come and pick me up all the time was not part of the deal. On the drive home she'd make it pretty clear she was annoyed and then she'd sit me in front of the TV and tell me not to disturb her until Dad got home from work at the *Advertiser*. I loved it because I would watch movies like *Rambo*, *Bugsy Malone* and *Star Wars* over and over again. I was learning more about cinema and I would absorb the movies like a piece of bread soaking up gravy.

When Dad came home he'd help me go to the loo, as Mum was busy. He sometimes ended up cooking dinner while Mum was being 'creative' in her study. We would then eat as a family and if there was one rule in our house, it was that the TV was switched off and we would all try and discuss our day. That was the theory. The reality was Geoff and Kerry would talk about work, and either the problems he had at the paper or how she was trying to find an original angle for an article. Myles, Sia and I wouldn't say much and gradually my parents' conversation would turn into an argument that would go on for hours.

Myles would usually tuck me into bed and, on rare occasions, Mum and Dad would come and do the Joan Crawford act – tiptoeing into our bedrooms, asking us individually how much we loved them. I found it quite horrifying, and I could smell the alcohol on their breaths. I don't understand their insecurity because they already had our unconditional love.

After about twelve weeks, Mum finally received one call too many from Belair Primary. When she picked me up she was furious and told me she couldn't take the constant distractions anymore.

The next morning as I lay in bed I overheard my parents having a huge argument.

A little later my dad walked into my bedroom. I was scared at what was coming but shocked at what he said. He told me that he and my mother had put so much of their lives aside for me for the last ten years that they had forgotten who they were as a couple, they had forgotten who they were as parents and they had forgotten who they were as individuals. Something had to be done. Dad told me that I had to make the sacrifice and go to the Regency Park Centre for the Young Disabled again. But this time I wasn't going to be visiting. I had to stay. I was to be there five days a week but would come home every weekend. There was no song to soften that message.

I didn't understand what I had done, why I was being pushed away. Dad explained it as if I was going to boarding school, a magical place where I would get to make new friends, but I wasn't buying it. I had already stayed at the centre so I knew what the place was like and knew how people were treated. It was an institution for disabled people, it wasn't a nice place. It was horrible.

I still remember that first night back at Regency Park. I didn't have just a few clothes with me this time. I had a full suitcase with my battery charger and a couple of toys. I remember Dad saying goodbye and telling me that it wouldn't be permanent, that he'd get Mum to change her mind so that I could come home.

At first I was allowed to call home every day. I would tell Mum and Dad about my day and ask about theirs, but it became too painful for them to keep talking to me. So once a day became once every other day and then eventually not at all.

Dad would pick me up on Friday evening and they would drop me back at the centre on a Sunday night. The place was terrible. If I didn't eat my vegetables every night I was either force-fed them or my wheelchair would be strapped to the table and I wouldn't be allowed to leave until I had eaten them. That was fine if you enjoyed the food, but most of it was boiled and horrible. I remember being force-fed brussels sprouts on more than one occasion. Even now if I see or smell them, or even get a hint that they're near, I get a lump in my throat as if I'm going to vomit.

When I went home on the weekends there wasn't much for me to do. Myles had soccer practice on Saturdays and Sia had started a childhood modelling career as she was (and still is) a very beautiful young woman. Mum dropped Myles at soccer practice. Dad took Sia to modelling school, leaving me at home alone with Mum. She'd be locked away in her study and I'd be instructed not to disturb her, which left me once again in front of the TV watching cartoons with our little chihuahua, Pepper. It would be okay when Myles came home because then I had someone to talk to. We'd play games and we'd watch WWF professional wrestling. He would playfully (and very carefully) pretend to body slam me on the couch or give me soft clotheslines or elbow drops. He would be the Iron Sheik and I'd be Hulk Hogan, or he would be 'Macho Man' Randy Savage and I'd be Ricky 'The Dragon' Steamboat. One night we were allowed to stay up and watch *Wrestle Mania*. We both loved the spectacle of WWF with all the pomp and ceremony, and I'm still a fan. But it was also a way of bonding with Myles, a way of having a continuing relationship with him.

After a few weekends of coming home and having to fit my presence around everyone's commitments, Mum and Dad thought it would be best if I stayed at Regency Park full-time and came home only for school holidays. I know my dad felt guilty about this, because he arrived out of the blue one morning and took me out for a day of what he called 'you and me'. As we drove away from Regency Park he said I could do whatever I wanted. My dad had never done this before.

Dad had to make a quick stop at the *Advertiser* and it was the first time I'd seen his office. It was amazing: typewriters every-where, new computers and old journos with cigarettes hanging out their mouths. Dad introduced me to a journalist by the name of Shirley Stott Despoja, whose daughter happened to be there on the same day, a beautiful sixteen-year-old named Natasha Stott Despoja, who would become an impressive Australian politician.

Once we finished at the office, I suggested that we go to the movies. My dad had only ever taken me to the movies once, to see *Star Wars* when I was about three years of age. He said I could pick whatever movie I wanted, and I picked *Gremlins*.

The childhood film about cute Mogwai suddenly turned into a horror movie about gremlins and scared the living crap out of me. Dad didn't like it but he sat through it and then took me to McDonald's afterwards. It was quite a day. As he dropped me back to the centre he shed a tear as he said goodbye and gave me a huge hug. He knew the sacrifice I was making for the sake of his marriage and I knew that he hated to let me go. It was pretty emotional and he told me, 'I just can't bear to lose her Quentin. I'm sorry.' Then he drove home and I was on my own.

For weeks on end I would not hear from them or see them. I became my own person, with no real parental control other than a house parent. Everyone has heard stories about places like the centre and, let me tell you, those stories are true. If you were weak, you were vulnerable. I had to stand on my own two feet (so to speak) and I became brash and arrogant to protect myself. People at the centre had judged me as someone who thought he was better than everyone else because I was on TV. I didn't think that at all, but after a while I started to act the way they expected. If that's what people were going to think of me, then sure, why not? I wasn't afraid anymore. I wasn't afraid to stand up for myself, I wasn't afraid to talk back to people, I wasn't afraid to do my own thing. No one else was looking out for me so I had to do it myself.

I was belligerent and nasty and talked back to the nurses, house parents and the other kids. If the kids rammed my wheelchair, then to hell with it I would ram them back, and I had a bigger, stronger wheelchair than they did. Pretty soon it was known that you didn't mess with Quentin unless you wanted to get your wheelchair smashed around. It wasn't as if they didn't try and hurt me either, but I was in a full-body brace covered in plastic. You can't mess with that.

There were other ways though and they found them.

Despite the book tour being over, Mum and Dad were still getting interview requests. Apparently everyone wanted to see another interview with me and Mike Willesee. It was the beginning of the 'chequebook journalism' era in Australia so Dad, knowing how popular the doco had been, asked for an appearance fee and Channel Nine was very happy to pay.

I was taken out of Regency Park Centre and brought home for a few days. I hated my parents at the time because they'd left me in that place alone, but I had to suck it up and pretend we were all happy families and that my mother and father were both good parents. I didn't think they were.

My mother had a penchant for my hair long. She said I looked like Beethoven when the reality was it was matted and knotted at the back. I thought it looked like a damn mess, but when Mike Willesee turned up we all put our smiles on. I answered his questions as well as I could, and 'the star Quentin' reappeared for a short time. My dad told me that the fee I earned would go into an account with other money that I had received. He and Mum opened up a bank trust fund and deposited the fee there. Once the interview was over and the film crew were gone, I went back to Regency Park.

It was the weirdest time because most days I was stuck in this horrible place trying to look after myself and then something completely surreal would happen. During one particular interview I had said that I wanted to go onto *Young Talent Time*. Somehow Johnny Young heard about this and he invited me onto the show to sing with all of the team. I wanted to do it, but I was nervous at the same time. My mother suggested that I sing 'The Rainbow Connection', because it was a positive, happy song that I used to sing when I was five and watched *The Muppet Movie*. I hadn't minded singing it around the McLeans, but singing it on TV was a little different. I found the song cheesy, but I thought, what the heck, I'd do it. Mum had driven me, Myles and Sia to Melbourne, en route to visit the McLeans in Queensland for a family celebration. We couldn't fit my big electric wheelchair in her small car, so took my smaller wheelchair with us.

Once we arrived in Melbourne, we met everyone at the studio. I was in awe because there was a live audience, a big production crew and all the Young Talent Team – people like Beven Addinsall, Vince Del Tito and . . . Dannii Minogue. We had a rehearsal and I quickly learnt that the Talent Team would pre-record their music and then lip-sync through the show so they had enough breath for the dance numbers.

I wasn't lip-syncing. I was going to have to sing live. I practised and practised and practised. But I didn't realise they had to cut the entire second verse of the song and go straight to the bridge because of time constraints, so when it came to the live recording I lost my way and stuffed up. I had to pick up the song again quickly without looking like too much of a goof. I was mortified and afterwards I was backstage, crying. In one of the breaks, the kids all gathered around and someone came up with an idea to cheer me up: a little game of truth or dare. Now what happened next is disputed by Dannii Minogue but, as it happened, Dannii chose a dare and that dare was to kiss me. I forgot all about messing up the song because at the age of ten my first kiss was with a gorgeous fourteen-year-old Dannii Minogue. My first kiss was with a Minogue sister! Dannii may vehemently deny it happened, but as if I'd ever forget such a monumental moment.

After that, we made the long drive to Queensland to spend some time with the McLeans. I always loved it there but when we drove back to Adelaide I returned to Regency Park. After a few months I started to make some good friends there and, though I went home for Christmas that year, I didn't really hang out with my family a lot. I felt isolated and a burden so I kept to myself in my room. After a little while I asked to be taken back to Regency Park as they had activities for kids who had been left behind on holidays. I thought I'd be better off not hearing my parents argue while Myles had to look after me the whole time.

At the start of the 1986 school year I was given the chance to go to a regular, everyday primary school – Croydon Park Primary. It was a multicultural school with kids with Greek, Italian, Indigenous and Asian heritage all under the same roof. There were no racism issues, no nasty comments, and that inclusive attitude helped make the school a great place for me.

Croydon Park worked in cooperation with Regency Park so a lot of the disabled kids from the centre could go to the school and either stay in a special class or be integrated into the wider classrooms. When we needed to go to the toilet all we had to do was leave the classroom and ask a staff nurse to help us. There was no drama. I was really happy at Croydon Park and it turned out I was quite popular. I had girlfriends and was well known for doing the old 'pash and dash' behind the taps. I also became quite the master (or cheat) at marbles.

But other problems began. I had started to upset quite a few people at Regency Park – older, stronger kids – and one fateful evening I got into a fight with a kid who punched me in the arm and broke it. I screamed. I screamed for hours. At first the centre staff didn't believe that anything was seriously wrong and so they just took me to the infirmary. But when they realised that the pain wasn't going away they called an ambulance and I was taken to hospital.

Usually if your child suffered a broken arm, you'd rush to the hospital to be with him, to comfort him, to take care of him and then to take him home to recover. That's not what happened with me. My mother and father decided that I'd be okay by myself. After all, it wasn't like I hadn't broken an arm before. If anything went wrong, they figured the doctors and nurses would be there to look after me. I was stunned. It was the first time that I had been to hospital in years and my parents didn't bother to show up. How could I think anything other than that they didn't care about me anymore?

That was it. I hated them. I hated them with a passion after that. Everything I had ever thought about them had been a lie; all the good they'd done in my earlier years had been thrown out the window. They didn't come the next day or the day after.

I was taken back to Regency Park Centre and didn't see my parents for a full two weeks. When I did, my father rocked up one Friday night to pick me up and he was obviously drunk and reeked of alcohol. The house parents decided that he was too inebriated to drive and they wouldn't let him take me with him. Dad got angry and said they couldn't stop him, as he was my father. The house parents threatened to call the police and that was it. Dad went home without me.

I didn't mind. I didn't want anything to do with Mum and Dad. It seemed to me that all they cared about were their careers. Mum was a respected travel writer and was jetsetting all over the world. Dad was a lead writer and columnist for the *Advertiser* and he was busy too. Sia and Myles got to stay home with Dad or they stayed with relatives if Mum and Dad were ever away at the same time. I was stuck in Regency Park. I didn't want to talk to my parents on the phone, I didn't want any part of their lives. Not anymore.

CHAPTER 10

The prime minister, the billionaire and me

The thing about families is that they are all dysfunctional. I read a quote somewhere that said 'a dysfunctional family is any family with more than one person in it'. By the time I was eleven I knew my family was not exactly *Brady Bunch* happy. I had a lot of conflicting emotions about my parents. Mum and Dad were still battling each other, which I hated, but I had to admire the way they could put all their angst aside when they needed to step up for a cause.

One afternoon in 1986 my father raced over to Regency Park Centre to pick me up straight after school and take me home. I was still angry with him for not visiting me, among other things, but I wanted to see Sia and Myles. When we got home I saw a copy of the *Advertiser* Mum had left out for me to read. She pointed out an article about how funding for the disabled was about to be cut by the Federal Government. I was a bit 'whatever', but I read it and Mum and Dad explained to me that if the money was taken away, Regency Park Centre would close and a lot of my friends would have no place to go. That made me feel differently and I fired up. I decided I would try and do something. I know I was only eleven but despite being only a kid, I had a media profile and I wanted to do something positive because of that.

I asked if I could call Mike Willesee. When I got hold of Mike, I told him what was going on, how upset I was and what I thought we should do so funding could be restored. Mike listened and together we came up with a great idea: get little Quentin, the 'Great Aussie Battler', on TV duking it out with the then Prime Minister, the Hon. Robert James Lee Hawke.

It didn't take long for Mike to get things happening and the next day my dad and I were flown to Sydney. I appeared on a live TV broadcast with Mike Willesee to discuss the situation. I'd talked through everything with Dad beforehand and he'd helped me understand all the ramifications of the funding cuts and he'd also helped me nut out discussion points. On TV, I was articulate and impassioned because I firmly believed what was happening was wrong. I challenged Prime Minister Hawke to debate me, with him sitting in a wheelchair. It was publicity gold. The most well-known disabled kid in the country taking on the prime minister. You couldn't make it up.

•

After the interview, we got word through Mike that the prime minister wanted to have a chat with me alone, over the phone, and so Dad and I went back to the studio. I was placed in a big boardroom with a couple of toys to play with by myself. After about thirty minutes, a huge, towering man walked through the door. He looked at me. I looked at him. He said gruffly, 'Do you know who I am?'

I did. I said, 'You're Mr Kerry Packer, sir.'

'That's right,' he replied and then he asked, 'Do you know what I do here, son?'

I said, 'You own everything.'

He laughed. 'Very good kid, I like you. I think we'll keep you round for a while.' Then he said goodbye and left the room.

At the time I didn't think much of the encounter. A little while later, I went down to the studio to talk to Bob Hawke on the phone.

I was so nervous. As far as I was concerned he ran the entire world. I picked up the phone and the PM's secretary or security person told me that they would be recording the conversation. I said that I didn't really care, but fair enough. Then the prime minister got on the phone and asked me first off if the whole thing was a publicity stunt. I told him it wasn't, of course. I explained that I didn't understand why money for disabled kids and disabled people was being taken away. He tried to explain that in every fiscal year, changes are made to a budget and that the government takes some things from column A and gives them to column B and then, after a while, they reinstate that money back to column A. This time around column A impacted on disabled people. I asked him if that meant services would be cut and people left without support and he assured me that they were just cutting out middle management and not hurting the people who received actual care. I didn't believe him. We to-ed and fro-ed for about ten minutes, then we said goodbye.

I was immediately rushed downstairs to the studio. 'He asked me if I was doing a publicity stunt,' I told Mike Willesee on air.

Mike said, 'Was it?'

'Of course not,' I said. 'This isn't for me, this is for the other kids like me who need assistance, who need help.' I believed this wholeheartedly; heck, it was my life.

I flew home the next day and went straight back into Regency Park, but I watched *A Current Affair*, or *Willesee* as it was known in those days, and the very next night I found out that Bob Hawke and the Labor Government had decided not to cut funding for the Health Department and disabled people. I was really happy and I hoped I'd helped play a part in that decision.

After that, news crews and journos wanted a reaction from me. I even received a phone call from Sir Joh Bjelke-Petersen, who was the premier of Queensland at the time. I got to go home that weekend and everyone was proud of me, even my mum. She gave up time in her study to spend two days with me. Towards the end of that weekend Mum and Dad sat down with me and said that what had happened meant something, that as a disabled person who appeared on television I had the power to help people. They told me I had a responsibility to use that power as much as I could to give voice and attention to those who were often ignored.

At first I was more than willing to do this. I became the face of the Crippled Children's Association and the face of Regency Park Centre for the Young Disabled. Even though I knew abuse and bad behaviour occurred at the centre, by both staff and kids, I kept on smiling and waving for every photo and interview. I was even on the cover of the *White Pages* in 1986, quite a feat as far as I was concerned – me and Fat Cat (the TV character) right on the cover.

It was around that time when I found out that to own an electric wheelchair in South Australia you needed a licence to drive it. I thought this was absolutely stupid. You didn't need a licence to walk and my wheelchair wheels were my legs, so I didn't see why I or anyone else should need a licence to use them. Dad explained to me that with a licence came third party insurance so if I hurt or hit anyone with my wheelchair I would be covered.

Even so, it still felt like a compulsory licence discriminated against all disabled people. You didn't need a licence to ride a pushbike or skateboard, and you could hit people with them as well. Licences cost money, and meant time and visits to a motor registry, which would be too hard for some disabled people. I decided to 'run' the eleven-kilometre fun run marathon to the 1987 Glendi Festival as a protest against the licence regulation.

At the time, my mother was the public relations officer for Glendi in Adelaide, the biggest Greek cultural festival in the Southern Hemisphere.

On the day of the marathon, I lined up with everyone else and raced off, but my wheelchair was relatively slow and I steadily fell behind. After a while the police ordered me off the road and out of the race. I was mortified. But then the officers changed their minds and I was given a police escort to finish the race. Despite their change of heart, I still felt like a nuisance. I realised the reality was I had very little power and only had a voice when others allowed me to speak.

After that, I kept on as the face of the Crippled Children's Association for a while, but it seemed the fundraising events that I was involved in weren't funnelling money back to the grass-roots, the people I thought needed it, but rather to the increasing infrastructure and wages of the executives in charge. I don't begrudge anyone being paid for hard work but I wasn't sure research trips and large office spaces were helping kids like me. Ah, the 1980s, where the rich got richer and the disabled people went without. Actually, now I think about it, the more things change the more things stay the same.

•

The next few years settled into a pattern of intermittent visits home but then suddenly, in early 1988 when I was thirteen, Mum and Dad's attitude to my absence changed. I knew the guilt of leaving me at Regency Park weighed heavily on Dad but it seemed Mum started to feel the same. They also discovered that a bus drove kids from Regency Park to their homes, so I could be picked up and dropped off from school to my house every day. This made their decision to bring me home much easier.

I'd always assumed that I would go to Croydon High School with my friends, but my parents had other plans. They thought that I had become a little bit belligerent. I'd started spiking my hair and had a rat's tail. I'd pierced my ear and I didn't mind cursing back to them whenever I felt the need. In their eyes, I'd become a little bogan and they wanted me to clean up my act. They decided that I would follow Myles and go to Mercedes College, a prim and proper secondary school that only rich people went to. I guess we could afford it.

Leaving Croydon Park Primary was one of the hardest things I had ever done, and that is saying something! I'd made so many wonderful friends. Not to mention the girls who had kept me company behind the taps. Saying goodbye to everyone was tough. The teachers had also been good to me at that school. They'd known how to give us individual attention and how to spend time with each and every one of us. Even in a classroom with thirty or forty kids, I never felt left out. I remember crying on my last day, hugging everyone and promising that somehow we would keep in touch. Sadly, I didn't. When I got home, still visibly upset, my mother and father said that part of my life was over. It was time to move on.

CHAPTER 11

Playing the cards you're dealt

Well, we're ten chapters in and it's all been pretty dark, but my life was filled with a lot of pain back then. I'd spent a great deal of time either in hospitals or institutions and it was very lonely at times. But for every Yin there is a Yang. For every bit of darkness there are beams of light which poke through.

Despite the pain of my operations and the hurt of my parents leaving me at Regency Park, I also had some amazing experiences. It was never lost on me that I was doing some incredible things at a young age. By the time I was ten I had travelled some of the world, I'd met famous people and been in and out of radio and TV stations. For a while, at age eleven, I had my own Adelaide radio program. I'd even met a billionaire in Kerry Packer. You don't meet men like him very often.

What I didn't know about that brief conversation was that after I talked to Mr Packer, my dad, Mike Willesee and Kerry Packer had a meeting and I was signed to a deal where I would appear on a Channel Nine show every year from the age of eleven to the age of eighteen and I'd be paid well for doing so. Loyalty was a big thing with Kerry Packer. He could see I was bringing in viewers and that meant ratings (ratings and making money were also important to him) and he thought I should be rewarded for appearing only on the Nine network. Whenever Channel Nine needed a ratings boost, or whenever viewers wanted to know what was going on with my life, they would get a dose of Quentin. I would be rolled out on this show or that and I would explain what I was doing at that point in my life. It was kind of cool, actually. I was flown to Sydney every now and then, put up in a fancy hotel, and then I would spend twenty minutes being interviewed. I met people like Kerri-Anne Kennerley and Jimmy Barnes, and other Channel Nine personalities.

Being at home with my family again was good. I haven't spoken much about my sister Sia because it was hard when she was little for me to relate to her (and also because she didn't want to be mentioned in this book very much) but, when I was thirteen, our relationship changed. Sia and I were both home from school one day, faking being sick. The midday movie was *Beaches* and Sia and I watched it while we ate frozen cheesecake until we both really were sick.

One of the characters in *Beaches* is CC Bloom and for some reason I started calling Sia CC. It is still my pet name for her, little CC, the one who has the smile that blooms but who could also call a spade a shovel and give as good as she got. That's my sister!

After our *Beaches* cheesecake binge, we'd sing songs together and I'd help Sia choreograph dance numbers. Of course Sia and I fought a lot and she would whack me across the head with magazines and things, but I will always have a special place in my heart for her.

While I have a lot of angst, anger and resentment towards my parents, there is still a lot of love, too. They kept me alive, fed and protected me, and they also taught me a lot as well. My dad once said to me, 'Son, you don't have legs, you don't have strength, so you're never going to be able to do regular things like other kids do, but what I am going to teach you is how to be confident, how to stand tall, and how to stay strong. I'm going to teach you how to go into a room, work out who the most important person is and then work out how to steal the show from them, command attention, become a leader.' And my mum was tenacious, which rubbed off on me. That and the fact she was always correcting our grammar and spelling, making sure we spoke 'correct' English. After a while Myles, Sia and I knew how to speak properly, but we would often say 'ain't' instead of 'isn't' or 'carn't' instead of 'cannot' just to infuriate her and also make her laugh despite herself.

She said to me early on: 'I cannot give you legs on which to walk. But I will try to give you wings of imagination and creativity on which to fly.'

One of the things of which I was most proud was when Mum became a published children's author. She created a book called *Red and the Heron Street Gang* that was loosely based on her childhood in Mildura, Victoria. It was a really good book. The publishers had loved it. Another book she wrote was called *By Lexie Roberts*. It was about a young girl who was an aspiring writer. She had to deal with her crazy parents while becoming a successful romance novelist. Mum wrote it in three days. That's right, three days. She had this flash of inspiration driving back from Victoria, where she'd been to instruct Western district students how to write. Mum is a qualified teacher and remains so in South Australian adult education. She burst through the door telling us that she'd had an idea for a book and that the thousands and thousands of words were just on the tip of her fingertips and she couldn't wait to get them down on a computer.

I'd never seen such determination before, such ability to have a command of the English language so readily available. Mum locked herself into her study and when she came out she read the first chapter to us. It wasn't like any of her other books. *By Lexie Roberts* was mesmerising. It was like watching someone create a fairytale and I was there to see it happen. We'd sit waiting by the door until Mum had finished the next chapter and read it to us. It was so good. When she finished the story, she sent it off to the publisher and we all crossed our fingers hoping that, like us, they agreed it was a magnificent book. Fortunately, they did, and *By Lexie Roberts* was soon published. In my opinion it's one of the best children's novels I have ever read. Well, maybe not as good as Harry Potter, but it's up there. I own the film rights and have always wanted to make it an Australian coming-of-age drama, but unfortunately I haven't made that happen yet.

•

Every year, whether I was at Regency Park Centre or at home, I'd go to Oakbank Camp after Christmas. The camp was organised by the scouts, and disabled kids would camp out at the Oakbank racecourse with scouts, rovers and venturers (the older scouts). I always went with the Clovelly Park Rovers. The scouts would be allocated to a different child with a disability and they would help look after them for a week. It taught them responsibility and camaraderie and meant they would get to make new friends with people they would never usually have the opportunity to meet. For me, it meant making new friends and having new adventures in a safe environment with people who wanted to spend time with me.

Each year the camp was terrific. We'd play poker and stay up late at night watching movies, we'd go swimming in the Oakbank school pool, we'd race around the Oakbank racecourse, we'd sit in the stands and pretend to watch the horses go by and, if we were lucky enough to get up at 5 am, we could see the horses training for their latest race. The person who ran the camp, a guy named Jack, would walk to our tents every morning and say, 'Wakey, wakey, hands off snakey. You've had your sleep, you've had your time, time to get up and don't start a whine.' That was his call for everyone to get into gear. Aside from learning how to play poker and blackjack, the camp taught me how to make friends with people who were different to me. I started going at the age of ten and kept going until I was eighteen. On my last year I became a camp leader and helped the scouts run everything.

The last event of the camp every year was to have a water fight with the Oakbank Fire Department. The fireys would turn up with a full truck, hoses, backpacks full of water, water pistols and bag after bag of water bombs. If you get an electric wheelchair wet it's bound to short-circuit, but as kids we didn't care. We filled up those water bombs and water pistols and it was on. Scouts, disabled kids and firemen up against each other in a no-holds-barred water battle that usually lasted about two hours. We would race through the fireys' bombardment on our wheelchairs to see who could survive getting wet, we would pelt water bombs at each other, and blast each other with water pistols until they were empty and then run the gauntlet to refill our guns and bombs.

At the end of the two hours we'd be dripping wet and we'd have little bits of rubber from water bombs plastered all over our bodies. Some wheelchairs would inevitably be short-circuiting and need a few blasts with a hair dryer to dry out the wiring. Some kids would be rushed to the bathrooms to be dried off quickly so they wouldn't catch a cold or pneumonia. But the chance for us to just be kids was precious. We didn't have to worry about our disabilities, we didn't have to worry about sickness, and for those two hours we were able to share a moment like every other kid. The simple act of getting into a water fight was so freeing, so liberating, it brought everyone together. Throughout my life there weren't enough of those moments and that's why I loved that camp so much and why I kept going back year after year.

It's funny but, looking back, it isn't the expensive hotels where I stayed, the celebrities I met, or the cameras and spotlights, that mean the most to me, it is those small moments that I shared with family, friends and other kids, having fun times. A lot of people at Oakbank Camp were going through the same stuff I was, or worse. A lot of the disabilities that the kids in Regency Park Centre had were terminal, so it wasn't uncommon for me to be chatting with my friends one day and going to their funeral a few weeks later. I lost about eight or ten friends during the three years I was at the centre. It was hard. As kids, it was hard to accept that someone could be there one minute and gone the next. If you're lucky, that is something you don't have to confront until you are older. But that was my life, our lives, and we just had to get used to it. So things like the camp, and the water fight or poker games helped us forget about that reality.

•

When I was thirteen my mother won a trip to Tasmania for the family. We travelled from mainland Melbourne to the Apple Isle on the *Spirit of Tasmania* ferry. Wheelchairs and ships do not mix, because when the boat rolls the wheelchair rolls with it. I was constantly trying to balance my wheelchair from one side of the room to the other without being smashed like a bug on a windshield, and I became seasick. But after a harrowing night of me waiting to re-enact *The Poseidon Adventure*, we docked in Devonport and picked up a car.

Mum and Dad drove us all around that great state. We probably had Devonshire tea at every little café that served it and we would rate the scones, jams and cream every time. We had fun playing I-spy until our parents were nauseated with the game. We fed animals like kangaroos, wallabies and koalas and then we went up to Cradle Mountain for three days and it snowed. It was the second time I had seen snow and while I couldn't actually play in it, I was happy to sit and watch Myles and Sia mess around in it.

Myles carried me out to the snow in a chair so I could almost be part of the action but while he was showing me his favourite athletic moves he slipped and fell on the ice and hurt his back quite badly. I was stuck in the chair so I had to scream loudly to get Mum and Dad's attention to come and help Myles. He was pretty sore for quite a few days. He couldn't lift me or carry me, which meant that my parents had to do it. While my carers weren't around, they were still heavily reliant on Myles to do a lot of the lifting as my mum had a sore back and Dad had started feeling the effects of his constant cigarette smoking. I wasn't pleased that Myles had hurt himself but I was glad he didn't have to look after me all the time.

During those evenings at Cradle Mountain we would go to a viewing area and watch possums and other wildlife come down to feed on fruit. I saw an owl for the first time. I love watching nature, and observing animals in their natural habitat. It's something that has always been a part of me and so those moments with my family on that Tasmanian trip are another wonderful memory I still carry with me.

It is the small moments in life that matter and I think we'd all be much better off if we remembered that.

CHAPTER 12
You said . . . what?

Before we knew it, we were at the end of the eighties. A time when the economy was still recovering from the Wall Street crash, a brand new Batman and Indiana Jones were about to hit the silver screen and I was starting my first secondary school year at Mercedes College. Mercedes College was the polar opposite to Croydon Park Primary: it wasn't multicultural, and it didn't have people from the lower socio-economic end of the street. It was upper class, what you'd call the silver spoon area of town. It was the school you went to if your parents had money, big houses and fancy cars. Despite Mum insisting I cut off my rat's tail, I didn't fit in at all.

And, even worse, there were no teachers' aides to help me, so going to the toilet became an issue again. I had to learn to hold on all day. I would try and go early in the morning and then wait till three o'clock in the afternoon when I got home. It was frustrating. It seemed I was the first person that many people at the school had met or seen in a wheelchair and they didn't know what to do. Not knowing what to do isn't a problem. All you have to do is ask if you are uncertain, but no one there – neither teachers nor students – ever did.

It was difficult to make friends because I had to constantly ask people to carry books from one class to the other for me. As much as people didn't mind doing that at first, it seemed to become an ordeal to be stuck helping me all the time, so I was always on the back foot. I felt bad asking people to help and it made me hold back on making friends.

Mercedes College had talented teachers, though. I had a fantastic home room teacher called Mr Peak, and a wonderful drama class. Mr Peak knew that I wasn't skilled academically, but that I had a good imagination for visual art. He would spend a lot of time teaching me how to draw, and how to cut things like vinyl with a scalpel, and he showed me how to think visually rather than through words. He also taught me about the great artists of the world, like van Gogh, da Vinci and Michelangelo. I loved anything creative.

One thing I struggled with at Mercedes College was the way religion was forced upon me. Talking about religion was not something that I was comfortable with. Even though I had read the Bible and had studied religion in primary school, I didn't consider myself a religious person. I'd been dead, I'd seen what was out there, and I didn't like it. I was angry at religion, particularly with God. I'd seen too much not to be. If God was such a benevolent entity then why was there so much suffering? Why did he make me disabled? Why did I regularly break bones and why was I constantly in pain? These are questions I still ask, but back then I decided that if God was going to punish me then I was going to hate him back. So when people asked me about God, my answer was always, 'I think the Bible is a good book, I think it tells a great story, but it's not for me.' As you can imagine, that kind of attitude didn't go down too well at a Catholic school.

I might have settled in better at Mercedes College if I hadn't had to take an extended break from the place because of a serious injury. One winter day when I was turning a corner into the courtyard, a kid raced up to catch a football. He was concentrating on the footy and not looking where he was going so he crashed over the top of me and we both tipped over. I ended up with a badly broken leg. The ambulance came and I was taken to the Royal Children's Hospital in Adelaide where it was discovered that my leg had broken below one of my rods and that the rod was sticking out of my ankle. Needless to say, I was in a lot of pain. Mum and Dad had to ask Sir Dennis Paterson to reinsert a rod into my left leg. They couldn't leave the rod sticking out of my ankle otherwise it would've become infected and I could've lost my leg.

Because of the need for haste, the surgery was done relatively quickly and, once again, I was in plaster from the hip down, which made going to school quite difficult. Both my parents were busy working so they encouraged me to get back to school as quickly as possible. I ended up going back with plaster still on my leg, which made getting around even more difficult, so I was happy when the school holidays rolled around.

During the break, it was arranged that us three kids would visit our brothers Shawn and Christopher in Melbourne. We hopped on the overland train and shared a sleeper until Shawn met us at the train station.

I was still in plaster, so we spent most of the visit sitting around watching episodes of *Blackadder, The Young Ones* and *Are You Being Served?* It was like a crash course in British comedy. Shawn and Christopher are vegetarians, so I had to go without meat for a couple of weeks but I offset that by eating copious amounts of Shawn's famous potato chips that he would make up in vegetable oil. They also took us to the museums and art galleries of Melbourne, and the two weeks went too quickly. It was great getting to know Shawn and Christopher better as we hadn't spent much time together.

Before I knew it, it was time to go back to school. I still didn't feel comfortable at Mercedes College. I missed my old friends from Croydon Park Primary and the college grounds weren't wheelchair friendly so it was hard to be independent. It was pretty frustrating because it was the same at home, so I spent a lot of time in my chair staying close to my classroom or my bedroom and I didn't move around much. I felt locked in. Trapped. The only reprieve I would get would be if my dad decided to take me somewhere.

One day my dad drove me to get my wheelchair repaired and, on our way home, he parked next to an odd-shaped building with a red light in front of it. I was fourteen. I asked what the place was and he said, 'That place is a brothel' and then explained exactly what a brothel was. Talk about embarrassing! No fourteen-year-old wants to talk about sex with their dad. And then it got worse. He said basically this: 'Quentin, if I train you correctly the world is going to love you and people will love you and you will always be taken care of, but unfortunately you will never be loved the way you want to be. You're not Harrison Ford, you're not Sean Connery, and you're not Batman or any kind of superhero. You're going to have to wake up to the realisation that you're three feet tall and most people see you differently. No woman is ever going to be able to see past your disability, so women like the ones in this brothel are the only contact you're ever going to hope for.'

I got really upset and depressed because my father had just told me that no woman would ever see the true, real me, and as much as I fought it, every love that I had would be unrequited. I stayed quiet that whole day and probably a few others, just trying to understand what he meant, because up until that time I had never seen a pornographic movie or understood what a prostitute was. I understood how sex worked and where babies came from, but what my father had laid out was quite confronting and damaging. I had hopes and dreams and ideas that one day I would get married and have 2.3 kids and a white picket fence, so to be told at fourteen that that was never going to happen was devastating. It was the first time I felt the black dog bite hard.

If that wasn't enough to cope with, when the plaster came off my leg, it turned out there was a small problem. My left leg had become an inch and a half shorter than my right leg. Now I wasn't just three feet tall, I was three feet and lopsided!

From that moment on, the idea that I would walk had to be abandoned. The reality was that I would be stuck in a wheelchair forever. This wasn't actually such a bad thing, because I didn't much like walking anyway. It took me at least half an hour to get from one side of the house to the other and it required a lot of effort. Heck, I'm just a little bit lazy so I was happy to say goodbye to the walking frame and say hello to the wheelchair.

I could no longer stand in the Big Green Machine, the wheelchair that my father had built with Wally Motloch, so it was time for something new. The problem was, Mum and Dad said we didn't have enough money for a new wheelchair. It turned out that the extra coin I thought they had was all going to school fees and there wasn't any spare. There was my trust fund, with the money I had earnt from interviews, but I was told that was to be kept until I was eighteen. With my parents' encouragement I wrote a letter to Mike Willesee to ask him to help out. He did. Thanks to him, I got a new wheelchair and it was a beauty. It was called an Everade Turbo. It was an English machine and had a hydraulic lift built in, which meant the seat could go as low as the floor and then as high as a person standing. It even had a spare seat at the back that could be used as a boot or for someone to sit on. And it was pretty. It was flaming red, had hubcaps, lights and if you screamed at a high pitch it would shut off automatically. Basically it was the duck's guts.

The wheelchair was delivered after about a nine-week wait and my father, Myles and I immediately took it out to a giant car park to give it a once-over and test run. I had never had a front-wheel drive wheelchair before, so the controls were different and it was like driving in reverse. I had to learn to drive all over again. It had good range though, so even though we lived in the hills I could take the wheelchair down to the corner shops on a Saturday. The only problem was that it stuck out a lot and exposed my legs, which meant that it wasn't good for taking to school, so I had to use the wheelchair I'd had from when I was three at college. It was kind of cool, I had one wheelchair for school and one for fun, like having a sports executive car that you used on the weekends.

•

At the end of that year I don't think anyone was too surprised that I didn't do very well at school; my grades weren't that impressive. It could be because I'd had so much time away with that busted leg and partly because I wasn't comfortable at the college. But things were about to change, and I was about to go on a big adventure, bigger than I ever thought possible.

CHAPTER 13

Blood doesn't mean you're family

At the end of 1989, the McLeans, who owned the Susan River Homestead, invited me to spend a year with them on the farm. We'd stayed in touch and they must have known things were difficult. They suggested I go to school in Maryborough in Queensland while Myles completed his last year in high school back home. It was a way for him to have some peace and quiet to concentrate on his studies, without the stress of having to look after me. At the same time, it would give my parents some respite and hopefully give me an extraordinary experience. It was such a wonderful and kind offer and it couldn't have come at a better time for me. There was a lot of fighting going on between the entire family in my house, so when I was asked if I wanted to go I jumped at the chance.

Dad was a little more tentative about it so he threw in a caveat – I had to take Sia with me. I didn't care as long as I got the hell out of South Australia, out of Mercedes College and away from my parents for an entire year. Sia was almost twelve and liked the idea of being away from the folks too, but she enjoyed her life in the city and had a fledging modelling career so she wasn't as enthused about staying in Queensland for a year, but she chose to make the best of it. Faye and Norm McLean weren't worried they were getting two of us instead of one, so it was all organised.

Both Sia and I were anxious getting on the plane. I hadn't been to Susan River since I was eight years old. I didn't know what would be expected of me or Sia: whether we had to work on the homestead, how we would be treated, and what we'd do when we got to school. It was going to be quite an eye-opening experience.

The matriarch of the family, Faye McLean, picked us up at the airport with her youngest son, Guy. Guy was my age; our birthdays are only a few days apart. I was going to share a room with him. We hopped into their van and headed three hours north to Maryborough. On the way there, Faye was welcoming and kind but she told me that she wasn't going to put up with any of my city-slicker crap. Apparently my father had told her that I had gained quite an attitude for talking back and being rude to people and she told me that wouldn't wash among country folk. I didn't appreciate Dad painting me in that light but Faye's upfront manner was good because I felt I knew exactly where I stood. I liked her.

When we got to the homestead we were reintroduced to the whole family. There was Glen, who had married a lady by the name of Louise and had a little baby daughter, Caitlin, who I would end up babysitting a lot. Then there was Cameron, who was always in a tractor or on a horse dealing with the farm side of the homestead. He was a man of few words, but when he said something you listened. Next was Scott, my brother from another mother. He and I would end up bonding and we remain close to this day, even though we had a rocky start. Then there was Travis, the prankster, who was always getting up to mischief and trying to get me into trouble. Last but not least were Guy and their daughter Skye. Skye had just turned eleven so was about the same age as Sia.

We were given a grace period of about two weeks to get ourselves settled.

A few days after we arrived it was New Year's Eve and we went to a drive-in cinema to watch the dusk-till-dawn session: four movies all night long. The McLeans did drive-in cinema a little differently. We drove up in a big rig, an eighteen-wheeler flatbed truck which we parked in the back row. The flatbed was lined with deckchairs and eskies full of cold drinks and chips. We sat watching movies, wrapping ourselves in blankets when the night air started to get cold. The smell of the bush as I watched Batman chase the Joker at one o'clock in the morning was a beautiful experience. There was a scent of eucalyptus and, whenever Danny Elfman's soundtrack quietened for a moment, there was the sound of crickets and mosquitoes all round. People were whispering and crunching on chips. It was a truly fantastic cinematic experience and one that I will never forget.

After the two-week honeymoon period, my attitude became an issue. Basically I thought I was top shit and better than everyone else and I didn't mind telling anyone either. At first the family ignored this behaviour, but after two weeks it was decided that something had to be done. So, whenever I got a bit uppity, the family, any one of them, would unplug my battery and walk away from me. It didn't matter if I was in a paddock, the lounge room, the kitchen, the bathroom or by the pool, if I pissed anyone off they would just unplug my wheelchair for ten minutes and walk away. The ultimate timeout! I would scream and yell and say, 'You can't do this to me, I'm going home, I'm telling my father.' But we all knew that was a lie because going home meant going back to my parents fighting and Myles having to do more than he should, and I didn't want that. I pretty quickly learnt to shut my trap and get with the program.

Faye and Norm knew there had to be something else fuelling my anger and outbursts so they arranged for me to have hypnotherapy to work out the reasons why I was so upset all the time. This was my first experience of therapy and it gave me a chance to tell someone what had happened to me at the Regency Park Centre. The force-feeding, the times I was beaten up or other kids used me as a battering ram, the times when my parents left me, the times where all I wanted was some emotional connection with someone but didn't get it. The hypnotherapist made me confront those feelings and then used a method to help me bury those thoughts and memories, and lock them all away so I didn't constantly access them. The idea was that I wouldn't have to feel defensive, or as though I had to prove or justify myself, or fight everything that was put in front of me. I could shut those memories off and not think about them ever again. For a while, it was absolutely brilliant. I was a changed person. I didn't feel angry anymore, I didn't feel the need to act out, I didn't talk back, I was just happy to open myself up to the affection and love that the McLean family were offering me. It was a good time for me.

Every day at Susan River Homestead I would be woken by Norm, who would help me have a shower and get through my morning routine. I would then quickly rush to the kitchen and help serve breakfast to the guests at the resort before I'd get my own breakfast (fruit and toast) which was much healthier than what I was used to. Next I would take the morning tea saddlebags down to the stable yards where the guests would get on their horses and prepare to go for their morning ride.

I became attached to a small quarter horse named Stratus. He was a fourteen-hand chestnut who seemed rather curious and started coming up to me and sniffing and nuzzling my chest. The other stablehands couldn't believe that Stratus was so calm around me and didn't run off when he saw the wheelchair, like all the other horses did. I started walking him around the yard. When I stopped, he stopped and when I moved, he moved.

And when I went up to him and patted him, he wouldn't veer away, he would just look into my eyes, bow his head and let me scratch his forehead. It was amazing. The stablehands told me that I could look after Stratus when he was in the yard with me. I had my own horse. I thought that was extremely cool.

After the guests had left for their ride, it was my job to help Travis or Scott sweep the decks of the front yard. We would end up talking about our future, or share jokes that we'd heard or things that had happened the day before. Once the guests were back from their ride, we'd serve them lunch and then we would eat our own. There was usually a short break when guests would do their own thing, like have a nap, and then in the afternoons everyone would go waterskiing or parasailing. I would babysit the children who were too young to participate in the water sports. I usually ended up letting the kids climb all over my wheelchair, or I'd take them around the paddock, or watch *Barney the Dinosaur* with them. In the evenings we would have to wash up, put good clothes on and then help serve dinner to the guests before we had our own dinner and went to bed. That was pretty much the pattern of our days until school started.

My first day at Aldridge High, I was really nervous. I had never been to a country school and I thought it would be different to Mercedes College. It was, and I was very happy about that! It was more like Croydon Park Primary: down-to-earth folk, kids who I understood, people from hard-working families who didn't have money or ego attached to them. I got along with the kids there.

I met my first real girlfriend at Aldridge High. Her name was Jodie Reed and she was the daughter of the maths teacher. Jodie and I would hang out during lunchtime, holding hands and talking about our day, and then she would go off to her class and I would go off to mine. After a while, my grades were better than they had ever been in Adelaide. Aldridge had a school choir which I joined and I enjoyed singing in. The time flew by and, in the blink of an eye, Sia and I had already been there three months. I hadn't spoken to my parents much in that time. They would ring up every week, but I would make sure that I was never near the phone.

There are so many wonderful stories that I could share about that year in Queensland. Like the time the stars of *Home and Away* stayed during a promo tour they were doing around Queensland for *A Country Practice* and *Home and Away*. I was so excited to see TV stars I had grown up watching staying at the homestead that I wanted to wait on them hand and foot and make sure their every need was met.

Other memories that I love to talk about are the ones involving the cattle dogs. There was Spur, the labrador blue heeler that would howl every time the dinner bell rang. There was Clancy, the blue heeler that nobody messed with; if you touched him you knew you were going to get bitten. But if you needed to muster up the horses or cattle, he was the dog you took.

One day Cameron asked me to go out and round up the horses for the morning ride. I didn't know the first thing about how to round up horses. I had seen others do it, I had even seen little Skye do it, but I had never done it myself. I mean, how could I? I was in a wheelchair. But Cameron said, 'Just take Clancy and he'll do it for you.' I was pretty sceptical at the idea of getting a dog to round up twenty horses, but off I went. I wasn't sure that Clancy would follow my orders as he never even blinked an eye at me unless I had his tennis ball, and then it was on for young and old. But as soon as he locked eyes on those horses, he was off.

'Get around, get around, get around,' I said. 'Drop, move forward.' I didn't know what I was doing, but I pretended I did. Luckily, Clancy instinctively knew where to go and how to drive the horses straight into the yard. Thanks to him, I looked like a freaking champion. Cameron brushed his hat off and, looking dumbfounded, said, 'Far out. I can't believe you did it.' I was as proud as punch. I had finally earnt a bit of farming respect.

But every bit of respect you earn can be lost the next day. One day I pissed Cameron off. I can't remember how but I remember him getting me to scrape mud out of bulldozer tracks for three whole hours with a screwdriver. Gosh that was boring, dirty and painful. But I did that like a champion too!

One special moment I remember clearly is a conversation I had with Scott at the homestead. I was all of fifteen and he was eighteen and a half, but we sat there one afternoon and decided that we would both be famous actors and work alongside each other on a big movie set with directors telling us what to do. We were certain we'd one day see our names next to each other on the Hollywood Walk of Fame. It was big, lavish pie-in-the-sky stuff. But it was a conversation and a dream that stuck with me and, in some ways, it came true. Scott became one of the most sought after and well-respected stunt men in the entire country and he was in Hollywood movies such as *The Matrix*, *Star Wars* and *Superman*. He was doing so well but he was horrifically injured when a stunt went wrong in December 2011 on the set of *The Hangover Part II*. Scott is facing permanent disability and battling seizures because of what happened, but I know he won't give up on reclaiming his dream.

A couple of years ago Scott came to visit me on the set of *Mad Max: Fury Road*. More on that later, but I was so proud he was there to see me acting in my first big Hollywood movie. We both shed a few tears when he saw me in makeup getting into costume for the first time. He gave me a huge hug and said, 'See, mate, I told you we'd both end up doing it'.

I have always looked up to Scott, and still do. Here was a man who had lived his dreams and conquered the world, only to have it taken out from under him. Seeing him struggle with the transition from a healthy, strong, able body to a damaged, not-so-strong one was hard for anyone who loved him, but to have Scott share that moment on set with me, something we had both imagined doing when we were just kids, was very special.

•

Since things were going so well at Susan River, and so well between myself and the McLean family, Norm and Faye asked me and Sia if we wanted to become a permanent part of their family. It was a huge decision. I thought about it long and hard, about what it would mean. I wouldn't be in the limelight anymore. I would just be Quentin, a country kid going to the local high school and hopefully chasing my dreams afterwards. I'd have Sia with me and Myles would have the freedom to live his life without the burden of looking after me. It seemed like a wonderful dream coming true. I jumped at the chance. I wanted to stay, I wanted to be part of that family and I wanted to just be Quentin.

When the McLeans spoke to my father about it, he got really angry and then very drunk and demanded that I get on the phone with him. I refused and for eight weeks I ignored his phone calls. But when he threatened to fly up to Queensland himself, I finally got on the phone to him. The conversation went something like this. He said, 'So I hear you don't want to come home, you ungrateful little bastard', and I said, 'No, I'm tired of your crap. I'm tired of listening to your fights. I'm tired of hearing you guys drink and cause us distress. I'm not coming home and I'm going to remain a McLean forever.' I continued, 'I'm fifteen now and I can emancipate myself and do exactly what I want.' He said, 'You're right, son, you can, but your little sister, she's only thirteen and she doesn't have that choice so if you stay I will drag her back to Adelaide and I can guarantee you that I will make her life a living hell.'

I didn't know what that threat meant exactly, other than that he would probably be constantly verbally and emotionally abusive to Sia. I had to weigh it up. Did I stay and be selfish or did I go home and protect my sister? I told my father that at the end of the year I would return home with Sia and live once more in Adelaide. I hung up the phone and I was gutted, completely defeated. The McLean family was bereaved too. They had embraced us as a son and daughter and I had fallen in love with all of them. They had become my family.

We decided to make the best of the last of our stay at Susan River Homestead. It would be nothing but love and fun. There was still always work to do, chores to finish and guests to look after. But everything else was about bonding and having fun.

During the week, the entire family played indoor cricket and I'd go and watch their games. Win or lose, it didn't really matter because it was about sharing the experience together, all of us jumping in the car and racing down Ghost Hill to Hervey Bay or down the highway to Maryborough to the indoor cricket grounds to watch the boys slap around the leather ball. During those last few months, we were always in the pool or around it. I swam in some crazy floatation device that Faye had invented for me out of pool toys. Scott would pick me and the device up and throw me in the pool just to see if I would float or sink. It was his joke, knowing that he would always rescue me if I started to drop to the bottom.

The thing that I loved was just how much the McLeans made us feel like a family. Even though they had six kids already, Sia and I never felt left out or unloved. We always felt as though we were included and a part of the family, part of the fabric of the homestead that made it tick and made it fun and appealing for the guests to come and spend time with us. Sometimes Sia and I would just sit and reminisce about what life used to be like, how different it had become and how much we dreaded going back. We'd discuss what we had to go back to and how we had to mentally prepare ourselves.

I can honestly say that every life lesson I learnt during that year was about how to be a good person. How to be selfless and kind and how to not let your ego get the better of you. How to just sit and be in the moment. I learnt how to meditate and how to calmly deal with my memories and the pain I had gone through as a child with my broken bones and surgery. How to calm my mind of the things that had happened to me at Regency Park and how to basically forgive my parents for the things that they had done to me. I was trying to become more adult in that year and to see things for what they could be, not what they were, so that I would leave the McLeans with a sense of hope that I could forge a better relationship with my parents and a brighter future at Mercedes College.

The final two weeks at Susan River Homestead were emotionally tough because I was going to have to leave it all behind. We were all trying to make it the best two weeks ever and the family decided to have a huge bonfire party. Now, I know people have probably been to a bonfire where you get a bunch of branches and the fire burns for a few hours. Well, this was nothing like that. This was epic! Cameron went out on his bulldozer and bulldozed five trees, then chopped them up with a chainsaw and stacked them on top of each other. Then Travis walked over the mound of trees splashing them with diesel fuel and walked over it again with a can of unleaded before running the petrol trail thirty feet back to us. I remember him just looking at me and smiling as he said, 'Well shit's gonna go down!' He lit a match and held it down to the line of fuel. I watched a flame dance along the line back to the huge pile and when it hit the timber a huge mushroom cloud of fire and smoke suddenly whooshed up and the heat bounced back and practically singed all our eyebrows off in one go. Travis leapt back and said, 'Whoops, that was a bit of a fuck-up. Ah well, didn't need eyebrows.'

We'd invited our friends and basically half the classrooms of Aldridge High to the bonfire party, but I pretty much just sat with Jodie the whole time. We told stories, held hands and, for the first time, she kissed me. I thought the night couldn't get any better after that. When she left, she cried and said that she loved me and that she would write to me and that I would see her again.

I wish I could tell you that Jodie and I stayed in touch but after a while our letters stopped. Years later I found out that Jodie passed away from diabetes complications. She didn't live to see twenty-five. When I found that out I was deeply saddened; she was my first real love.

A few days after the bonfire, Sia and I had to say goodbye to people we loved and a place that will always be in my heart. I can never thank the McLeans enough for the way they took us in and helped me at a time I really needed it. We got into the car and Scott and his girlfriend drove us to Brisbane where we got on a plane and flew back to Adelaide. Going home was as bad as I had thought it would be.

CHAPTER 14

My own worst enemy

It was the beginning of 1991 when Sia and I returned home and for a short time Mum and Dad tried to be calm, loving parents. They took us on holiday to Port Lincoln, on a yacht, for an entire week. I don't want to sound ungrateful but the trip was fun for everyone, except me. Mum and Dad were trying, but because I was in my wheelchair the only places I could be on a boat were either inside the cabin or sitting on the deck. The deck wasn't a good option during the day when we were sailing as it was too bumpy. I liked it when we were actually moored someplace as I could sit on the edge of the boat and fish and soak in the tranquillity. There was a spot in Boston Bay, where the water was crystal clear and I could watch the colours of the water change as the clouds moved overhead. I took my video camera and made short movies about Boston Bay, and ended up catching quite a few whiting there which we ate for our dinner. That holiday was one of the last times I remember my parents being together without having a complete rip-roaring argument.

When we returned home, the holiday ceasefire ended and Mum and Dad's fighting intensified. It got so bad they decided to separate. In most separations one parent would leave the house and the other would stay and never shall the twain meet again. But my parents never walked the expected path. Mum and Dad had been working together for about thirty years, so their assets, finances and work were all intertwined. They knew that they couldn't get out of their working relationship easily – and it was actually still pretty good; it was the personal one that was in tatters – so they decided to divide the split-level house into two and both keep living there.

My mother decided that she wanted the downstairs area – it had its own bathroom, lounge room, kitchen and study, so it was good for her. Mum decided that the big space next to her study would become her bedroom, and that my father would stay in their master bedroom upstairs. The upstairs area also contained its own bathroom, lounge room, kitchen and bedrooms for the rest of the family. Myles had just turned eighteen so my parents converted one of the garages into a bedroom to give him his own space. It had insulation, electricity and all the things he would need to make it comfortable. I got the bedroom that Myles and I used to share. I went from a bunk bed to a hospital bed, which made it much easier for the support workers to get me in and out of bed in the morning. The hospital bed had a hand crank so the bed would go up and down, and the back rest had settings that could be utilised as well. It meant that I didn't need to have a pillow.

When I turned sixteen my father suggested that I apply to get the disability support pension so that I could pay rent and help support the household, despite the fact I was still at school. I wasn't too sure about this idea, because Dad was proposing to charge me 50 per cent of my disability support pension, which at the time was $140 a fortnight.

At sixteen, however, the thought of earning even half of that pension meant my hesitation didn't last. I agreed, but on two conditions. I told Dad that if I was paying rent, I should be treated like an adult and that I would no longer accept the rules for a normal teenager. It meant that I was leasing my room from my father and so in order for him to enter it he had to ask my permission. (I didn't have to worry about Mum as she was living in her downstairs area.) And, secondly, I wouldn't have to explain to him where I was going or what I was doing, my time was my time. I could go out till any hour of the night. He agreed so that was that.

I told my mate Andrew, or The Beast, as we called him, that I didn't have a curfew anymore and that was all the reason we needed to run amok, or at least try to. Andrew was a friend of my brother's who had repeated a year at school so he was now in my year. We'd quickly become best friends. The Beast and I decided we should go out and stay out all hours of the night, so we hit Hindley Street, the heart of Adelaide's nightlife scene, with that in mind. We went to the movies and afterwards we thought, what should we do? We quickly realised that we were both under eighteen and didn't have any adult ID so couldn't get into any nightclubs. Even if we did have fake ID, everyone knew who I was and knew that I hadn't hit eighteen so they weren't going to let me in anyway. There wasn't anything to do but go home. When we got back at eleven o'clock, my dad laughed.

The good times at Aldridge High were just memories by then, and settling back into Mercedes College wasn't exactly smooth going. I was having trouble keeping up with the rest of the class. I couldn't write as quickly as everyone else and I couldn't memorise all the notes on the blackboard which needed to be taken down. In fairness, Mercedes College tried to help and they found a retiree to come in to take notes for me. He was a sweet old guy named John. John did his best to listen and take as many notes as he could. The problem was that his handwriting was so scribbly, and written so quickly, it would take me at least an hour and a half every day to decipher what the poor guy had written. I tried to talk to him about this and he didn't take it well (which I can see now was partly my fault; I wasn't what you would call tactful about his poor penmanship). He quit. After that, my parents bought me a laptop with some of my pension money. I was one of the first kids in South Australia to go to school with a laptop. It was actually a lot of fun, because when I needed to take notes I was able to type pretty quickly, and when I got bored I would simply play a computer game during class and pretend to be working. Andrew and I were both in Business Maths, and we would just sit there and play Dungeons & Dragons to our hearts' content. If the teacher came up to see what was on the screen I would simply close one window and open another and a Word document would pop up. Ah, the joys of Windows 3.1. I loved those days.

Before I knew it the school year was over and I spent the summer holidays with Andrew and our other friend Sebastian, going to the movies religiously every week. Gaining a film knowledge and learning about film-makers, editing and directing was important to me and I started collecting books about various directors. I would buy the novelisations of movies which had already been released and compare the two. I studied up about acting; I learnt about Stanislavski, Lee Strasberg and the method acting technique, and how acting was taught at New York's Juilliard School. Then I watched movies with actors who used those methods such as Marilyn Monroe, Robert De Niro, Harvey Keitel and, of course, Al Pacino. I spent the Christmas school holidays making it my mission to learn everything about how to create characters and a story structure. The problem was that my finished stories never matched up to what I thought they should be so I had to keep pushing myself to do better.

The first term back at Mercedes College in 1992 wasn't good. I didn't feel I was keeping up with the class. It's an awful feeling. I wasn't stupid, but I physically couldn't keep up. Just getting around with all the books I needed was hard. It all became too cumbersome and stressful.

One afternoon after school in March 1992 I was going out to meet The Beast. I was in a hurry and I asked Mum to help me get a jacket on. Unfortunately, when she slipped my hand through the sleeve she got my thumb caught, and instead of stopping and waiting for me to adjust my finger she kept going and bent my thumb back and broke my arm. My thumb practically hit the inside of my elbow. Both bones had snapped in two and I was in excruciating pain. I went off to Flinders Medical Centre straightaway and staff put my right arm in a plaster, but instead of using actual plaster they used a fibreglass cast. It was meant to be lighter and stronger. When I got home, I lay around for a few days and then one evening I was arguing with my father about something trivial, I can't remember what. He was drunk, so the argument was going nowhere and I was so angry about everything I picked up my portable CD Walkman and threw it across the room. The effort that it took to throw the machine caused my left arm to break also. Another trip to the Flinders Medical Centre and another broken arm in plaster. So there I was, sitting at Flinders Medical Centre feeling very sorry for myself with two broken arms.

I was stuffed! I couldn't lift anything, I couldn't move properly, I couldn't write or type, I couldn't take myself to the toilet and, most importantly, I couldn't feed myself. I was completely dependent on other people. I was horrified and I wasn't sure my parents could look after me. Luckily Flinders Medical Centre and my GP decided that I should be transferred to Blackwood

Hospital for rehabilitation, where I could stay until both my arms were healed and I had my independence back.

Going to Blackwood Hospital was a godsend, because I had my own room with a television and they had a little controller that I could operate with my toes to call a nurse or use the TV. The nurse would come and help every day with my food, drink and going to the toilet, but for the most part I was left alone. The Beast would sometimes come after school, and every Saturday afternoon he would be there without fail. Most of the time we would just sit and talk and tell jokes. I was grateful to him. He didn't have to spend his afternoons sitting in a hospital room with me, but he could see I was down on my luck and feeling awful and needed some cheering up. I don't think I ever properly thanked him for that time, so I'll say it now – Beast, thanks buddy.

When I was in Blackwood I received a phone call from the vice-principal of Mercedes College. He suggested that I take the rest of the year off as it would be difficult for me to complete the year without the teachers taking time out of their schedule to help me. I assured him that it was only April and that I would definitely catch up on my own time and that my commitment to school was solid, but I don't think that was what he wanted to hear. It wasn't a pleasant conversation and before I knew it things escalated and I found myself telling the vice-principal to get fucked. His reply was along the lines of, 'Well, this makes everything a lot easier and I am now expelling you. Thank you very much.' Everything went silent. It was like a bad movie playing out before my eyes. What was my father going to do to me? What was I going to do? I'd just been kicked out of school for telling the vice-principal where to go.

When I told my father he took the news pretty well. He said, 'Don't worry, son, I only finished year 10 and look at me, a 45-year career in newspapers and printing. We'll get you back on your feet.' What I didn't know at the time was that Myles had started a PR company called MKA Communications. It was owned by him, but run by my father, who had retired from *The Advertiser*. Everything was in my brother's name, supposedly to give him the best start at a successful future, so my father decided that, since I'd been expelled, I should join the family business. I was excited. I had a place to go and a purpose. That is all most people want, isn't it?

When I was out of plaster and back home, the first thing I did was dress in a suit – white shirt, black tie, black jacket, black leather shoes – and I went into Mercedes College to grab my things out of my locker, shake a few teachers' hands and say goodbye to friends. I don't know quite what possessed me but I then went into the vice-principal's office, saluted him and said, 'Mate, fuck you.' I left the place feeling like a superhero.

From there I headed to my new job. I didn't know anything about public relations, but I was about to get a crash course. The first thing my father did was give me the office address book and ask me to memorise every phone number in it. He told me he didn't want to have to open that book again. He wanted to be able to say, 'Quentin, what's that guy's number?' and have me roll it off for him. It took about a week for me to memorise it all, but soon enough I had over 200 phone numbers locked into my brain. I'm not sure what that added to the business, but I figured if that's what Dad wanted, then I'd do it.

Myles and Dad already had a couple of interesting clients and things seemed rosy. My father could see we were going to need a desktop publisher, and had the idea to train me up. My brother Chris, who was still living in Melbourne, had done a lot of work with Photoshop and had taken a break to work for Telecom. So I was sent to Victoria to learn desktop publishing from him on an Omega computer.

Chris is a lovely man, but for some reason when he started to teach me Photoshop everything he said went over my head, far too quickly. Before then, the only thing I had used a computer for was to type notes and essays, and play Dungeons & Dragons. Clicking layer here, layer there, draw circle, change fonts, change colours, save, flatten image – all that was new to me. I was feeling the pressure and I started to get sick. By the time I flew back to Adelaide I had pneumonia and so I went back to Blackwood Hospital. I spent two weeks recovering but it was a scary time, and that particular illness ended up making me more disabled. It was the start of a downward slide for me. And something else was starting to become a problem, not that I would see it as an issue for a long time.

I had been prescribed some powerful painkillers when I'd broken both my arms. I had a lot of pain afterwards, so my doctor prescribed codeine phosphate to take the ache away.

When I was in pain, I would take just a few millilitres of this drug and the pain would go away. At first I was taking it just once a day, which was sustainable, and I was getting on with my life pretty well. But about five months into working with my father and my brother, things started to go awry. Because my father was who he was, his habits didn't change now that he was working for himself, and nor did his temper and attitude. It wasn't uncommon for him to go out on a boozy lunch with the clients, get upset with them and tell them that he no longer needed to be working for them. Now this is okay if you do it once or twice, but if you do it four or five times, you suddenly realise that your client roster is diminishing quickly and so is your income. So my father approached me and said, 'Mate, now that you're nearing eighteen, I need to give you access to your trust fund, so that you can get it and help get the company out of hot water.' I was like . . . what? I'm not doing that! He told me that the business was in Myles's name and that if the company went under then Myles would either go bankrupt or end up in jail. I can see now that might not have been the case, but back then what choice did I have?

I went to the bank and soon discovered that there wasn't $17,000 as I had hoped, but a mere $7000. When I confronted my father about this he told me that he had taken money out back in the late eighties to pay for my mother's international holidays. I was so angry. As far as I was concerned, my father had stolen nearly $6000 from me to cover my mother's need to travel overseas while I was stuck in the Regency Park Centre.

I was beyond ropeable, but I didn't want Myles to get into trouble so I handed my father a cheque for $1000. That cheque lasted two weeks and then Dad came to me for another $1000, because he couldn't make payroll again. Back to the bank I went and back in his hand went another $1000.

Shortly after that I was told I had to bail Myles out of trouble again. I am not sure Myles even knew how bad things were until the very end because Dad was intent on looking after everything. I handed over another $2500, so that the company could be wound up and everyone's entitlements could be covered. It wasn't Myles's fault. Dad had built us both up, told us to trust him and then helped hasten the business's failure. In six short weeks I was out of a job and left with only $1500 in my trust fund. The future wasn't looking so bright.

CHAPTER 15
OCD overdrive

Being unemployed and broke was not in my plan when I'd left school, but that's how things ended up. I didn't feel so much like a superhero now. Myles was in the same boat, and perhaps even worse off because he had experienced the excitement of opening his own business only to see it dissolve. It was pretty tough for him and I think he felt a lot of guilt at the way my money had been used. Myles did his best to be out of the house most days. Sia was still at school so this meant that I was stuck in the house with my parents all day. Mum wasn't around much either, though. She was scoring more overseas writing assignments, so she travelled a lot. That left Dad and me alone together all the time. With my friends still at school, I had nothing to do all day. At this point it seemed I wasn't

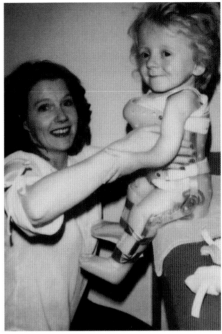

TOP LEFT: With Mum in front of the Great Pyramids of Giza, checking out the Sphinx. I was six months old.

TOP RIGHT: This was taken when I was seven. Mum is holding me while I am being fitted with braces. Around the same time, I took my new walking-frame Wally Motloch (*below left*) had made for me for a test drive.

BELOW RIGHT: With my favourite person, my brother Myles. I was two and he was four.

TOP LEFT: Me and Myles building spaceships out of Lego.

TOP RIGHT: In my mean, green machine that Dad and Wally Motloch had worked on. I really did feel like the Bionic Man. Here I am holding my certificate after my First Communion.

BELOW LEFT: Not sure others appreciated my musical gifts, but I wasn't one to hold back – on anything. Here I am letting it rip during a *Woman's Day* photoshoot in 1985.

BELOW RIGHT: Dad, Mum, Myles, me and Sia – the Kenihans all gathered in all our glory, for Sia's First Communion.

TOP: This was me surrounded by the *Young Talent Time* team. You'll have to read the book to find out what happened backstage! That's Dannii Minogue on the bottom left.

BELOW: Sia (*far left*) and me (*far right*) with the McLean family in 1990, probably the BEST year of my life was spent with them.

TOP: After a few months with the McLeans I settled in to farm life really well. And thanks to the cattle dogs, Jessie, Spur and especially Clancy, I was an expert in rounding up the horses.

RIGHT: Celebrating my 21st birthday, I looked so young and carefree. You'd never know I was a recently recovered drug addict.

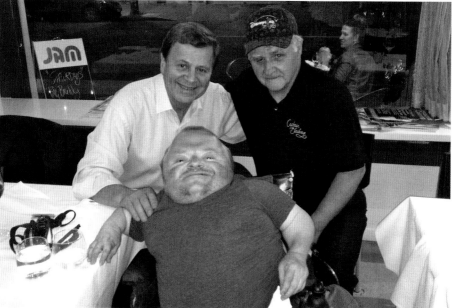

I thought appearing on Mike Willesee's episode of *This Is Your Life* (*top*) would give me a chance to apologise to him, but I never got the chance.

Mike (*top left*) and Ray Martin (*below left*) are two men I feel very lucky to be able to call friends.

I thought the concept was genius! *Quentin Crashes Hollywood*. What could go wrong? Well ... lots. But running over Jennifer Lopez's dress was pretty epic. Jenny from the Block wasn't happy, and her bodyguards even less so.

TOP: Me and my support worker Elisa Rouvray meeting Jean-Claude Van Damme at the World Music Awards in Monaco. This was surprisingly poignant. He is a great guy and I really liked his honesty. Maybe I shouldn't have shared details of my sex life, but he asked! And meeting the gorgeous Kristanna Loken (*below right*), who played a terminator in the third movie of the franchise, meant a kiss I will always remember.

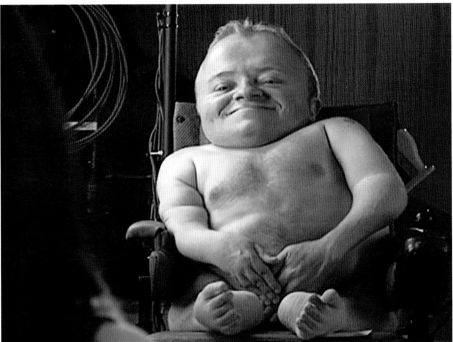

Appearing on *Australian Idol* was pretty full on, but appearing on *Big Brother Uncut* was even more revealing!

qualified to do anything except appear on television every so often.

Dad started to get into the habit of heading off to the pub or the RSL at about ten in the morning and he'd come home at around three in the afternoon. Three things invariably happened when he'd get home. He'd either go straight to bed, stay out of my way or try to engage me in some bullshit story he'd heard at the pub. If it was the third option we'd end up fighting. We fought a lot. I was so bored and pissed off, and we both felt stuck in the house so we would take it out on each other.

Despite his emphysema, Dad was still a chain-smoker and so the house was constantly filled with smoke. I had only recently recovered from pneumonia, so it wasn't surprising that the smoke affected me. I developed asthma. The constant coughing then caused me to break ribs, which in turn made me increasingly susceptible to lung infections. It was a hideous time and hospital-isations became more frequent for me, about once every month. The strange thing was that I started to enjoy being in hospital as it meant escaping from Dad, loneliness and boredom. In hospital, people came in and out of my room and, when not in severe pain, I talked to them. I ate three good meals a day, a welcome change from the junk food continuously supplied by Dad. I know I was almost an adult by then but I couldn't go shopping on my own so I was still reliant on him. All of this added up to me becoming even more dependent on painkillers in greater and greater quantities.

At first it wasn't a problem. I took codeine only once or twice a day and it made me feel fantastic. My doctor was not responsible for my growing addiction. I lied to him about the extent of my pain. If I were lucky, I'd be able to get my hands on some marijuana through former schoolfriends and combine the two. At first I'd have adamantly disagreed with The Verve's song 'The Drugs Don't Work', because mine were bloody great . . . in the beginning. The pain in my body would disappear, along with my hatred of living in that house and my dull, mundane existence was not as depressing. I started taking codeine more regularly and bought more pot.

I made sure that I was straight during meal times so Myles and Dad wouldn't suspect anything but, other than that, I was regularly off my face a lot of the time. For the first three months of my addiction, everything was fine. However, it didn't take long for the lines of reality and paranoia to become blurred.

It all started one night when I was watching a medical documentary highlighting a condition called Progeria. Progeria causes a child to age prematurely. It is a terrible disorder affecting a small group of kids. I gained the delusion that I had the condition. I began constantly looking in the mirror and counting how many lines were on my face. I'd then check the elasticity of the skin on my hands and feet to see how quickly it would revert to its original shape. At first I did this when I felt anxious, but soon I was checking all the time. I tried hard to keep my OCD paranoia secret but it soon became evident to Myles and Sia that I was acting strangely. I carried a mirror around with me so that I could see my reflection frequently, covertly pinching my skin at least once or twice every five minutes. I didn't want to go out anymore or, if I did, it had to be in the mornings when there weren't many people around. I confided in Sebastian and Andrew about my fears and they were supportive but also concerned. They had not supplied me with any drugs and they tried to talk me into getting help.

To reduce my anxiety, and hopefully escape my delusions, I took more drugs. That only made me worse. I started to believe that my parents were plotting to kill me and that I should avoid them. Except for meal times, I attempted to stay at least ten feet away from them. In my mind, this was a safe distance.

In the meantime, I was trying to keep busy. Sebastian and I had started the Australian fan club for *The Rocky Horror Picture Show*. *The Midday Show* got wind of this and I was asked to appear on the program to speak with Ray Martin. Sebastian and I both thought it would be good publicity for the fan club so I agreed. The day we were due to leave for Sydney, I experienced a delusion that if Sebastian and I boarded the plane, it would crash and burn. I became so anxious at the airport that I rushed to the nearest disabled toilet and vomited. I was gripped with irrational fear and I didn't know what to do. Sebastian begged me not to freak out. He really wanted to go to Sydney and so did I. Consequently, I did what I knew would calm me. I cracked open a codeine packet and took a good dose. Boy, did it work.

I spent the whole flight off my pickle. I felt great again. But the itinerary wasn't how I'd read it initially. Instead of going to the hotel to freshen up, or in my case, come down from my high, we had to go straight to the studio to go on air. That was not good. I was pale, clammy and buzzing out of my brain. I was all over the place.

We were unable to go backstage at the studio because they had a surprise for me, so Sebastian and I were asked to sit with the studio audience and wait for our segment. I tried desperately to pull myself together. I was positive that people could tell I was off my face. I asked the producers if I could have some makeup (to try to hide my drugged complexion) but they said that I looked fine. For twenty minutes, I attempted to focus on reality, put aside my irrationality and become the old Quentin whom people had grown to know and like. I didn't want to stuff up and I didn't want to insult Ray Martin. I knew him as a caring man. For many years, he'd phoned to wish me happy birthday.

Miraculously, like a light bulb being switched on, I snapped back into television mode. For fifteen minutes, I held it together with Ray. As a surprise, producers had brought Alyssa-Jane Cook, who was acting in the stage version of *Rocky Horror*, to meet me. She'd been hiding backstage. I made people laugh and was entertaining. No one knew that I was completely stoned. The rest of that day went without a hitch. Flooded with relief, I was able to keep my obsessive-compulsive behaviour, like checking my face in the mirror constantly, to a minimum and had a good time in Sydney.

That night Channel Nine put us up at the Sebel Townhouse. It had been a long day and I took more codeine to get to sleep.

But there was a lot of noise coming from the floor above so even with the drugs I couldn't sleep. I called the front desk, and the night manager said that Metallica were staying and they could do whatever they wanted. Sebastian and I were enraged and wondered why a rock band could get away with depriving others from sleep by making noise and trashing their rooms. Even Metallica! I then came up with an amazing idea: what was good for Metallica was good for us. I decided to trash our room. I am ashamed to write about this now but I was still under the influence of too many drugs and clearly not thinking properly. I flung tomato sauce at the walls, threw the furniture about and knocked over the TV. I considered throwing it from the window but even in my state I knew that was going too far. The next day, we were asked to pay the cleaning bill which came to over $300. My reply was to charge it to Channel Nine.

When I returned to Adelaide, the situation worsened. My obsessive-compulsive behaviour went into overdrive. I retreated from people, certain everyone was out to get me. For over a month, I visited my doctor every second day about problems and diseases I was sure I had contracted. But they were figments of my imagination. In and out of hospital constantly, I went from one doctor to another for prescriptions for my habit. I travelled by Access cabs for the disabled and didn't have one constant driver. The doctors knew me from television and they knew that I fractured frequently. They didn't query my requests for painkillers after I'd spun a story. I am ashamed to say I became a very good liar.

One day I was on a real bender, cowering in a corner of the lounge room, crying. When Dad tried to approach me, I screamed fearfully, sure that he intended to kill me. He became worried and asked me to voluntarily admit myself to the teen psychiatric ward at Flinders Hospital where he hoped I could get help. He later said he suspected that I was on drugs but wasn't sure. He thought I'd suffered a nervous breakdown, and in many ways I had.

I admit I did several very silly, stupid things in adolescence. But karma came to me. Just after turning eighteen, I became a clichéd teenage celebrity in rehab. I had hit rock bottom.

My first night in the ward of the psychiatric hospital was the coldest and loneliest night I'd ever spent. It was worse than when Mum and Dad first left me at Regency Park. Three other patients shared the room but I had no wish to talk to them. I was still paranoid but I felt a strange calm flood over me, as if the hospital walls would somehow keep me safe. The next day I had my first session with a young psychiatrist named John. He started trying to convince me that I wasn't suffering from Progeria nor dying of any other strange disease. He encouraged other doctors to run tests on me just so I knew it for sure. Once that had been proven, John set about trying to work out why things had become so bad and to understand why I had alienated myself from the rest of the world. Sometimes we would talk about family and sometimes about life in general.

One day, Dad visited and I became badly behaved again. I yelled at the staff to give me my drugs back. I wanted them – no,

I needed them, or so I thought. John told the staff to administer me some. But I was unaware that his instruction included adding something which would make me very sick. After I took the drugs, for two hours I zoomed around the ward off my head, having a fantastic time. Then, suddenly, I felt rotten. I vomited as never before for a good half-hour and then passed out, only to wake up a day later not wanting to ever touch a drug again.

Physical recovery from my addiction was the easy part. Coming to terms with the psychological side of it was the hard aspect. After a few days, the drugs were out of my system, I wasn't sweating or craving them. But I still felt I needed them. Over a week of intense therapy, John and I discussed what was at the root of my problem. After five days of soul-searching, we both concluded that I was a figurehead with no place to go. To the public, I was a boy who could do no wrong. I was perceived as a young man with high moral values, expected to be triumphant and successful but, at that time in my life, the opposite was true. In my mind I was only known for one thing: being cute on TV. To everyone outside our family, my parents were the paragons of virtue, the brave couple raising a disabled son, when at the time they were more dysfunctional and more abrasive than I had ever been. With John's help, I realised that I had been manifesting all the angst of being a teenager, all the pain of my disability and all the issues to do with my family upon myself.

I had become a person racked with guilt, fear and anger. John made it clear to me that at eighteen years of age it was okay to have fear, angst and anger. They were human emotions that I should be able to feel without worrying about the repercussions of what people would think of me if I let them out. We then had to deal with my obsessive-compulsive behaviour. Even as I write this, the urge to become obsessive-compulsive is returning but I realise that this is only because I am dredging up memories from the past. John pointed out that I wasn't going to die today and I probably wasn't going to die tomorrow and it was highly unlikely that I would die next week, next month or next year, and if I felt anxious or afraid and as though I'd have a panic attack, then I should go ahead and let it happen. In the end, whether I pinched myself or not, the feeling would remain. The issue was to accept it, process it and learn from it.

We took a few days off from therapy and I sat in the courtyard of Flinders Hospital feeding the birds and trying to avoid as many people as possible. When it came time to return to therapy, John suggested that I face my father so that I could find out if I could be in the same space with him without wanting to run to my obsessive behaviour and addictions to hide. I wasn't ready, but is anyone ever ready to face what they don't wish to do? So Dad came to the hospital to see me and for the first time I saw him with different eyes. I didn't see a man who got on my nerves or who fuelled my anger and rage, I just saw an old man confused by his own problems and issues who was trying to make the best of life in the only way he knew how. I felt sorry for him. No, I pitied him, and then, suddenly, it was all okay again.

That night in bed, I cried, thinking about my future and where I should go from there. A bloke in the bed next to mine had been transferred from the cancer ward. He heard me and asked why I was crying. I told him my problem and that I didn't know what my future held. Then he asked a question no one had asked me in a while.

He said: 'What's your dream?' (I am pretty sure he wasn't talking about the one I had which included Teri Hatcher and a jar of honey.) He meant what was my dream for life. I said I didn't know. I asked him what his was. He said: 'Kid, I'm dying and all I ever wanted was a loving wife and to raise some kids. I've done that so I can die in peace knowing that I accomplished my dream.'

I asked him what his big dream was. He replied: 'A dream doesn't have to be big or small. You just have to want it. It doesn't matter if you ever achieve it because it's the journey that's most important. It's like going on a yellow brick road and not knowing where you'll end up.'

He was a wise man.

'What was the point of the dream, then?' I asked.

'Without a dream, you cannot start on a path so it's important to find that dream,' he told me. 'A dream can take a day, a week or a lifetime to find, but eventually, you'll wake up one day and you realise what that dream is.'

He said I had nothing to worry about because, soon enough, I would discover my dream, begin down a path and never look back.

A week later I was discharged. I re-entered the world in complete sobriety. It took me a few weeks of watching my favourite movies to realise what my dream was. For my whole life, whenever I'd been sad, upset, even stoned, I could watch a movie, escape and become another person. I could be the guy who saved the day, got the girl and had a happy ending. I realised that this was a special gift. To be able to allow someone an hour and a half when they could escape the bullshit of life is inspirational and it's something that I desperately wanted to give to others. I decided I wanted to be a film-maker. I didn't know how to start or where to go but at least I knew what could lie ahead on my yellow brick road.

I returned to the hospital to thank the man in the bed next to mine but I was told that he'd died. I was pleased to hear he'd had his family by his side. Even to the end, he was living his dream. I decided to do the same. I wanted to become a film-maker and while I was sure I'd never make it up there with Steven Spielberg, I had chosen my path and that was the main thing. Thanks in large part to that man in the hospital bed next to mine, the road to recovery was the first direction I'd taken.

CHAPTER 16
Moving out

Once I had my life back, I couldn't wait to get on with it. I was free of drugs and I wanted to move ahead with my dream of becoming a respected director.

I was eighteen and had no clue how to start, but my father convinced me that if I were to become a film-maker I should learn how to be a businessman first. Dad didn't have a great track record on a lot of things but he was a good motivator when he set his mind to it and he pointed out that film-making was not the cash cow that Hollywood makes it out to be. He added that without a Higher School Certificate it would be difficult for me to get a good job. He wasn't instilling me with hope, but he then told me about how he'd started at *The News* alongside Rupert Murdoch and how Rupert had to start at the bottom, learn the business and work his way up, just like everyone else. Dad said that I should do the same. I told him that it was a little different when your father owned the newspaper and the trust fund wasn't depleted but he ignored the barb and told me to discover what I was good at and what I enjoyed doing. He suggested that I call the Commonwealth Rehabilitation Service (CRS), a government organisation which helped people with disabilities and injuries find work, to see if they could help me.

Through the CRS, I did a course in job-seeking and interview skills and also had counselling sessions with them. My case worker, Mary Burfield, discovered that I could remember hundreds of phone numbers easily, which helped me gain work experience at the Flinders Medical Centre as a telephonist. It felt strange because only four months earlier I had been in the centre for a drug addiction and now I was working there. Each morning, from 9 am until 1 pm, I manned one of the centre's phones. There were more than a thousand phone extensions in the hospital and I was only able to remember a few hundred, so I constantly had to look numbers up. Most days the job was boring but one day was particularly dramatic.

A call came through to me that there had been a hydrochloric acid spill in the hospital, which meant that I had to co-ordinate all the communications to deal with the emergency and to help evacuate parts of the hospital. It was a real challenge but afterwards I felt I had done something positive. Due to my quick thinking and ability to organise things along with other staff as part of a team, no one was hurt in the spill. I returned home on top of the world.

My work experience ended all too quickly. I was now a trained telephonist and Mary sought to get me more work. She tried hard and it wasn't easy as, when she made suggestions, Dad would contradict her and try and tell me what was best for me, which most of the time was best for him. It wasn't a good time at home. Most of the time Mum remained locked away in her study, where she thought no one would find her. With the house segregated into 'Mum' and 'Dad' zones I hardly saw her, except when she ran upstairs to scream at Dad. Myles wasn't around anymore, but Sia was and it was really tough for her. In their effort to protect Sia from the family's woes, our parents had ended up neglecting her and she had to raise herself. She was doing okay despite it all and becoming quite a successful young model in Adelaide. She even scored a role on TV. If she had grown a few inches taller, she may have graced the catwalks at French fashion shows because she is beautiful. I was proud of her.

Sia and I both looked for any excuse to get out of that house, but while she was busy, I was finding it hard to get a job.

Despite Mary Burfield's help many companies didn't want to hire me because I was *the* Quentin Kenihan. In the end, Mary suggested that I take a test through the Department of Labour so that I could apply for a traineeship in the public service. So I did. I received 81 per cent for my exam and was given a state public service traineeship. This meant that I would work somewhere in the government three days a week and study at TAFE for the remaining two. As it happened, I was sent to work at TAFE.

On 17 January 1994, I started at the Douglas Mawson Institute of TAFE, Panorama Campus. I loved it. People treated me as a regular employee. I began as the relieving telephonist and had a lot of fun. The only problem was that the greeting was a bit of a mouthful. 'Good morning, Douglas Mawson Institute, Quentin here. How may I direct your call?' But I got the hang of it quickly.

I made some wonderful friends there, whom I still see today. Penny Finch, Michelle Bullen, Paul Utry, Paul Wilson and Jenny Cooper all became really good mates. We hung out together during lunchtimes, depending on our rosters. I had a carer who helped me with the toilet after lunch. It was a good set-up.

My studies at TAFE were also progressing well. I finally felt I was working in a job at which I could be competent. It wasn't film-making but I was taking my first steps into a larger world and it felt good.

I worked hard but I didn't get it right all of the time. I remember being told off quite a few times for making mistakes. As I was working for a government department, there were many policies and procedures I needed to adhere to and, because I was learning all of these and not accustomed to authority, I took a bit of time to adapt. Most of the other trainees transferred between departments, but I mainly stayed at the switchboard.

After about eight months, I got itchy feet. I wanted to do something more, something different. A new unit, called the Quality Management Unit, was being established to assist the campus in getting its quality assurance. Sue Bertossa was running it and she let me work for her as her personal assistant. It was like someone taking in a stray puppy, but I was grateful and determined to do well. The unit's first priority was to create a policy and procedure manual for every function of TAFE, so Sue and I investigated every department to learn what everyone did. The most bizarre thing I wrote was a procedure on how to change a nappy for the TAFE childcare centre. I'd never changed a nappy before so I had to watch people doing it so that I could write the step-by-step guide.

If you asked Sue what kind of personal assistant I was, I am sure she'd say that I was terrible but enthusiastic. Despite wanting to do my best, I was still a bit of a brat at times. I spent too much time on the phone with friends. I even got busted for looking up the Playboy website on the net. I was only reading the articles!

I eventually graduated from my traineeship, and the only person to show up to my graduation at the Hilton was Sue. My parents couldn't even be bothered to turn up, which was disappointing but not surprising. While I may not have been the best assistant, Sue said I was fun to have around so she continued to keep me on after my traineeship. I was given a temporary contract, which meant I was a full-time employee of TAFE.

While this was going on at work, big things were happening at home. Sia left school and moved into her boyfriend's house and Myles finally tired of our parents' continuing battles and decided to move out with Andrew and Sebastian. I begged Myles to take me with him. He agreed to let me come on condition that I spent time learning to look after myself. My father tried to put the guilt trip on me that he would be all alone if I left, but I was unmoved.

Despite only being sixty-six, Dad's health had deteriorated and he had to use a scooter to get around because his lung capacity was so compromised. Luckily for him, it wasn't far from the car park to the front bar. Harsh, but true. When he begged me to stay, I asked him to give me one good reason why I should. He couldn't find a reason so, at twenty years old, I moved out of home.

Myles, Andrew, Sebastian and I found a house in Adelaide's suburban Clarence Park. We each had our own space and it was fun to be venturing out together. Our house became the focal point for socialising and our friends would get together there every chance they could. We were closely knit and, after work, I usually found part of the crew at our house, watching TV, enjoying PlayStation or cooking. If I ever tired of my friends, I simply went to my room, shut the door and zoned out in front of my TV.

My government carers were happy about my move as Clarence Park was less distance for them to travel. I have to give a special thank you to Julie, Fiona, Mary, Tracy and Vicki for looking after me all those years. They were fantastic carers.

I was busy socially as I spent a lot of time out with my friends from work as well. It was around this time that I got really drunk for the first time at my friend Penny's house-warming party. On arrival, I was given a vodka and I congregated with a group of people in the kitchen. I'd only had a few sips but started to feel hot and light-headed, then very drowsy. Something was wrong. Alcohol didn't normally affect me so quickly! Then somebody noticed that there was a smell of gas in the air. It seemed that Penny had turned on the oven but it had failed to ignite. As I was at a lower height than everyone else, and closest to the oven, I realised I was being gassed. We panicked, opened all the windows and doors and made a mad dash to other parts of the house. I had a huge headache so I got drunk to take the pain away. I don't remember much of the rest of that night or how I got home.

•

It had been a while since I had been in the public eye. For over two years I had escaped the spotlight and the scrutiny of public opinion. I thought my television days were well and truly over, so when I got a call from a producer at Channel Nine asking if I'd be interested in being part of Mike Willesee's episode of *This Is Your Life*, I was unsure. It's not that I didn't want to help celebrate Mike's achievements, or thank him for paying for my new wheelchair, but I felt guilty. When I was addicted, I was sick and tired of being recognised and, in my drug-induced state, I blamed Mike. When I was really out of it, I wrote him a nasty letter. Thankfully, he never replied but I was apprehensive about what he would say if I saw him again. I told the producer that I wasn't sure how my relationship was with Mike and that maybe I wasn't the right person to be involved. He told me that they couldn't do the show if I wouldn't do it. He likened our bond to that of Abbott and Costello, Martin and Lewis, or Gilligan and the Skipper. That was pretty funny, actually.

He went on to say that people would always remember Mike's documentary on me and that we were forever linked. After listening to him for a while, I agreed to appear. I was nervous about what would happen. All I wanted to do was go to the studio to apologise to Mike for being a complete arse.

A few days later, a researcher named Antonia rang and gave me different details to those the producer had given me but, instead of being calm and sorting it out like an adult, I once again put my foot in my mouth and became obnoxious.

A week later Myles and I were flown to Sydney. By then, I was mortified at how I had reacted on the phone and intended to apologise to Antonia when I saw her in Sydney. (I was starting to build up a list of people I had to say sorry to!) On arrival the most stunning woman I had ever seen in my young life walked up and introduced herself. 'Hi, Quentin. I'm Antonia Kidman.'

The name whizzed around in my head and suddenly the penny dropped. I had been a complete shit to Nicole Kidman's sister. Myles knew what I had done, leaned down and whispered, 'Smooth moves, man. Smooth moves.'

I didn't feel good about myself, that's for sure, and I was pretty quiet for the rest of the day. I was feeling bad about being rude to Antonia and I was nervous about seeing Mike again. There were many other celebs to talk with and I tried to focus on them and not on the fact that the last time I'd been in that studio I was stoned off my head.

The studio audience filed in and the show began. When it was my turn to appear, I realised I'd worried for nothing because, as the old saying goes, the show must go on, no matter how you are feeling. My bit went off without a hitch except that I couldn't look Mike in the eye. After the show, a party was held and I wanted to talk with Mike but he had many friends and family around him so I didn't feel it was appropriate. I mingled with Myles and some of the crew. We left but I felt something was missing. There were two people to whom I hadn't apologised and I wasn't sure when I'd next get a chance to do it.

Not long after I returned to Adelaide, *Woman's Day* magazine rang me and asked if they could interview me about my work at TAFE. They were willing to pay so I agreed. It was a disaster. The reporter somehow knew about my drug addiction and instead of focusing the interview on my work, she asked me about my personal life, and my lack of a girlfriend. She then asked if I'd have my photo taken holding a rose. I refused but it was pointed out that, as I was being paid for the interview, I should do what I was told. Uncharacteristically, I did!

When the story was published, I was mortified and so were the senior management of TAFE. It was a bad piece that didn't show me, or my job at TAFE, in a good light. I was brought before the director of the campus and given an official warning stating that publicity like that was not welcome and, if I were to continue to work there, I would have to consult with them before I agreed to do similar media. I was so upset, I sulked for days and regretted agreeing to take part in the interview. My friends supported me and Sue was wonderful too, but it took a few months to put the incident behind me and get my confidence back.

A while later, TAFE planned a promotion to try to gain more enrolments. The executives thought this was my chance to make up for the magazine interview and do some good with my celebrity status. So I was taken out of Sue's department and put into the marketing department on a temporary basis. While there, I was asked to help create a television commercial to promote an information day. I was thrilled to finally have a crack at making something on film. I helped write and produce the piece and it went to air. It was a low-budget educational commercial but I felt like Steven Spielberg after it was finished. In my mind I had taken the first step down the path to becoming a film-maker. It felt good.

Not long after this, Sue left to have a baby and I was returned to the switchboard. I didn't love it but I knew exactly what was expected so I settled back into the job. I was happy to take my time developing my skills and get ready for my next film opportunity. I should have realised my life is never drama free!

CHAPTER 17

Snap, crackle . . . pop

On 27 February 1996 I turned twenty-one. Turning twenty-one is a big celebration for most people and I wasn't any different. My mother had returned from a trip to Austria just before the party. I was angry with her for always being away and so I asked that she not sit by me nor speak to the media at the party (Channel Nine was covering the event). I still wanted to punish her and Dad back then.

In the photos from that night I look so young and carefree. You'd never know I was a recently recovered drug addict dealing with a dysfunctional family and bouts of depression. It is an important lesson. When you see photos of friends or celebrities you might think they have shiny, happy, sparkling lives that are much more interesting and fulfilled than your own, but no one really knows what is going on in other people's lives behind their Instagram or Facebook pose.

After the party, life went back to normal and worked ticked on. I was occasionally getting an extremely sore back from sitting in the same position in my wheelchair for hours a day but I'd take some Panadol and it would usually ease off. One afternoon I got home tired and grumpy because the Panadol hadn't worked so I decided I should lie down and rest. Myles was home so I asked him to help place me on my bed. As he did, his hands slipped and my body folded in on itself, causing the muscles around my vertebrae to tighten and spasm around the bone. My bones gave way and I broke my back.

I knew what had happened because the lower half of my body went completely limp and numb. I couldn't move my legs. The most blinding, sharp stabbing pain shot through my back over and over again. I screamed as loudly as I ever have in my life and I started to go into shock. The thought that I might become a paraplegic consumed me. I don't think I've ever been so scared. I thought over and over that it would be better to die than to suffer from two debilitating disabilities.

Myles immediately rang for an ambulance and then tried to calm me down so that the spasms might ease. It was no use. I just kept screaming. I knew that I had to relax my body, so I breathed out as hard as I could and then held my breath until I knew I could control it. Once I had my breathing under control, I attempted to move my legs. I started with my big toe. I couldn't feel it but Myles said it was moving. I then tried to move my feet and legs and realised I could move them but I couldn't feel myself doing so. I was slightly relieved. The minutes waiting for the ambulance seemed like hours. The pain remained even though the spasms were diminishing. I started thinking about pain relief, good hard narcotics which could drop an elephant.

After the ambulance arrived to whisk me to hospital on an immobilising spinal board, an inexperienced intern greeted me. It was her job to do the first examination. Her technique was terrible and, when she lifted my leg upwards, the spasms recurred. I was in so much pain, I did the first thing I could to make her let go of me. I hit her on the arm and told her to 'Fuck off and get me a real doctor'.

Tears welled in her eyes and she ran off. I know what I screamed was terribly wrong but, at the time, I felt neither guilty nor concerned for her. At least the orthopaedic registrar arrived more quickly. He took one look at me and ordered full back and neck X-rays as well as agreeing to give me pain relief. Pumped with morphine, I was soon pretty drowsy. This made my muscles relax and, to my extreme relief, the sensation returned to the lower part of my body. I lapsed into unconsciousness soon after.

I came to three days later. A drip was in my arm yet the pain was still intense. I was flat on my back and couldn't see anything except the ceiling. A team of doctors entered and told me that I had fractured my L4 vertebrae and that a pinched nerve caused by the muscle spasms around the injury had caused temporary paralysis. They said that for the first week or two I would be regularly sedated and it was important that I move minimally.

In other words, my back was broken.

In those first few weeks I was dependant on nurses for everything. They fed, washed and toileted me, and rolled me on to my side twice a day so that I wouldn't develop pressure sores. Instead of feeling depressed, I was relieved. I felt I had dodged the biggest bullet of my life. I had been knocked down harder than ever but now had the chance to overcome it. Dad, Myles and Sia were frequent visitors but, because of the drugs being pushed into me regularly, I wasn't really aware of their presence. I hardly noticed Mum's absence. She was working in India and knew nothing of what had happened. After about three weeks, I was slowly weaned off the painkillers so that I would be more alert and ready for the weeks of rehabilitation ahead.

It's quite weird to wake from a semi-conscious state after so long. I realised that the world had passed me by. I began to care about the small matters of life again. How was the weather? What time and day was it? When could I eat that pile of chocolate people had sent me? I wanted to see my friends and find out how they were. I sought a familiar face to tell me I'd be okay. Unfortunately, I would have to wait until I was a little stronger. So with a KitKat in one hand and the television remote control in the other, I decided that I would not become depressed and convinced myself that it would be okay for the world to pass me by a little longer.

A kind of formulaic monotony kicks in when you are in hospital for so long. The days were completely the same except for what television shows were on. The nurses woke me and prepared me for the day at around 7.30 am. I watched television until 10.30 when doctors arrived to assess me. Then more television until lunch, which would only be disturbed if a medical student wanted to conduct a case study on me. It was surprising how often that happened. Lunch was at noon, more TV until 2 pm, nap till 4 pm, then dinner at 5 pm was followed by prime time viewing. My schedule was full.

The evenings were loneliest. The hustle and bustle of the hospital quietened down. If I was not careful, this was when depression could creep in. Every day, I hoped that someone would visit me after they finished work. I imagined what I would be doing if I wasn't in hospital. I'd think about what movies I was missing at the cinema; what my friends were doing without me. But I tried not to let big issues enter my head. In the end though, they did.

The big questions were how long would I be there? Would I be able to sit again and drive my wheelchair? The major question was how would this setback affect my growing independence? Would I be able to function as I did before the accident? Would I be able to return to work? My mind was filled with too many questions and too many 'what ifs'. This is why I have to shout a big thank you to Bert Newton, Oprah Winfrey and the makers of *NYPD Blue* for keeping my mind occupied enough so that these questions and depressing thoughts weren't consuming me twenty-four hours a day.

By week six, the real battle began . . . rehabilitation. I was scheduled to see Kerry, a physiotherapist, every day until I was discharged. It was her job to get me functioning on all cylinders. It was tough. Some of my muscles had frozen and some had atrophied or knotted into balls. Kerry massaged my frozen muscles so that they could start to move. She focused on my legs and lower back, the region of the injury. She then gave me differently weighted bean bags and told me to lift them as often as I could throughout the day.

At first I could only lift the very small weights and the massaging hurt terribly, but I knew it would help. I was determined to persevere. I made my exercise routine a game. I lifted the weights five times during the television commercial breaks and rested after 6 pm. Slowly my strength increased. Friends began visiting regularly at night so my loneliness wasn't as bad. Mum returned from abroad. I asked her to bring me some decent food. I couldn't stand the hospital stuff.

After I'd been in my hospital bed for eight weeks, Kerry said that I was ready to return to my wheelchair. I was terrified. I was scared that my back would break again and that I would be permanently incapacitated. She showed me a way of bracing my stomach muscles when I was lifted to protect my back. With a deep breath and a nervous smile, I allowed a nurse to place me in my chair. As soon as I was upright, I felt dizzy and panicked. But Kerry assured me that this was because I had been lying flat for so long and that it would take a while for my body to become accustomed to sitting.

She instructed me to make sitting in my wheelchair part of my daily routine and to try to stay in it a little longer each day until I was able to stay upright for five hours. This was a battle as there wasn't much to do but roam the corridors and feed the birds in the courtyard. In total, I was doing about four hours of strength-training a day and gradually sitting upright more and more.

Eleven weeks after breaking my back, I was ready to go home from hospital. I was happy and apprehensive simultaneously. I wanted my freedom, my own bed, my friends and food that wasn't served on a tray. On the other hand, I was anxious about how I would cope. When would I be strong enough to return to work? And there was the question of Myles. Would he be willing to care for me if the need arose?

When I got home from hospital I asked Myles how he felt. Rather than carrying a huge load of guilt about my accident, he was more worried about me and my wellbeing, which made me feel much better. I asked him if he was confident enough to pick me up again. He wasn't sure. I then described some new handling techniques which Kerry had shown me and asked him to test them. Nervously, we both braced ourselves and Myles successfully did it. That part of life was back to normal.

I spent the next few weeks pottering around the house and becoming stronger, ready to take on the world again. I spent time reflecting on what had happened. It was an incredibly amazing experience to fight my way back from a horrific injury. I had battled depression, loneliness, fear, anxiety and pain and overcome them all (or at least learned to live with them).

Since that time, I have tried to protect my back as much as possible. Unfortunately, I have developed a lordosis, or inward spinal curvature, from osteoporosis. This will only worsen over time. I'm heartened that there are medications being developed that will slow the process.

I'd broken bones, been injured and come through long surgical procedures in the past but my broken back was different. It was terrifying. It was also the first time I'd had to make life and death choices myself. Before I turned eighteen, my parents had made decisions for me. Now, I faced quandaries on how I would live and how I could potentially die. I also knew I'd have to face the prospect of being confronted with these issues again.

In the meantime, I had to focus on returning to work, my friends and the life that had passed me by for months. However, when I returned to work, things had changed. I was transferred away from the switchboard to work in the Wool Education section at a different campus. The wool section was where farmers and shearers were taught about the different types of wool and how to grade and sell them, and basically everything to do with what came off the sheep's back.

I was keen to be back at work but what the hell did I know about wool? I asked if I could go back to a more familiar section but nothing happened. I talked to my union rep and asked him to help but that failed too.

I gave the wool section a try but I couldn't physically do the job. Half of my duties meant removing samples of wool from large cabinets and cataloguing them on the computer. I simply couldn't lift the samples. I raised the issue of a transfer again but I was told that the wool job was the only position available at the institute and that if I couldn't do it my contract would not be renewed at the end of the year. I reacted with my trademark lack of maturity at the time and said if I wasn't to be renewed then I wasn't working.

The response was that if I didn't work, I'd be fired. It was a stalemate as far as I could see. I couldn't do what they wanted me to do so I simply couldn't work. But I was pissed off and decided to test the theory that it was almost impossible to be fired as a public servant. So every day I turned up at 9 am, surfed the internet, talked to friends and took long breaks until I left at 5 pm. It became my full-time job to avoid work. I suspect my friends disagreed with what I was doing but I believed I was being discriminated against and I had to take some sort of stand. This went on for more than two months until 20 December 1996, my last day working at TAFE.

It was the day of our big Christmas party, where the director of the institute thanked everyone who was leaving TAFE to pursue other opportunities. They all received a gift and a cheer. Unfortunately, I was not included in this group. Apart from my friends, I'm not sure I said goodbye to anyone. I just packed up my desk and left. The strange thing was that even though I was upset, I still felt positive. I believed it was the dawning of a new time in my life. I would finally be free to become a film-maker.

CHAPTER 18
Dick Smith to the rescue

After three years in government employment, I was happy to put the working world behind me for a while. Our shared house continually buzzed with activity as friends visited almost daily. Having a group of friends on whom I could rely meant the world to me. Andrew and Sebastian were like brothers to me and I think Myles felt the same. At the time, we were all experiencing different changes in life and heading down our own paths.

I still wanted to get into film-making. My father recognised that entering the film industry was a difficult process and that I should have a back-up plan, so suggested that I study marketing and advertising. He wasn't being discouraging but he wanted me to keep my options open, pointing out that my public relations knowledge had helped me produce my first TV commercial for TAFE and that marketing study could lead to other things. I didn't need much convincing and quickly enrolled in a course at TAFE's city campus.

Although Dad and Myles had already taught me many of the principles of marketing and advertising, I found the course absorbing. It was a good feeling as I hadn't really challenged my brain for a few years.

One lunchtime I came across a place called the Media Resource Centre – a not-for-profit organisation designed to help emerging film-makers. Sebastian had told me earlier that the centre could help people enter the film industry but I lacked the courage to go in. Although my friends were supportive of me, they weren't sure if the knowledge I had accumulated as a child on television could transcend into some sort of film-making talent.

After a few false starts, I decided to take a deep breath and enter the centre. But when I was confronted by two flights of stairs, my eagerness evaporated. I turned away. Luckily a man was walking down the stairs. He recognised me from TV, introduced himself as Kanesan Nathan and we talked. I told him about my desire to make films and he told me about a short film he was making for the South Australian Film Corporation. It was called *I Was A Teenage Child Bride*, a comedy about arranged Indian marriages. It sounded fantastic. I was talking to someone who was actually fulfilling his dream. Kanesan was creating entertainment for an audience and I wanted to do the same. He said that the best person for me to talk to was Philip

Elms. I thanked Kanesan, took his number and promised to communicate with him once he finished shooting his short film.

The next day, I made an appointment to meet Philip to chat about my ideas. He was really welcoming and actually took my desire to make films seriously. At first he tried to talk me out of entering the industry. He explained how hard it was and how few people made it. But I think he recognised that I was determined to have a crack anyway so he told me that the most important thing was the story. If you didn't have a good story, you had nothing. He advised me to go home and write a script. It didn't matter if it was big or small. The important thing was that I should write the story down on paper. I left the meeting on a huge natural high. I couldn't wait to write. Over the next two months, I wrote a script called *Love Bites*. It was about an assassin who received jobs over the internet and killed people for money.

Sebastian, Andrew, Myles and my other friends read it. Everyone gave it the thumbs down. I thought it was brilliant and told them that they wouldn't know a good script if it hit them in the face. But then Philip read it and, sadly, he too thought it was crap. I was heartbroken. All that work, all my ideas, and everyone else thought they weren't fit to use as scrap paper. I felt like giving up. 'If you ever have a good idea, I'll help you by working on it,' Phil said.

He also said he'd train me in some film-making techniques, particularly editing. Back then, people didn't really edit on computers as they were expensive. They used what is called a linear-editing suite, commonly known as a tape-to-tape system. At first, I re-edited old short films and eventually I started editing people's show reels and wedding videos. Initially I didn't charge people as I was still learning, but eventually I was competent enough to charge $25 an hour.

When I was editing, I wasn't treated as Quentin, the celebrity; I was just Quentin, the editor, which was fantastic. People hired me for what I could do, not who I was. To me, that meant everything. I also continued to attend my marketing lectures to maintain good grades. The pressure was on and my time began to thin but I pushed myself because I was loving doing it all. But by September 1997 things came to a head. My body didn't like being pushed too hard and my health started to decline.

I caught a cold. Over the next two days I worsened. It was becoming harder to breathe and I lost all desire to eat. On the third day I started coughing up large amounts of blood. Something was very wrong. I knew it was bad so Myles took me to the emergency department of Flinders Medical Centre. After examinations and X-rays, I was told I had pneumonia and that only 5 per cent of my lung capacity was working. If I had not gone to the hospital I could have died. I was administered a variety of antibiotics and anti-inflammatory drugs to assist my lungs. I was shocked to hear I had been close to death.

At first I didn't tell Mum and Dad as I didn't want to worry them unduly. It may seem strange to most people not to call your parents when you had almost died, but for me near-death wasn't a one-off occurrence. Thankfully, the staff at Flinders Medical

Centre wove their medical magic and allowed me to cheat death once more. Once my condition had stabilised, I was transferred to Blackwood Community Hospital in the hills, closer to my parents and my doctor. There, I discovered that my father had been admitted to hospital as well and also had pneumonia. His emphysema had worsened; he could only walk short distances and was using oxygen most of the time. I couldn't believe that he was still smoking. The staff asked if I wished to share a room with him but being roomies only lasted twenty-four hours. My old man snored dreadfully!

Over the next three weeks, the physiotherapist worked on clearing my chest. The treatment unfortunately caused me to break five ribs but it couldn't be helped. All my friends visited and smuggled in Hungry Jack's whenever possible.

It was a strange feeling to know that I'd escaped the big beyond several times. It made me wonder if the next hospital-isation would be my last. Escaping death so many times gave me a superiority complex, as if I were Superman and nothing could kill me. I may have taken that notion just a tad too far because when I was discharged I went to a tattoo parlour in the city and had the Superman 'S' inked on to my left shoulder.

Dad was out of hospital before me and I went to visit him. I showed the tattoo to Mum. She scrubbed steel wool on my arm thinking that it was a big inked hoax. Dad just smirked and said, 'You are probably right, son. The only thing that will undoubtedly kill you is kryptonite and we are in short supply.'

It became a bit of a joke, which he used to regale his mates with at the RSL. That hospitalisation had blessed me with one important thing though: an idea. I looked at my father and myself and wondered what the effects of his constant cigarette smoking had done to both of us. I knew smoking was on the rise with young kids. I decided to make a documentary about the dangers of smoking on young people; I called my concept *A Different Perspective*. I needed $20,000 to lift the idea off the ground. I approached the Anti-Cancer Foundation and was told it was a great concept which they'd like to support but they had to spend their funds where they were needed most.

I met up with a friend, Nick Bevan, who was working as a financial planner. He said I needed a proposal and a business plan outlining how I could raise the money. He signed an agreement to help me. It took time to get the business plan together as I was receiving advice from both Nick and Phil separately on the best ways to write it. After about two months, it was ready to market. Nick sent the proposal to many people; I was surprised he was so determined to help me but I was also grateful for his support.

I wanted a celebrity to speak in my documentary as I knew that would appeal to kids. Not just any celebrity, I wanted a big name. When Kylie Minogue came to Adelaide, I contacted her. She remembered me from when I appeared with her sister Dannii on *Young Talent Time*. Unfortunately Kylie declined to appear in my documentary due to touring commitments but she suggested that I try Dannii as she would be in Adelaide for a production of *Grease* later on in the year. Kylie was so wonderful and gave me front row tickets to her concert. I took Penny and we loved it. Kylie is one of Australia's great talents and she is an equally fine person.

When singer Tina Arena, also formerly a *Young Talent Time* star, came to town, I asked her if she'd be in my documentary. She too declined but also gave me tickets to her concert. She gave me a big hug and spent about half an hour talking to me. Her concert was awesome and, when she sang 'Amazing Grace', I think everyone at Adelaide's Entertainment Centre had tears in their eyes. I sure did.

I checked with Nick regularly but no one would fund my show. We began to think that the project would never succeed. Then he got a call from adventurer/entrepreneur Dick Smith's office. Dick had read our proposal and seen the value in it for kids. He said that if we made it with the full support of the Anti-Cancer Foundation he'd be willing to fund it. I was gobsmacked. Someone actually believed in my idea and, more to the point, believed in me.

When I rang Phil, the first thing he said was, 'Oh, shit.'

He hadn't thought I could get the money but was pleased just the same. He and I began work immediately.

We purposely scheduled filming around the time that *Grease* was appearing in Adelaide so that we could hopefully persuade Dannii Minogue to be in the show. We conducted pre-production, including hiring a crew. This was my first big directing gig and I was as nervous as hell, but Phil was there to mentor me through the process. He also agreed to shoot the documentary so that I could learn lighting and camera techniques. We started filming but left the celebrity shoot until last to give us time to make it happen.

We started the documentary with a profile on Dad. His emphysema was now really affecting him and he wanted to get the message to kids that they shouldn't start smoking or they'd end up the way he had. I thought it was brave as he opened up quite a bit to the camera and let the audience understand his distress. It was hard to film him like that as it wasn't the lasting memory I wanted of him. I wanted to remember him as the journalist dashing around at a million miles an hour to chase down a story and file it before hanging out at the pub.

Next we interviewed people from the Anti-Cancer Foundation. Filming them was smooth too. It was coming together and all we needed was a celebrity to hang it off.

I'd somewhat misled Phil by letting him think a celebrity had already been locked in. I didn't like being dishonest but I was determined to back myself and I really thought I could pull it off. He was unhappy when I told him the truth and he gave me the first of what would be many lectures over the course of our friendship. He means well when he takes me to task and it only happens when I've really stuffed up. Nonetheless, we both rocked up to the Hotel Hilton International to try to lock in Dannii.

I had contacted her but she hadn't replied. I'd even sent flowers to her room but they failed to get her attention. Despondently wheeling through the hotel's foyer, thinking all was lost, I ran into Craig McLachlan. I'd met him in 1990 when I was filmed in a scene for *Neighbours*. Yes, I once visited the set of Ramsay Street and shot a scene at the Robinson house with Alan Dale. I was fifteen – and a terrible actor. My scene was cut but during the shoot I met and became friendly with actor and rock singer Craig. At the Hilton, I told him about the documentary and my need for a celebrity to feature in it.

Without hesitation, he offered to be interviewed. All I had to do was clear it with his manager and we could shoot the next day. I was stunned. Phil called me the luckiest bastard on Earth. I was starting to agree with him.

In the morning, Craig was tired after a late night of partying. I guess what they say about the rock star life is true. I was grateful he was there. He was not feeling too well but as soon as the camera rolled, Craig fired up.

Turning on his charm, he soon had the crew in stitches of laughter. His answers to my questions were well considered and spoken in a language young kids would understand. He let me interview him for more than an hour. He was a true professional and added something special to the documentary. After he left, the crew was on a high. We realised that Craig had made the show funnier and given it an edge. We shot the rest of my pieces to camera and some random comments from people we approached in Rundle Mall. My friends Lee and Tanya also agreed to be in the program. Filming was wrapped and we were all pleased with the result. I was stoked!

Then the hard work began. Every day I met with my editor, Ryan Howard. Ryan was a patient person because I could be

demanding. I'd have crazy ideas about the documentary's potential. He would listen and then try out what I wanted. After a
lot of work, *A Different Perspective* was finished and we were
all proud of it. I was so grateful to everyone who had helped
me. I decided that a big launch would be appropriate to kick
it off, followed by large distribution to potential broadcasters
and festivals.

The ABC had rung me and asked if I'd appear in their
Australian Story episode about Mike Willesee. We decided to
launch our film in conjunction with the filming of the show.
That way, the ABC would be able to shoot something interesting
and my documentary could gain some free publicity. Invitations
to the launch were posted and mostly everyone replied yes. Dick
Smith couldn't make it because he would be away on business.
I could understand that, but then my dad declined, which I
wasn't expecting.

Since his condition had worsened, Dad had become
agoraphobic and germ phobic; he was paranoid that the air-
conditioning at the cinema would spread germs which would kill
him so he decided to stay at home. I was upset. My father had
been the catalyst for the whole documentary. Strangely though,
my anger didn't last. In the end, I just felt sorry for him.

The day of the launch arrived and we filmed the material for
Mike's special. I finally apologised to him in person for the harsh
letter I'd sent him years before. I was so sorry for the things that
I'd said. He told me it was okay and he'd guessed that I'd been

going through rough times when I wrote it. I was relieved that he accepted my apology, as it was genuinely heartfelt.

As guests arrived for the launch, my nervousness grew. I'd invited all my friends, family and work colleagues. Too soon, it was time to show the finished documentary. The first half went well but then an audio glitch occurred and the sound went dead. Phil and I just looked at each other. We stopped the film and checked it. It seemed there was a problem with one of the master tapes and I apologised to the crowd. We eventually fixed the problem but people's reaction to the show was mixed. I knew that it wasn't great and, if I knew then what I know now, I'd change the whole thing. My mum loved it, as mothers should. Mike told me it was a good effort for my first time. I knew that I could have done better but I put that disappointment behind me and enjoyed the rest of the night.

Over the next month, I tried to get the film out to broadcasters but it was rejected by them all as, deep down, I knew it would be. I am pleased to say that the Anti-Cancer Foundation used it as a resource and that made me happy. I hope that it benefited some people. At the start of the project I had known nothing so it was a huge learning experience and one I was very grateful for. We can't all be Matt Damon or Ben Affleck and win an Oscar with our first film!

CHAPTER 19
Never tip the waiter!

Midway through making *A Different Perspective* the lease on our share house expired. We'd been in each other's pockets for over three and a half years and it was time for us to go our separate ways. Myles also recognised it was time I looked after myself. This meant living without him to do things for me. Even though I was apprehensive, I knew he was right.

I'd been on a waiting list for a new place specifically designed for me in Adelaide's city centre by University of South Australia architecture students, but building had been delayed. It would be six months before I could move in. I was allocated a government-subsidised Housing Trust house in suburban Plympton Park.

In less than two hours, I knew I hated my new house. On that first day, the next-door neighbours jumped the fence and stole the pilot lighting mechanism to my gas water heater. Not long after that, I discovered that drug dealers lived two doors down. I watched as they did deals openly in the street. They were loud and screamed and fought and the whole atmosphere of the neighbourhood was charged with a feeling of danger.

A few times I came home to find that people had broken in and taken a look around my house. I called the police but they never found the culprits. I decided to buy an emergency alarm and was glad I did because one morning at 3 am, a stoned guy started bashing on my door, demanding to be let in. I was scared and upset at being alone. After that, I begged Myles to stay with me and he stayed a few days but he said that it was important for me to learn to live by myself.

One day my friend and taxi driver, Dave Hope, mentioned that the police had taken over a house down the road and were watching my street. I was angry when he told me. Why didn't they bust these people then? The next day, I drove my wheel-chair to the surveillance house and was greeted before I'd even knocked. At first, the guy denied he was a cop but I told him to stop lying. I knew the truth and asked him if he'd seen what had been going on in the street. He said he had. I asked him why he hadn't busted these bastards.

He told me he was sorry but they were after bigger fish.

I stormed off more furious than ever.

Things were going from bad to worse. I had just started dating a girl who I thought might act in a short film that Kanesan and I were writing. A dancer, she fitted the role perfectly. One evening, I took her out to dinner. And she went home with the waiter. I was crushed.

With the stress of creating my first documentary, drug dealers a few doors away, living in fear with sleepless nights and my girl running off with the waiter, I went into overload and stupidly started taking pills to take the pain away. For two weeks I went on a big binge. The paranoia returned after only a week.

I knew I was in trouble and needed help but I didn't have the time nor the inclination to return to rehab. I rang my friend Lee to explain my problem. He told me to grab all my medications and meet him in Rundle Mall. When I did, he said that for one day, we would party hard. We'd drink, get stoned and have a great time. At the end, any remaining drugs would go down the sink and that would be the end of it.

So that is exactly what happened. We partied, laughed, cried and got really messed up. At 5 pm, we entered a local cinema toilet and flushed every remaining drug away. It was the best thing. Lee then told me that if it happened again, he wouldn't help me. I knew he was right. I had to take control of myself and my emotions. I had to look after myself and learn not to rely on anyone else. I realised one valuable lesson: if you are an addict, you are always an addict. You may be clean and sober but addiction never goes away. You make a choice and I knew then that I would have to spend the rest of my life trying to avoid the bad path. I know now I can do it because since that day I haven't used drugs. But I also know I can never let my guard down.

When I received the call that my house, a two-bedroom apartment in the city, was finally ready for me, it was like a huge turning point in my life. I could start all over again. I couldn't get out of that drab Plympton Park cottage quickly enough. I didn't bother saying goodbye to the drug dealers, but I waved goodbye to the police.

Moving to the heart of Adelaide couldn't have been more perfect. I didn't need to spend money on taxis every day to travel, so I finally had money to buy real food. My friend Samantha stayed for the first four weeks but then she and her soon-to-be husband decided to live together. I was sad when she moved out but it was lovely to see her so happy. The other units in the complex were occupied by students and we all spent the summer together. There were numerous parties and I had a lot more visitors because I lived centrally.

The unit designed for me included cupboards and a stove installed at a level I could reach. All the doors were wider than standard size for easy wheelchair access. The apartment was modern and sleek and an easy place for my care workers to maintain.

The new place gave me a new attitude and I decided to make some other changes. I was only one subject shy of gaining my marketing diploma but I had tried and failed the accounting component twice. I knew that no amount of study would make me understand it so I decided to ditch the diploma for something more film focused. Some people may call that quitting but I see it as knowing your limitations and strengths.

I took a test and was accepted into university to study for an arts degree, majoring in film and drama. Almost too excited for words, I was finally about to concentrate on the subjects I loved most. When I started, I was so nervous. Every day, Dave drove me to Flinders Uni and I was unsure initially if I fitted in. But, after a month, I realised that I was in the right place. I made some fantastic friends and learned about different aspects of cinema, about Russian, French and Australian cinema and the encroachment of Hollywood around the world. I was even gaining distinctions for some of my assignments.

While my days were filled with study, nights concentrated on partying. My friends and I liked Tuesday karaoke nights at the Hilton International. I loved singing. Often I'd wake up on a Wednesday morning with a hangover saying I'd never do it again, but by the next Tuesday those words were forgotten.

I was still spending time at the Media Resource Centre. Phil and I were becoming friends outside of work hours and I started to create more films. My first was called *Dumped, Thumped and Nauseated*. It was a short film about a guy from England who meets an Australian girl over the internet. He flies over to see her and, over twelve days, gets dumped, thumped and nauseated. It screened with some other short films at the Mercury Cinema as part of Adelaide's 24-Hour Film Festival. I felt it was a real accomplishment as it was my first fictional piece and a work which I wrote, edited and directed.

Phil liked the way I wrote comedy and asked me to write a short film for a class he was teaching. The only problem was he asked me on a Friday and the class started on the Monday. I racked my brain and came up with a film called *Tomorrow I am Klingon*. It is about two men dressed as characters from *Star Trek* and what happens to them on the way to a convention. My mates from uni starred in the film and Phil's students made it. It remains one of the funniest and most enjoyable productions I've written and been involved in.

Life was sailing along well. Uni, my home and my health were good. Heck, I was even dating on a regular basis, though nothing ever went too far. A lot of the time women walked away when the physical relationship moved beyond kissing. Things all changed one day when I went to see Phil at his office. I was just about to cross a major intersection in Adelaide when a car rounded the corner and struck me. I had the 'walk' signal but the driver hadn't looked.

My leg and wheels were caught up and I was spun full circle yet, amazingly, I wasn't thrown out of my wheelchair. It was badly damaged, however, and my knee hurt. I took the man's details and then slowly drove my damaged wheelchair to see Phil. He took one look at me and suggested he call an ambulance. The Royal Adelaide Hospital was nearby so I said I'd drive myself. When I arrived, my wheelchair collapsed and my knee was three times the size it should have been. I was in a lot of pain. X-rays revealed a crack in my hip and one in my kneecap. I had also torn cartilage. The police came to the hospital to take a report. After being in emergency for five hours I was sent home, but I was in too much agony to move.

I rang my doctor and he said I should come into Blackwood Hospital again until my knee had settled. Dave, my taxi driver, suggested I find a lawyer. I spent the next two weeks trying to get better and working out what to do next. Luckily I didn't need my wheelchair while I was in hospital so it was repaired by the time I was discharged. I was fortunate it could be fixed.

After the accident I had a lot of trouble sitting up straight for long periods of time. Uni became impossible. I tried not to let depression overtake me. It was hard not to. After two weeks at home, I was contacted out of the blue by Network Ten's show *The Panel* asking if I would be interested in being on the program a week later. You bet I would! Making connections with successful production companies like Working Dog, who made the show, could possibly help me find film work. You never know what can happen if you put yourself out there.

A week later, although still in a lot of discomfort following the accident, I flew to Melbourne with a carer and appeared on *The Panel*. It was a big success. People saw me differently, not as the cute kid from the past. It was funny and the team at Working Dog invited me to a barbecue at their office the next day. I thought this was an honour as I had been a fan of theirs for many years. (They had written a few jokes about me when they did *The Late Show* on the ABC.) At the barbecue I chatted to their executive producer, Michael Hirsh, about my aspirations for a career in the industry. I was surprised when he said that my ideas were good and suggested that I should talk with Network Ten's head of programming, David Mott.

I was apprehensive at the thought – I'd sent David Mott a copy of *A Different Perspective* and had had no response – but Michael said it couldn't hurt and he rang David for me. He told me that Motty, as everyone called him, would contact me a few days later.

A few days after I returned to Adelaide, Motty did indeed ring me. He said he knew that I had some ideas and that I had twenty minutes to impress him. I was taken aback but couldn't miss out on this opportunity. Over the next twenty minutes, I rambled on about all of my ideas, trying to pitch something that would interest him. After my time was up, he said, 'They're not bad, mate, but what I'd love is a sequel to the Quentin documentary.'

I'd been offered big money in the past to do a sequel, but it would always have been under others' control, someone else putting their spin on my life. Every time I had refused.

Motty said, 'What if I asked you to do it? You're a film-maker. You should know enough tricks of the trade to do it yourself.'

I was shocked. The head of programming at a major Australian television network was actually encouraging me to make a documentary myself? It was too good to be true. He ended the conversation by saying that if I came up with the right package for the documentary, I'd have a deal. A deal, my first big deal. It was incredible.

I was excited but not enough to be stupid. I knew I wouldn't be able to do the documentary by myself, and I didn't think Phil would have the time, so I took the idea to my friend Grant

Anderson. For as long as I've known him, Grant's nickname has been Skip. I had met him through *A Current Affair,* where he'd been a producer, but he'd left to work at a company called Banksia Productions. Banksia had been in business for years and was based in Adelaide, so it seemed perfect. Skip and I were enthused about the prospect of working together. I developed the story elements of my life and he and his colleague Tony Agars worked on them.

Banksia was a big company, and it was difficult to make the project profitable for them within the budget drawn up. In the end, they had to pass it up. Skip and I were disappointed as we wanted to work together. We vowed that it would happen one day. I was anxious as I thought that, without Banksia, the deal would break apart. I called David Mott.

'Don't worry, mate,' he said. 'We can still do this. I'll give you fifty thousand dollars to make the show yourself.'

'Oh my god! Fifty thousand.' I must have sounded hysterical because he replied, 'Steady on. Fifty thousand is not a lot of money in television.' He continued, 'Quent, if you make a success of it, I've only spent fifty thousand. If you stuff it up, then I've only spent fifty thousand. I think you are worth the risk.'

I couldn't believe it. The deal was done. All I had to do now was convince Phil.

When we started discussing it, Phil was concerned that I wouldn't be objective making a documentary about myself. I told him this was all the more reason for him to help me. I needed someone looking over my shoulder to check that I wasn't glorifying myself or exposing too much of my family or my own life. I needed someone who'd tell me to pull my head in when it was needed. I offered him the role of associate producer and the opportunity to shoot some of the program as well. He finally agreed on the proviso that I would always listen to his advice and that any arguments we had at work, stayed at work. When the clock struck 5 pm, we would leave our differences behind. It was a deal.

We assembled a wonderful crew and the next big hurdle was convincing everyone, mainly my family, to be in the documentary. My parents agreed without hesitation and even gave me a thousand dollars to start up my own company, Q Productions Pty Ltd. Convincing Myles and Sia was harder. They'd never liked me being on television. Not because they were jealous but because they felt that I had been exploited by TV networks and they were fearful that it would happen again. I reassured them that I had complete creative control. Myles made me show him the contract to prove it. Once their fears were assuaged, I approached Mike Willesee. Surprisingly, it only took one phone call for him to say yes.

Everything was set, the network was happy, the treatment (or planning) had been approved, pre-production had gone smoothly and it all seemed too easy. Is it Murphy's Law that decrees 'anything that can go wrong will go wrong'? I hate Murphy!

On the day filming was due to start, my father was rushed to hospital with pulmonary oedema. He was immediately taken to intensive care and placed on a respirator. I was shocked.

I wasn't sure if I should cancel everything or continue. I sat by Dad's side for quite a while. He woke up, gave me a strange look and then with a lot of difficulty asked me what I was doing there. I told him that I'd put the shoot on hold. He took his mask off for a second and said, 'Son, you have a job to do. Don't sit here. Do it!'

I knew he didn't want me to worry about him; he just wanted me to succeed. I realised that was all he had ever wanted for me and I now had the opportunity. Although it pained me to leave, I pushed my feelings aside and began making *Quentin, World At My Wheels.*

Production started with an interview with my mother. I'd employed Chelsea Lewis, a reporter from Network Ten, to interview everyone so that each piece had objectivity but my parents insisted that I interview them. My mother was unusually nervous but, in the course of the interview, she warmed up. At this point, I no longer judged either of my parents for what they had done or how they had acted when I was younger. For my own sanity I'd had to let my anger go a few years before and so it was easy to look back and see the good as well as the bad. I needed to focus on the good.

When Mike Willesee came to town, I was really anxious. It was a weird experience for both of us as we'd completely switched roles: the reporter had become the subject and the subject had become the reporter. I decided to interview Mike myself and it was like being in the twilight zone. I had flashbacks of being seven years old when he'd had to bribe me for answers. I hoped he wasn't going to be as belligerent as I had been to him. I was pleased that Mike adapted and he gave a great interview. We laughed a lot and I was still able to bring a tear to his eye. When I took him back to the airport, he said that he was proud of me. To hear that from him meant so much as Mike was the person who had ultimately set me on this career path.

The next obstacle we had to overcome was to show me actually working as a film-maker. I'd written another short film, a comedy called *The Audition*. It centred around a girl having a bad day on her way to a theatre audition. We gained some funding from the Media Resource Centre to make it and shot it at the same time as the documentary. If directing one project was hard, doing two at once was almost impossible. However, the crew made it easy and, with the help of my uni mates, we completed *The Audition*.

The next thing I had to do was the hardest. Dad wanted us to film and interview him after he was out of intensive care and back home. I was not sure if it was the right thing to do, as I didn't want to show him in a bad state at home, but he insisted. He said that, if I were to make an accurate biography about myself, I had to stay true to those around me. I felt uncomfortable but respected his wishes. First, we filmed him in the hospital. The doctors didn't let us stay long and only Phil and I were allowed into his room. We remained about fifteen minutes but this was long enough to get what was needed. When Dad was discharged, he was weak. I wanted to cancel the filming but knew this would stress him more. Instead, we helped him sit behind his desk, propped him up and rolled the camera. He was on a lot of medication so when I asked questions, he'd focus for about thirty seconds then go off on tangents. In some answers he rambled for fifteen minutes about nothing. He even started talking about his father in World War I. After ninety minutes, the tape ran out but instead of stopping Dad, we let him talk. He seemed proud of himself and announced, 'There you go boys, a better class of interview.' We thanked him and assisted him back to bed.

The final hurdle was interviewing Myles and Sia. This was the most nerve-racking for me because I knew how they both felt about the media. Now I was on the other side! We flew Sia in from Sydney, where she was living, and put her up at the Hilton for a few days. I thought it best that Chelsea interviewed my siblings. At the start of their interviews, each seemed a bit tight-lipped. I took some red wine from the minibar to relax them. They'd asked me not to be present at their interviews so I disappeared for a few hours. When I returned, the crew was happy. The documentary was wrapped.

We only had five weeks for post-production as Network Ten was excited about the project and wanted it on air quickly. Ryan and I edited during the days and into the nights. It was rare that either of us saw more than a half-hour of daylight, we were so fixated on the project. This affected my eyes so I started wearing sunglasses everywhere, day and night. If I wasn't being objective about a shot or if Ryan and I had a disagreement, Phil arrived to give a judgement call.

The biggest argument we had was over a piece of archival footage. It was necessary to show some of my most memorable appearances on TV from the past. The problem was we didn't have the money to pay for them. When I asked Channel Seven for footage without charge, I entered a big debate with the then head of programming and was forced to pay full price for what they agreed to share. Channel Nine was a whole different story. David Leckie, who was head of the network then, replied to my request for some footage with, 'You know, Quentin, you've been good to us. When we've rung you for a story, you've done it without big demands and you have always given us exclusives. You can have all the footage you want at no charge. Good luck, son.' He had obviously studied at the Kerry Packer school of loyalty.

I couldn't believe it. They had remembered me and what we had done together. David gave me thousands of dollars worth of footage and never sent me an invoice. Johnny Young was the same when I needed footage from *Young Talent Time*. It gave me a warm feeling to know that these high-powered people had acknowledged my contributions and paid back in kind.

The main disagreement I had with Ryan and Phil was about that episode of Channel Nine's *The Midday Show* when I'd taken too many drugs. I didn't want to include it as it would potentially give kids watching the program a bad example. I asked the crew to give their opinions and they all said the same thing: 'It happened, it is a reality and part of your past. Have the guts to show your failings as well as your triumphs.'

I was ashamed and scared about what people would think but knew the crew was right. The segment stayed in the final cut.

The crew banded together for little money and helped me finish the show. I was grateful to everyone for their efforts. We had a small celebration after the documentary was finished but then I had to go straight from the edit suite on to the publicity trail.

Publicising the program was fun. I appeared on *The Panel* again and also Bert Newton's morning TV show. He is the only person with whom I feel nervous when being interviewed because he is a legend and knows just about everything in the television industry. His timing is impeccable. I have the highest respect for him yet always felt butterflies when I'm on his set.

Mum told me that Bert's wife Patti was an entertainer on the ship which took my parents to Europe years before my birth. She confided to Mum about her engagement to Bert in Tahiti and Mum wrote an exclusive article for *TV Week* with Patti's consent. Patti and Mum never met again but Bert and Patti have become part of my family's mythology.

The Ten network wasn't expecting big ratings for my documentary but put it against *Friends* in the hope that if it did well it would take some shine off that show. I was apprehensive the night it aired. The crew and a few friends were at my house but I spent most of the time hiding in my bedroom. I was just too worried what viewer reactions would be. It turned out the locals loved it and the rest of the nation did too.

I was told that 1.9 million viewers tuned in. It was the highest-rating Australian-made program for Network Ten that year. I was on my way again.

CHAPTER 20
Red Carpet ready

After the success of the documentary I went back to the negotiating table with Channel Ten. I had proved I could deliver so
I was hoping I'd now have more leverage over the size of the
budget and the scope of what I wanted to do when I pitched
concepts. I sat down with David Mott and went through a
number of what I thought were good ideas but none grabbed
him. I was going to have to think of something else. At the end
of the meeting David asked me what I was up to and I told him I
was off to the set of *Star Wars* to visit my friend Scott (McLean),
who was a stuntman on the movie. David told me he'd tried
incredibly hard to get cameramen and reporters access to the
Star Wars set but he had failed, so he wished me luck in my
opportunity. The next day Philip Elms and I ended up on the

set of *Episode II: Attack of the Clones*. We were shown around all the sets and we got to see Scott dressed as Jango Fett's stunt double. We even got to meet Sir Christopher Lee and George Lucas. Honestly, it was one of the greatest days of my life. I'd love to say more about what we saw and did but non-disclosure agreements with Lucas Films have no use-by date. All I can say is . . . it was awesome.

A few days later, David Mott rang me at home. He'd been thinking and he told me he was impressed by my ability to get on a set that his employees hadn't been able to reach. I didn't tell him that being very good friends with one of the stuntmen helped. (Why pull yourself down a notch if you don't have to?) David asked me if I'd enjoy doing it for a job. I wasn't sure what he meant at first but then replied dumbfounded, saying, 'I'm not sure George Lucas would want me and a TV crew there.'

David laughed and told me his idea. 'You see, Q, people engage with you in a different way than they do with reporters. They've never experienced a legitimate correspondent in a wheelchair. What if we sent you to the hottest parties, the biggest events in the world, uninvited, and see how much access you could get? It would be something fresh for audiences and it would be a first as you'd be the first person with a disability to have his own prime-time series of specials.'

The idea was amazing. Why not turn a wheelchair into an asset! David was not only entrusting me with his idea but he was banking on me with a real budget behind me to deliver it. We agreed that Phil and I could do it ourselves if we took on a Network-approved producer and director of photography. It was all agreed. When I told Phil, he was as excited as I was and came up with the title of the show. It came to him at breakfast at the Park Royal Hotel. It came to him over eggs. It was genius. *Quentin Crashes Hollywood.*

I was up for that!

My then agent, Mark Morrissey, introduced us to producer David Sheridan and, after a meeting with him, we knew he was good for the project. The network approved him and then put up Roman Baska as the director of photography. He'd won an Emmy Award for the powerful documentary *Exile in Sarajevo* and more recently he'd been working with Val Kilmer on a documentary about Mars. I didn't get to meet him before he was locked in. The next major decision was who'd be the executive producer. David Mott introduced me to Tim Clucas. Tim and I hit it off from the start and so that was a done deal.

The first big thing we did was put together a plan to try and schedule an interview with Drew Barrymore in Los Angeles when I arrived. Drew and I had some things in common. We were both famous at a young age. We'd both had teenage drug habits and problems with our parents. And we were both trying to redefine who we were as adults. It took two weeks of phone calls to her agent, publicist and production company, Flower Films, but we secured an agreement to meet with Drew. It was a great starting point and from there I knew it wouldn't be hard to make up the rest as we went along.

You'd think travelling to LA would be a breeze but it wasn't as simple as getting off the plane and picking up your lone suitcase. When we arrived our gear was seized by customs as we were told we hadn't declared our equipment properly. David and I had to pay a customs broker thousands of dollars just to get it all back. It wasn't the impression I was wanting to give Roman when I first met him and I could tell he wasn't impressed. I noticed his annoyance as I took in his Polish accent and the fact he was very, very tall. We got over this initial hurdle and pushed ahead.

The next day we set up cameras at the hotel to record me calling Drew Barrymore's publicist to arrange a time for filming. I was shocked when the publicist told me that Drew was unavailable and wouldn't be granting me the interview that had been promised and I had counted on as I travelled over 12,000 kilometres.

To say I was disappointed was an understatement. Booking the interview with Drew Barrymore was my task and my responsibility and I had been sure I had everything in place. I was letting everyone down. David Sheridan instructed me to ring Tim Clucas back at Channel Ten to tell him what had happened.

Tim wasn't just disappointed, he was flat-out angry. He told me he was going to ignore the conversation we'd just had for five days. That's when he had to report in to David Mott about what we'd been up to, so I had five days to shoot some great stuff . . . or to hide. He then said it wouldn't matter what country I tried to hide in – Motty would find me and tear me a new one. I am paraphrasing but you get the drift.

I tried to give Tim the best pitch of confidence I had, but I don't know if I was trying to fool him, or myself. It was a pretty depressing start but, rather than lose focus, Phil suggested we spend a few days shooting stock footage of me around Los Angeles while we worked out Plan B. He then casually suggested that we try to gatecrash the Academy Awards. This had never been done successfully before as far as we knew, so we all questioned it at first and then realised . . . it was the scathingly brilliant plan we needed.

There was no Ellen on the red carpet back then and no reporters doing shots of tequila with nominees. The organisation was all pretty straitlaced so having me rock up uninvited to gain access was not only going to be unusual, it was going to be damn-near impossible. But impossible is my middle name (actually, I have two, Alexandros Charles, but you already know that).

We decided we first had to test if celebrities would take to me interviewing them on a red carpet. We needed a dummy run. To get some information on the closest Hollywood party happening that night, I tipped the concierge of our hotel $100 to find out where and when it was. He slipped me the information and we were set. That evening, I donned a suit and rocked up with the team to a charity function for paediatric cancer that was happening on Robertson Boulevard. We were greeted by the organisers, who were more than happy to let an Australian film crew cover the event. Things were looking good.

And then along came Anthony Michael Hall. For those who don't remember him, he was the nerdy one from *The Breakfast Club* and the romantic comedy *Sixteen Candles*. Being a huge fan of John Hughes (the film-maker who directed those movies), I knew exactly who he was so I started asking him questions about the charity and about acting. He was polite and nodded but didn't reply. I was starting to get worried until he looked at me quizzically and said, 'You seem like a really nice little guy, but I can't understand a word you're saying.'

AHHHH!!!! The old Aussie accent dilemma. I asked if he would prefer I talk with an American accent. I said that in an American accent. He said yes (Myles would have hated it!). Suddenly, I was speaking his language. I'd never realised it, but it seems an Ocker Aussie accent is amplified tenfold to uninitiated Americans. After that elocution lesson, the rest of the night went quite well. Anthony showed us around a wheelchair-accessible chemotherapy unit for children – a place where low-income families with sick kids could stay in their homes and be given the same medical treatment as those with high-cover health insurance. I was impressed and flashbacked to some of the kids I'd met all those years before at Ronald McDonald House.

We had succeeded and I started to feel less anxious about being able to deliver. The next day, we headed to the Airport Marriott Hotel to apply for media accreditation for the Academy Awards. Because of the time difference, we weren't able to get hold of anyone from Channel Ten to help us but we happened to run into long-time Channel Seven Los Angeles correspondent

Mike Amor, who vouched for us and helped us fill out the paperwork. It was nice to be taken seriously and to experience some camaraderie from the Australian media.

Once we had what we needed we hit the red carpet area of the 73rd Academy Awards to check it all out. It was the day before the ceremony and security was high. I found out later there were rumours of threats against Russell Crowe, who was nominated for Best Actor.

There were a lot of guys in dark suits, dark sunglasses and carrying guns under their jackets. Now we had some accreditation I wasn't worried but Roman had just spent the better part of eighteen months dodging bullets, mortar shells and rockets while making his documentary about Sarajevo, so he wasn't very comfortable around so many armed men. He expressed concerns about being on site and the whole idea of us trying to get more access uninvited only heightened his anxiety.

We made a plan that David would keep Roman company while Phil and I investigated how to get a permanent place on the red carpet before the ceremony the next afternoon. After rolling into a restricted area by myself, an Aussie floor manager by the name of Dean Madden introduced himself and told me that the CIA were concerned about what I could be hiding amongst the wires and batteries of my wheelchair.

I asked him if he meant the FBI. He told me that because there was an al-Qaeda threat, it had become an inter-agency collaboration and that every law-enforcement agency was there. I should point out, readers, that this was 2001 and six months after this conversation the World Trade Center in New York was destroyed when two planes flew into the twin towers, but it was obvious to me that tensions were heightened well before that. Dean told me to go back to the hotel and to be prepared to be vetted by one agency or another the next day. He was to call me with a time to get checked out.

The following day, when we rolled up, a guy dressed as a chef pulled all of us into a room where we were questioned for an hour about why we were there. We answered his questions honestly. We let him and his colleagues search our gear and my wheelchair was checked with a metal detector and by a sniffer dog. I am not sure what use the metal detector was, because my chair was metal, but when they were convinced we were telling the truth about why we were there we were allowed to return to the Academy Awards compound and continue filming.

I almost immediately ran into Channel Ten's Angela Bishop, who was more than happy to share information with me, given that we were both working for Channel Ten. Richard Wilkins also came up to me and asked to share information too, stating that I grew up with Channel Nine, so I should have some residual loyalty and be willing to scratch backs if we gained interviews. Normally I would, but Nine wasn't paying the bills so I had to tell him I would be keeping my cards close to my chest. He was still lovely but I could see a competitive edge creep in as he smiled and walked away.

I had to focus because I still had to gain access to the red carpet event when the stars arrived. The access we currently had ended at midday on the day of the ceremony. Then it hit me like a bolt of lightning. I looked around the bleachers, to all the fan access, and there was not one section allocated for people in wheelchairs. If I was ever going to make my move, it had to be then. With advice from the crew we all went up to the organisers of the awards and asked, quite bluntly, why there was no disability access in the public gallery section of the Academy Awards. We were told that no one had ever asked for it, so no one had ever needed it. I then pulled out all stops and said that the United States of America was part of the 1986 Accord which recognised people with a disability and that, where possible, people with a disability are to be given the right to attend and be part of all public functions. I told the organisers that I would hate to go home and make a big deal about how the most prestigious award show in the world failed to cater to people with a disability.

Within three hours a separate platform was built for me and any other person with a disability to view the red carpet event. From what I gather, the platform has been erected every year ever since. I was chuffed. All we had to do was go to our hotel, chuck our tuxedos on and get ready for the fun.

Late that afternoon we returned to film the red carpet event of the Academy Awards. The atmosphere had supercharged since the morning. We set David and Roman up on one side of the bleachers, while Phil and I remained on the platform. It was a lot of fun. We tried to get stars to come and say hello to us, but we weren't in the best spot to get their attention. I did catch

Russell Crowe's eye and he turned and waved directly at me. He went on to win the Best Actor Award that night for his role in *Gladiator*. Julia Roberts won Best Actress for *Erin Brockovich* but I didn't get a wave from her.

It was actually pretty funny seeing all these men and women dressed up to the nines at four in the afternoon. Everyone was in their best version of themselves and there were millions of dollars' worth of jewellery, sequins and silk on parade as the actors spruiked themselves and their latest movies. What they don't tell you and what you don't see on TV is how loud it gets. Thousands of people scream for their favourite stars, dozens of photographers scream for the optimum photo angle and reporters scream to get the attention of the A-lister who will hopefully provide a winning sound-bite.

Once it was over, all four of us got together again to plan which Hollywood parties we would hit up to get interviews after the ceremony had finished. We decided to go to chef Wolfgang Puck's party at his restaurant, Spago, and the *Vanity Fair* party at Morton's Steakhouse.

The first party was a trial of what I could do and what I could get away with. I got on the red carpet interview line and interviewed previous Award nominee Robert Forster and Tom Arnold (Roseanne Barr's ex) from the movie *True Lies*. I was going to interview David Hasselhoff, but when I greeted him he called me Mini-Me, in reference to Verne Troyer's character in the Austin Powers movie. It wasn't said with love and I didn't take too kindly to this. I replied, 'Fuck it, I don't have the patience for you, you useless Baywatch has-been.' We decided to bounce and move on to the *Vanity Fair* party.

When we got there, most of the journalists were hitting up invitees at the entrance to the party. I ran into Angela Bishop again and we made an agreement that she would cover the front of the party and text me the names of those leaving who I would then intercept. The first people I got to speak to were Angelina Jolie and her father, Jon Voight. They were very gracious and spent a lot of time talking to me about the movie they were publicising that was coming out in June, *Tomb Raider*. Jon said goodbye to his daughter, jumped into a limousine and went home; Angelina went back to the party.

I then got a text from Angela, telling me that she had mentioned to Samuel L. Jackson that I was at the exit of the party and that I had the same disability as his character in *Unbreakable*. Mr Jackson made a special journey around to meet me. I interviewed him for twenty minutes and it was brilliant; the icing on the cake of our show. I talked with him about our joint interactions with George Lucas and about him portraying someone with osteogenesis imperfecta – and how much research he had done for his *Unbreakable* role. He had met quite a few people with my severity level of the disorder so knew what he was talking about. All too soon it was over and he excused himself. But the fun was just beginning.

I ran into Monica Lewinsky and cheekily offered her a cigar. It was a cheap jibe and I can't say I was surprised when the joke fell flat. We then ran into Geoffrey Rush. He was quite animated and talked about working with Susan Sarandon and Goldie Hawn in *The Banger Sisters*. Whether it was the Dom Perignon that was freely flowing or the fact that he was in a good mood I'm not sure, but he couldn't stop laughing about the double entendre of the film's title. He was good value. Then we saw Jennifer Lopez coming out of the party.

Gold! I had to talk to her. She was walking quickly and obviously not wanting to stop. I raced to catch up with her and I accidently ran over and tore her $35,000 Chanel dress. She stopped then. I was mortified and apologised profusely, removed my wheel from the dress and let her walk away. Once she was safely in her car, her five bodyguards came back to have a 'talk' with me. Things got very heated very quickly. Suddenly my three crew became my own bodyguards and Australian gossip columnist Peter Ford stepped up to intervene.

What started as a verbal altercation quickly deteriorated into pushing and shoving. The bodyguards were trying to lift me up in my chair and carry me across the road. My crew were trying to stop them. Luckily, a county Sheriff witnessed all of this and ordered the bodyguards back to Jennifer's car and then told me and my crew to call it a night and go home.

Shaken up from the incident and happy with the material we had, we agreed. On the way back to our car we ran into Angelina Jolie again. She was signing autographs for what seemed like hundreds of fans. I went up to her and said, 'Angie, why are you here? It's more fun at the party.' She replied, 'I can go to a

Hollywood party anytime I want. These people pay my bills. It's only fair I come and thank them when I can.'

This was kinda cool. None of the other stars had taken time out for their fans like she was doing. I walked away thinking very highly of her.

Just as we were about to get to our car, a woman fell out of her limousine near us. Roman rushed over and helped her get back in her car and we followed him. It was Whitney Houston. The man she was with, Bobby Brown, got our attention while she straightened herself up and wiped a smear of something off her top lip. Bobby asked us where we were from. We told him and he declared how much they both loved fish and chips and that they couldn't wait to get back to Australia.

I didn't know it then, but Whitney's dishevelled appearance that night foreshadowed the downward spiral which would ultimately cost Whitney her life eleven years later. It is sad to think that her daughter, Bobbi Kristina, who was eight at the time I met Whitney and Bobby, would eerily suffer the same fate as her mum.

The rest of our trip was equally as successful. We filmed all around Los Angeles and, a few days after the Oscars, I found out that Drew Barrymore had eloped with Tom Green, which explained why she was unavailable for our interview. I guess love waits for no one.

We flew back to Australia very pleased with everything. David and I mapped out the show and decided it would all hinge on our interview with Samuel L. Jackson. It had all the makings of brilliance – the tie-in to my disability, *Star Wars* – it was a script that magically wrote itself. If only it had been that easy. Once our editor had digitised and reviewed all the footage, he told us there were only forty seconds of Samuel L. footage on Roman's camera.

Surely this was a mistake. I thought we must have misplaced a tape so I called Roman. He told me that forty seconds into the interview his camera battery had gone dead. Rather than break the interview and change the battery, he kept the moment going, figuring we probably wouldn't use all the footage anyway. He didn't know then that our whole concept hinged on this one moment. I freaked out but then pulled myself together to try and work out what to do.

Phil once again saved the day. He said, why don't you build it up to the moment you ran over Jennifer Lopez's dress? He even came up with the promo, based on a credit card ad that had made an impact. Electric Wheelchair, $10,000. Chanel Dress, $35,000. The moment wheelchair runs over dress. Priceless.

We pitched that ending to Tim Clucas at Channel Ten and I filled him in on all the rest. He wasn't happy with the loss of the Samuel L. Jackson interview but he knew that if we ran Phil's promo, it would work with the target demographic. After weeks of flailing blindly in an edit room, our editor Ryan, David, Phil and I cut the show together. It was done and I thought it was good, but I was nervous about what others would think of it.

It didn't take long to find out.

CHAPTER 21

Hanging with the Muscles from Brussels

When *Quentin Crashes Hollywood* aired, it did not rate as expected – 1.1 million viewers watched but it failed to bring on board Network Ten's key demographics, which advertisers were not enamoured about. A lot of people who viewed it simply didn't like it. On internet newsgroups, some horrible things were said about me. I wish I could tell you I shook the comments off, but I didn't, they stung.

What really hurt was that people on disability websites said that I was a joke (and not a good one), and a few said I was the 'Uncle Tom' of the disabled community. *Uncle Tom's Cabin* is a powerful anti-slavery novel by Harriet Beecher Stowe, but the main character's name has been appropriated as a negative slur to suggest a person of colour is only acceptable to the white community because they act 'white'. So I was somehow betraying the disabled community because I was . . . what? I wasn't sure.

I was devastated by people's reaction to the show. I'd wanted people to see that disabled people could do almost anything if they set their minds to it, and that just because we are a bit different doesn't mean that our contribution is less valuable to society. I hoped people would understand, but they didn't.

After the disappointing result, and at times harsh personal criticism, I suffered what can only be described as an emotional breakdown. I needed to disappear for a while and I turned inward.

I wasn't the only one whose life changed dramatically after our Hollywood trip. Phil's marriage broke down and he realised he had to focus on his own relationships more, so I stopped seeing him as often. Most of my friends from the apartment block were moving out so my little party group was gone too.

I retreated to my unit. I stopped answering the phone and dealing with friends. I stopped going out and I asked my carers to shop for me so I wouldn't have to talk to anyone. That black dog came back and pushed its way into everything. I sank into a dark depression. For three months, I watched TV and rarely left the flat. I couldn't shake the feeling that I had failed my audience, my backers and myself. I'd never felt more confused or alone.

Despite facing depression before, this time it seemed I couldn't pull myself out of the funk I was in, but then three events set me on to recovery's road. The first came from the most unlikely source: my father. He was totally incapacitated from his lung condition and would call me frequently. I knew he was living vicariously through his children and I am quite sure watching TV and staring at four walls was not the lifestyle he was hoping to hear about. We'd have long conversations and I told him that I'd decided I wasn't cut out to be a film-maker. I fully expected him to tell me to try marketing again, but he didn't. Instead, he reminded me that film-making had been my dream since I was young and that quitters never made anything of themselves. They just faded away. He gave me the same advice he'd given me all those years ago when I wasn't connecting with Mike Willesee: he told me to fix my bayonet, face the front, take one final look at the past and then look to the future and my next battle. The problem was, I wasn't sure what battles lay ahead. But, after he gave me the same advice in a few different ways, something shifted. I agreed I had to give my career one more try.

While most people had fallen away, or I had pushed them away, Kanesan had maintained contact. He visited every week and often our discussions veered into what movies we loved and then into what films we both wanted to make. We'd spark ideas off each other. One idea we had was for a film called *The Claw*. The storyline was set around a character, played by me, and what happened when I lost the claw I used to reach things with. It was just something we wrote on the spur of the moment; however, I saw it had potential. I fired up and told Kanesan that we should apply to the South Australian Film Corporation (SAFC) for funding. We'd submitted applications together before but none had been successful, so when I suggested we apply with this new script idea, Kanesan was apprehensive. I gave him the same pep talk my dad had given me and talked him in to at least giving it a go. I never expected it to be successful. But it was.

I was truly humbled. After the experience of *Quentin Crashes Hollywood*, all my past cockiness was gone and I was determined to do everything I could to make *The Claw* work. I was so thankful that the SAFC chose to fund the film, and that faith lifted me from my depression and helped me rediscover real joy in my craft.

Another project being funded by the SAFC was a short film called *Cat*, written by two aspiring young female film-makers. I found out they needed extra funding and resources so I suggested that we combine budgets and shoot the films back to back. Everyone agreed that was a good idea so first off the block was *The Claw*.

With little money in the budget, I had to find a crew willing to work for nothing. I was lucky enough to convince Gary Sweet and former *Neighbours* actress Monika Karwan to be in the film. I had my mojo back and so I asked an Adelaide agency, Actors Ink, to represent me. One of the agents, Angie Christophel, agreed to appear in the film at late notice when one of the original cast had to pull out. The director of photography, David Belperio, had a wonderful sense of humour which kept everyone in stitches and the mood light. As we got closer to our first day of filming my nerves kicked in, not because I had to direct but because I had my first kissing scene with Monika.

I talked to her about it and she said that if I was nervous, we should practise. Ummm . . . okay!

So, in-between shots while the crew was setting up, Monika and I went somewhere quiet – and practised. Strictly for professional reasons, I swear! When it was time to shoot the scene, David wasn't happy. Either the light was wrong or there was a boom in the shot. The scene had twenty-seven takes. I didn't complain and neither did Monika. She is a lovely person. I later discovered that David stuffed up a few takes for my benefit.

Shooting the rest of the film was fun. Gary Sweet is a known prankster but he is also extremely professional and generous. He gave me some good acting tips. After shooting was wrapped, there was no time to lose. I had to jump from one film to another as we started preparing *Cat*.

The creators directed the film and I produced. Some of the crew transferred from *The Claw* to *Cat* and Angie was cast with a bigger role. Phil had sorted out some personal things and so was back on the team with me. Everyone was stretched to the limit on *Cat*. The crew was huge. We had to set up at more locations which meant more problems that had to be sorted. Cameras broke down and local people, who were disrupted at some of the location shoots, became angry when we took too long filming. But we were having the time of our lives. I enjoyed focusing on production. It was good to try something new and the two directors did a great job. Working with all these amazing people and watching a screenplay come to life helped me rediscover my love for film-making and rekindled my desire to succeed.

We found a great young editor who cut *Cat* and *The Claw* back to back. Kanesan and I insisted that *The Claw* be cut first as we wanted to enter John Polson's highly regarded Tropfest short film competition. We spent ages making the film as perfect as we could. We were able to use a free online editing facility at a place called Imagination Entertainment. I had used them once before and they were wonderful. Towards the project's end, Kanesan and I remained indecisive about the music. We consulted with a sound engineer for hours, listening to a huge selection but, on hearing Tchaikovsky's Nutcracker Suite, we knew we had it. That score made the whole film sound and feel mischievous, perfectly in tune with the character I was playing. We were ecstatic when it was finished. We both felt we had created something special.

When both films were finished, we threw a huge party. I finally felt part of the film-making community in South Australia. Before, I'd felt unworthy; a hanger-on. Working on those two films showed me I could be accepted, and allowed me to believe I was headed in the right direction.

Kanesan and I sent *The Claw* to festival organisers around Australia and the world. We never thought we'd hear back positively from anyone so it was a complete shock when we were shortlisted at both Tropfest and the St Kilda Film festivals. I was thrilled. While we didn't make the finals or win, we were pleased that the film had been noticed above hundreds of other talented artists' creations. *The Claw* was selected in the touring programs of both festivals. That was honour enough for me.

We didn't need a fancy trophy or title. We were happy that Australians could enjoy our work.

When things are bad, every aspect of your life seems to turn bad. Well, the inverse is also true. Things were looking up. Life at home improved. One of the apartments in my block had become vacant and the landlord was looking for a reliable tenant. At just that moment, Myles needed somewhere to live and so he moved in. It was good to have him around again. Because we had our own space, we didn't feel as if we lived in each other's pockets. At times, I didn't see him for weeks. Other times, we met up daily. We helped each other if needed. In almost every way, being neighbours made us better brothers and more understanding of one another.

Around the same time, my doctor, Dr Adams, had learned of a new drug which could potentially harden my bones. He referred me to an endocrinologist to discover if I'd be eligible to take the drug. Up until then, it had only been successful for children, and doctors weren't sure if it would work on me. The drug stimulates the part of the brain that produces glycogen which hardens bones. My glycogen production hadn't functioned well for twenty-seven years, so the experts were uncertain whether it would work and what the side effects would be. In kids, it gives flu-like symptoms, but these pass in a few days. I was told all the potential downsides they knew of but I didn't care. If the drug gave me the chance to help reduce my disability, I'd take it. After many tests, I gained the go-ahead.

I was nervous as the nurse inserted the drip in my arm. It took three hours for the medication to be infused into my body and, when I left the hospital, I was all smiles. But the next day I knew something was wrong. I felt a little warm and my joints were sore. By noon, I had a full-blown fever and most of my joints had frozen. Dr Adams admitted me to Blackwood Hospital. After tests and examinations, it was concluded that I'd been administered too much of the drug too quickly and that future infusions would have to give me less medication over a longer period of time. The side effects lasted about five days and then I was discharged from hospital. At first, I couldn't notice if the drug had worked but after about a month something amazing happened.

For more than ten years I'd worn a protective brace on my right arm to help me use it, as the bones had been broken so many times and had been poorly set. One morning, I woke to find that my arm had grown too big for the brace. It wasn't that my arm had fattened; it was all bone and muscle. I removed it from the brace and . . . I could move it.

Even better, my hand co-ordination had returned. I could pick things up and bend my wrist without it hurting. It was a momentous day. Parts of the shackles of my disability were gone and the arm brace went into a cupboard, where it remains. Since then I have had more infusions and, although the side effects have meant hospitalisation for a few days, my fracture rate has dropped by 60 per cent. More recently, a weekly tablet has replaced the infusions and, while side effects remain, they only last a few hours instead of days. For any OI people wishing to know more about the drug, I suggest you talk to a caring GP such as mine. For me, it has made a huge difference.

In the summer of 2001–02, my work began to gain recognition. I was nominated for the Young Australian of the Year for my contribution to the arts industry. While I didn't win, it was still nice to be recognised. That same year the Adelaide City Council named me its Young Citizen of the Year. I wasn't sure who'd nominated me. I felt like the luckiest bastard on earth.

The confidence I had lost had returned and I looked towards the next project. Despite people's reactions, I started to think there was still life in the *Quentin Crashes* franchise. To regain Network Ten's attention, I sent a copy of *The Claw* to Tim Clucas. He had been promoted to Head of Factual Programming at the network and I wanted to prove to him that I wasn't just a one-trick pony. Tim called and we met when he was casting for the second series of *Big Brother.* He agreed with me that *Quentin Crashes* had a potential life and, in his opinion, the main reason my *Quentin Crashes Hollywood* didn't hit the mark was because I'd stretched myself too thinly. I was doing the job of four people – writer, producer, director and host. He suggested that I find a well-established production company willing to take on not only me, but the *Quentin Crashes* franchise. He also suggested that I speak to John Gregory, the co-CEO of Imagination Entertainment. Tim told me that if I wanted another chance at Ten I had to present a package on which David Mott would look favourably. I left our meeting enthused and hopeful.

Immediately, I rang my old mate, Skip. He had worked at Imagination. I asked his advice. Should I try to gain work there? When I mentioned John Gregory's name, he immediately said I should contact them. He added that JG was one of the most well-respected people in the industry and the only thing I had to lose was my sanity. I had everything to gain. I'd almost lost my sanity once before so I felt no fear about approaching the craps table of life and rolling the dice once again.

When I first rang JG in Sydney, I found out he'd been expecting my call. Apparently Tim had contacted him about the idea of my working at Imagination and the possibility of resurrecting *Quentin Crashes*. From the moment JG started talking, I started learning. He spoke to me about the commitment it would take, the hard work and the knowledge that I would have to absorb. He said that before things went any further I needed to speak with the founder of Imagination, Shane Yeend, and negotiate with him as JG was enthusiastic to employ me.

At our first meeting, Shane was amusing and charming. He said that while he was fond of me and happy to look at taking me on, business was business and I had to prove myself and fund my own income. Over the next three months, I worked with JG over the phone. We discussed program ideas and how I could be employed at Imagination. I then thought of asking for assistance from the South Australian Film Corporation, which had helped me in the past. It had what is known as an attachment scheme in which an approved person works on a film, TV show or production company in a specified position and the SAFC would pay a wage for six weeks. When I told Shane about it, he agreed I could be a producer's attachment. I submitted the application and was fortunate to be successful. I was now an employee of Imagination Entertainment thanks to the sponsorship of the SAFC.

The first two weeks were a super-charged immersion into the business. I learned about Imagination and what exactly a producer did on a day-to-day basis. I was lucky that Shane and JG had taken me under their wings and were teaching me the ropes. During my third week, Shane asked me if I'd ever considered doing *Quentin Crashes Big Brother*. I said, 'No.'

He replied, 'Pack your bags because that is exactly what you are doing.'

By the end of the conversation, the deal was done. The *Quentin Crashes* franchise had been resurrected and I was being given a new opportunity.

I knew nothing about *Big Brother* despite being a huge TV addict, so Shane sourced hours of footage from the previous series and told me to spend the week at home watching it. I was to produce a concept in that time because the following weekend I'd fly to the Gold Coast to create a show. We agreed that I wouldn't do anything I wasn't comfortable with and that I would have some creative control.

During that week Shane designed a new *Quentin Crashes* camera rig to fit on my wheelchair, while JG gathered a crew. Somehow I convinced Myles to accompany me but I have to admit it was a tough sell. He watches very little TV and once he saw *Big Brother* he hated it, but in the end he agreed.

While the experience at the *Big Brother* house was gruelling and tiring, it was an interesting project. Tim was there to see me in action so he could see exactly what I was doing and what I could offer. I made a good friend in one of the cameramen, Dion Isaacson. He understood the style of the *Quentin Crashes* series from the moment he began to roll tape. We created different camera techniques using different angles from my wheelchair and maintained a fast pace. We expected that the most memorable moment would be when I met the quick-witted presenter, Gretel Killeen, or the first time I entered the *Big Brother* house. Gretel is a lovely person and visiting the house was astonishing, but they weren't the highlights.

In my mind, there were three truly memorable moments, though I wouldn't exactly call them all highlights. The first was flying in a helicopter, which I'd done fearlessly before when I was very young, but that was before anxiety found me. As I grew older I developed a phobia of small aeroplane travel and I was hideously scared of the chopper flight. But Shane had paid a lot of money for a helicopter so that we could get shots of me looking down at the BB compound from high above. He was the boss and I had to do as instructed, so into the chopper I went and, although I was frightened, I was glad I did it.

The second memorable moment, which was even more traumatic, was appearing naked on the set. We had organised an interview with the producer of the adults-only, uncut portion of *Big Brother* and, thirty seconds before she was due to walk in, Shane told me to strip. He said that to interview someone about adult topics, I should be a little bit riskier and live on the edge. I trusted him so, begrudgingly, I did it, and again he was right as it became the most memorable part of the program for viewers.

My final, lasting memory was meeting the then Big Brother, Peter Abbott. Regarded as one of the most professional and creative people in the TV business, Peter had been told to be confrontational with me during the shoot so it would be in keeping with his *Big Brother* persona. I was taken aback at first, but it was enjoyable to watch him work.

Not everything went smoothly though. During the editing, the program's director and I were at odds creatively so Shane brought in a writer, Chris Hill, to work with us. There were only two weeks before the program aired. I contracted another lung infection but, because I had neither the time nor the desire to go to hospital back in Adelaide, I pushed through. I'd start at midday and work well into the night with the crew to complete the doco. It was a team effort on all fronts and I understood the commitment and hard work to which JG had asked me to aspire.

I was more worried about this program than any other I had made. It was make or break. There'd be no more shots or opportunities if this didn't work. Fortunately, the show rated 1.5 million viewers and captured the demographics required for Network Ten. *Quentin Crashes* was back. And so was I.

When I wasn't developing *Quentin Crashes* ideas, JG trained me in developing more television concepts. He'd explain the way they needed to be structured, how to cater to a network's demographics and how to utilise creativity to its full potential. JG was a good mentor and friend. I watched hours of television shows, breaking them down and then coming up with my own ideas. At first they were pretty awful but I eventually reached a level where JG thought they were ready to be pitched to different networks.

When it came time to develop more *Quentin Crashes* episodes, we left no stone unturned. I researched hundreds of possible scenarios, from *Quentin Crashes Michael Jackson* to *Quentin Crashes Parliament*. JG and I presented them to Network Ten but they were shot down quickly. Eventually, I was at a loss. I wasn't sure what was wanted anymore. Tim and Motty told us they wanted two more *Quentin Crashes* to be made back to back. The first would be *Quentin Crashes Australian Idol* and the next would be *Quentin Crashes the World Music Awards*.

The *Idol* concept interested me the most. I thought it would give me a chance to be a bit riskier and inject more comedy into the program. I planned sequences and comedic moments in advance. JG hooked me up with his new production executive Greg Quail and new director Sandra Fulloon. Sandra and I hit it off from the start. It wasn't that I didn't get on with Greg, but I just couldn't work at his pace and it often caused friction as I physically didn't have the energy to give him what he was wanting. The plan was to shoot the *Idol* show over a six-month period, finish it and then do the WMAs in a three-week burst.

Shooting *Australian Idol* was a lot of fun. I liked the concept and the crew. The people at Fremantle, who make the show, were also really welcoming. I think at first they were worried about what sort of program we'd present but, once they got a handle on my humour, it was all good. Andrew G. (now known as Osher Gunsberg) and James Mathison, the *Australian Idol* hosts, played along with my jokes and weren't afraid to make me the butt of their own. This was intended. I'm glad we made friends.

When I wasn't shooting the *Idol* show, my schedule was really full. I took weekly singing lessons so I wouldn't sound hopeless on the show. (I still remembered my *Young Talent Time* singing experience – I wanted to do better.) I was also developing other concepts for JG and was asked by an Imagination Entertainment executive to create low-budget television commercials for the company's clients. I was making at least one television commercial a week, depending on my commitments to JG and *Idol*. I flew to Sydney every six weeks and was in production with other things as well.

The biggest challenge JG gave me was to negotiate all of the music rights for my *Idol* show. This was a big issue when I had to do the closing song in front of an entire audience. I didn't have to learn one song, I had to learn three because we weren't sure which ones we'd get clearance for. It wasn't until the day of shooting that we found out the one I had the right to perform. It was 'Old Time Rock and Roll'.

When it was my turn to finally get on stage and sing, I felt sick with tension. Was it a good performance? Sadly, I have to say no. However, that was the intention. I was no musical genius and definitely not a threat to fellow Adelaide boy and winner, Guy Sebastian. *Idol* judge Ian (Dicko) Dickson verbally threw me off the stage faster than Oprah eating a deep-dish pizza (before she lost weight), which is the way I hoped it would go. When *Quentin Crashes Australian Idol* went to air, the show was viewed by 1.27 million people, another hard-won success for me and the terrific *Quentin Crashes* team. (Almost twelve years later, Dicko used my *Idol* appearance as fodder for his schtick on ABC2's *Story Time*. I wasn't happy at the language he used around disability and the way he slighted me. His version of backstage events and my version of events and production discussions were very different. I let him know I wasn't happy and Dicko apologised. I accepted that apology publicly but he is off my Christmas card list – permanently.)

We had a break between *Idol* and the *World Music Awards* and I was pleased to receive a cameo role in a feature film, *Thunderstruck,* during that time. It was my first full-length fictional feature and I told few people about it. I was flown to Perth and went straight to the set where filming continued through half the night. I played a disabled wheelchair rugby coach who picked a fight and swore. I was with well-known actors and director Darren Ashton, who were all relaxed and made my job easy.

Up until then, people hadn't seen me angry or swear in public so the role was a real change. I embraced it and, truth be told, the character probably resembled me more than I would like to admit, or so I thought at the time. It was my first attempt at method acting.

Once filming of my parts was over I went back to Adelaide with a secret project brewing in my mind. I'd met the producer of *Star Wars*, Rick McCallum, and had pitched to him the possibility of making *Quentin Crashes Star Wars*. To my surprise, he loved the idea and supported it wholeheartedly, however George Lucas had not been told about it at that point so I decided not to inform Shane or anyone else in case it didn't work out. Ideas for the show bounced between me and Lucas Films and eventually George Lucas encouraged me to fly to Sydney for interviews with him, Rick and the talented Ewan McGregor. Phil is a huge *Star Wars* nut so he came along too. We spent a day on the set of *Star Wars: Episode III*. I funded the covert operation myself.

I was no sooner off the plane from Sydney when I was back on a plane with JG flying to Monaco to film *Quentin Crashes the World Music Awards*. It was a terrible flight and I started to get ill; I'd developed yet another lung infection. When I wasn't needed on the set in Monaco, I was in bed with a bad fever and a wheezing chest. Fortunately, JG had spent many years working in Monaco and knew the principality well, so he was able to guide the crew around and I only had to be there when necessary. He had hired a co-host for this instalment, Fiona Argyle. Fiona had spent time in Monaco and spoke French but she preferred her dialogue to be scripted in advance whereas my humour was more reactive and created from on-the-spot situations. It was tough getting our two different approaches to gel but we got there, and Fiona scored many brownie points when she was able to get her, JG and me an invite to the music awards gala ball hosted by Crown Prince Albert. I was thrilled to interview Prince Albert, who was such a gentleman, and meet Pink, Mariah Carey, Macy Gray, Anna Kournikova, Kristanna Loken (who played a Terminator in the third movie of the franchise) and many more celebrities. I had definitely crashed into the big time.

During the dinner, the wife of the awards organiser grabbed the microphone and proceeded to roast everyone in the room. She questioned Pink about lesbianism, asked Anna Kournikova what it was like to sleep with Spanish men, and basically took obvious delight in embarrassing Europe's elite, rich and famous. Fiona, JG and I were gobsmacked and, by the time we'd left the dinner, I'm sure the night's exploits had been relayed to the world.

Then it was time for the actual awards. I interviewed international music personality Ronan Keating, and the 'Muscles from Brussels', Jean-Claude Van Damme. After his interview Jean-Claude hung around. He was interested in my disability and asked me outright how I could have sex. The cameras weren't rolling so I told him and he had a great laugh. Then it got serious. He put his arm around me and, in front of John Gregory, pulled me close and said, 'You and I, we are the same.'

I said, 'How Jean-Claude?'

He said, 'You and me, we both know pain.'

I said, 'I know I've had pain, but what about you? How's your pain?'

He said, 'The drugs, they take everything away.'

I knowingly agreed.

He said, 'I don't make good movies no more. I don't party no more. I don't dance no more. Heck, I don't even fuck no more.'

I looked at him in shock and sympathy and said, 'You can't fuck anymore?'

He said, 'No, the drugs, she takes that away from me too.' He looked down at his crotch.

Unsure of how to respond, I said the most Australian thing anyone can. I looked Jean-Claude deep in the eyes and said, 'You poor bastard!'

He hugged me and crumpled. After he composed himself he said, 'Don't worry. Like you, I will overcome.' (Jean-Claude was true to his word and has since gone on to bigger and better things.)

That night he told me if I ever needed anything I shouldn't hesitate to call him. He gave me his details before leaving.

As the party was wrapping up, I noticed Kristanna Loken standing by the balcony, all alone. I went over to her and asked why she was there by herself. She told me that she didn't really know anyone and kind of felt out of place.

'Are you kidding me! You're the most beautiful woman here!'

She replied, 'You're very sweet.' And then she kissed me. It wasn't just a peck on the cheek, either!

I couldn't believe it. I practically made out with a Terminator.

The next two days were spent filming transitional footage and some skits that would tie everything together. They were long days and by the end of the trip I was wrecked with illness and exhaustion, but I was pleased with what I'd done and hoped we had some memorable moments on film. I figured I could rest when I got home.

When I returned to work at Imagination Entertainment, my relationship with Shane took a turn for the worse. I was still feeling ill and I wasn't at my best but I'd also become too cocky again. In a series of emails, I said things I shouldn't have and Shane fired me. He had resurrected my career and given me a chance, and I repaid him by acting like a punk kid. I don't know what I was thinking! I should have shown humility, restraint and shut the heck up. *Quentin Crashes the World Music Awards* had not been completed and I had no one to blame but myself, though I couldn't see that then.

I was angry and upset but luckily JG's words got through to me and he convinced me of what I had to do to finish the production. But by the time the show was completed, too much time had passed since the award ceremony and it was never aired. I was devastated because I knew it was the end of *Quentin Crashes*, including my dream *Star Wars* project.

The universe spun and what had been good started to go bad again. *Thunderstruck* came out at the cinemas and, almost immediately, I started receiving death threats. Apparently there was one poor soul who had disliked my performance intensely, which wouldn't have mattered except that that person had also discovered my email address on the internet. The threats kept coming and they got into my head. I began to grow afraid of the outside world. I kept the death threats secret from everyone except the police. They told me that, because no physical act had occurred, they were powerless to do anything.

While I enjoyed being on television and appearing in films, I didn't think it was worth the price I was now paying. I decided to say goodbye to being a public face on television and focus my efforts on becoming a better producer and director. I pulled my ego back into line and focused on my work. I spent a lot of time creating concepts for companies around Australia and even did little bits here and there for Imagination. Eventually Shane and I made peace with each other and that made me feel a whole lot better as I owed him a lot.

I had to find new challenges but top of the list was learning how to hold my tongue. And to shake off the fear I was carrying. I decided to no longer be a victim.

CHAPTER 22

The phone call you never want to get

The year 2005 was set to be a monumental one for me as it was the year of my thirtieth birthday. And it started off okay. I'd walked away from corporate television and the high pressure demands that went with it and found work with a disability arts organisation called Arts Access SA. The organisation was designed to help disabled people gain a footing in the arts world through mentoring, assistance and education. I started off as a mentor in a program called 'Reins, Rope and Red Tape'. The premise was that we'd give you the reins, and enough rope and scissors to cut through the red tape. Well, that was the slogan, so we went for it.

At the same time, I was also trying to get my first documentary series without me in front of the camera off the ground. I went to the Australian Documentary Conference and did my best to pitch to people. I had spent five years learning how to pitch, and how to wheel and deal, and I had become pretty good at it. So it was not uncommon that if a television executive saw me they turned the other way and ran. Not that they didn't want to talk to me, but they didn't want to hear my lofty aspirations when they could just as easily do a deal with a more established film-maker.

At that conference, I tried to meet with a particular female television executive. Every time I saw her, she either gave me the brush off or walked the other way. At the final dinner, she was standing with a whole bunch of executives and, though I'd missed out on pitching to her, I just wanted to say goodbye and tell her I'd catch up with her another time. But when I moved towards her she looked to her group, rolled her eyes and said, 'Oh God, here he comes again.' I was absolutely mortified. She'd humiliated me in front of the other executives. I quietly said goodbye and shook their hands, but inside I wanted to cry. I left the dinner immediately and spent the evening feeling sorry for myself and cried myself to sleep. But, I moved past it and a week later I celebrated my thirtieth birthday.

I'd booked out a room at a café on Gouger Street in the centre of Adelaide and invited all the people who were special to me at the time. I invited my ex-girlfriends, Penny and the gang from TAFE, and all my neighbours. Scott McLean flew down from Queensland, my cousin Felicity flew over from

Melbourne, and both my half-brothers were there. So was Mum. The only person who was missing was my father, Geoff. He was in a nursing home, something he'd fought. He continued to smoke even though he was paying a heavy price for it. It was too late now. I'd spoken to him earlier that day and he wished me happy birthday and nothing but the best of luck.

I didn't party that night, or even consume enough food or drink to stay sustained or hydrated. The entire night I just ran around greeting people, hugging them, taking selfies and making sure that everyone was having fun. By the time 2 am rolled around, my friend Ben and I decided to go to the casino. When we got there we just sat and drank. When 5 am rolled around we were pretty boozed up. I went home, crashed for a few hours and woke up feeling very ordinary, which was hardly surprising, and I had what I thought was just a tickle in my throat.

The tickle didn't take long to develop into pneumonia and I was told by my doctor that I should check in to hospital to get better. I didn't listen to the doctor and I pushed on. Phil was getting married again and had asked me to MC the event and I was determined to do that for him. I arrived at the wedding in the Adelaide Hills dressed to the nines. I was also carrying a thermometer, a portable blood pressure unit, medications and enough Ventolin to last a lifetime. I was determined to make Phil and Emily's wedding special. I greeted the bride and groom as they came down the aisle, presented the cake for them and gave the best-man's speech, but every hour I would sneak away to take my temperature and blood pressure. Both kept going up. Towards the end of the night my job was done so I called my cab driver, Dave. I waved off the bride and groom in their BMW Roadster, jumped into the cab and asked Dave to take me straight to Blackwood Hospital so the doctor could meet me there.

When I arrived I was placed on a monitor and was told I was lucky I had got to the hospital in time. I thought they were being dramatic but it seemed I was in congestive heart failure because there was a lot of fluid around my heart. I was given a diuretic called lasix, which rids your body of excess fluid by making you pee it out very quickly. After that tablet I expelled over 1.8 litres of fluid in the space of two hours, not bad for a guy who is only three feet tall.

Dr Adams and the nurses decided it was time to have a serious talk to me about my eating and drinking habits. I didn't have a big drinking problem; well, not with alcohol, but I was drinking between three and five cans of Coca-Cola per day. Combined with an unhealthy diet, the result was that I had a stomach the size of a fully grown man's and I weighed over forty kilograms, far too much for a person of my size. Dr Adams said that if I didn't drop weight quickly I would die. From any other doctor I'd take that with a grain of salt, but Dr Michael Adams had been my family GP since I was eleven years old, so when he said it was time to shape up or ship out (literally), I knew it was time to listen.

He also referred me to a lung specialist, who put me on a regime of diuretics and steroids to strengthen my lungs. I'd never had to take diuretics in the past. I didn't know what time to take them, how quickly they would make me start weeing and how long their effects would last. When you're disabled, you need to have your toilet regime down pat. I only get the chance to do number twos once a day, so I have to have the timing worked out. If I don't, I've missed my window and I have to hold on or start wearing brown pants. As far as my bladder goes, if I'm going to be peeing in excess then I also have to time it well. So taking diuretics took a lot of getting used to.

I gave up Coke straightaway and switched to Diet Coke or water. I started eating things like steamed chicken and steamed vegetables. I had an appointment with a dietitian who told me that I had a calorie allowance of 1500 calories per day. But just to be competitive with myself I tried to get that down to 800 calories. I had this idea of eating a piece of toast for breakfast, some steamed chicken and rice for lunch and then a dim sim mixed in with chicken and sweet corn soup for dinner. I kept this regime of eating the same thing every day for two and a half months. After that time, I had lost seven and half kilos, but boy there were temptations along the way. I love junk food. If somebody said that I had a choice between a night at Jamie Oliver's fancy restaurant or a Big Mac, I'd probably take the Big Mac. Why? Because I don't know what I'm going to get at Jamie's restaurant, but I know that if I go to any McDonald's in Australia I'd get two beef patties, special sauce, lettuce, cheese, pickles, onions on a sesame seed bun. Since that time in America when

I am lucky, I have met some amazing people in my life. Like Prince Albert of Monaco (*top*), Ronan Keating (*middle*) and the most awesome and talented woman, who still inspires me every day ... Jewel Kilcher.

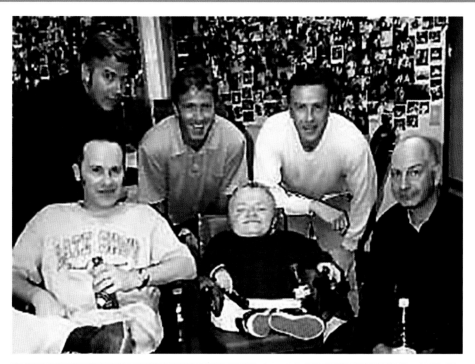

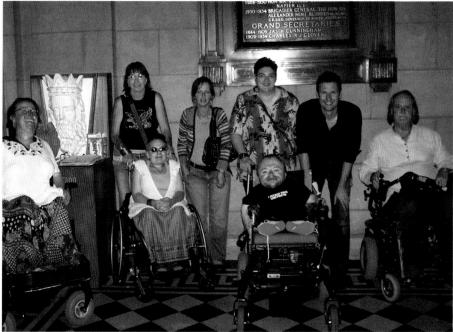

TOP: The team from Working Dog are my heroes. They make brilliant television and so meeting them and appearing with them on *The Panel* was an honour.

BELOW: I really enjoyed mentoring with a disability arts organisation called Arts Access SA. Here I am with some of the artists. That's Adam Hills behind me in the black shirt. We went to see Adam perform and caught up with him to talk about the potential these guys had to offer and the possibilities out there for them.

TOP: This is the crew from the documentary series I developed called *My Voice*, which aired on SBS as part of their interstitial programming. We were against a green screen as Catherine (*second left*) was filmed so we could show her interacting with an animated dog. I was very proud of this series. Sadly, Catherine died not long after.

BELOW: Filming *Quentin Crashes Australian Idol*, with the great Jimmy Barnes, who incidentally has his first book out at the same time as me. I am hoping we are both chart-toppers!

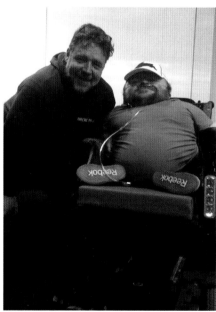

TOP: In 2007, I had a role in Rolf de Heer's comedy about the end of the world, *Dr Plonk*. The man is a genius.

LEFT: Russell Crowe. I am in awe of his talent but even more in awe of his heart. The man has been a huge supporter and mentor of mine, but also given me a kick up the arse when I sorely needed it.

RIGHT: She might be a megastar, but Angelina Jolie is without doubt one of the nicest people I have met. And she showed me those true colours long before her mega stardom kicked in.

TOP: The gorgeous Penne Dennison and Filip Odzark. Both true friends.

BELOW: The man who helped to change my life, someone I am proud to call my friend. And he is with my dog, Patchy, the Chihuahua that saved my sanity.

RIGHT: I was in intensive care here. This is how I look when I sleep. Perhaps not the most attractive device, but breathing is pretty sexy.

BELOW LEFT: The man! Dr George Miller. What can I say other than, thank you!

BELOW RIGHT: Here I am with Nathan Jones getting ready for my appearance in *Mad Max: Fury Road*.

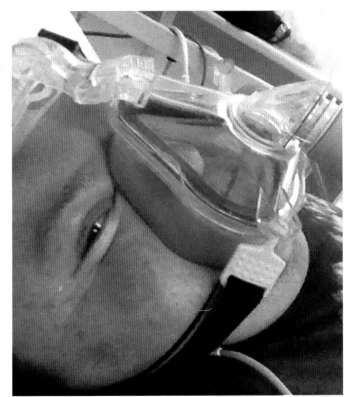

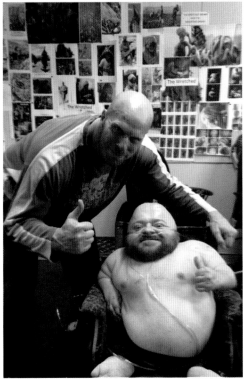

TOP: My dad (in *Fury Road*) the talented Mr Hugh Keays-Byrne aka Immortan Joe.

BELOW: The quick-witted and very intelligent Julia Gillard. Interviewing her kept me on my toes, that's for sure. She is a delight!

ABOVE: Me, Sia, Mum and Myles. We have had our bumps along the way, but I know my family will always be there when I need them. And I will do the same for them.

ABOVE RIGHT: Another major achievement ticked off the bucket list. My own one-man show that I tied to my 40th birthday. It was awesome!

BELOW RIGHT: And now, I am determined to keep writing new bucket lists. My health is always going to be a battle, but, as long as I can, I am going to be hanging with my friends and with Patchy and making good things happen. Stay tuned for my next exciting adventures...

Dad had let me eat junk food before my surgery, it had been my comfort food. But now it was time to say goodbye.

•

As if I didn't have enough good news to deal with, Dr Adams then sent me to a lung specialist who told me that my sleeping patterns were out of whack. They did some tests and it turned out that for twenty seconds of every minute I was sleeping, I stopped breathing. This meant that I wasn't getting enough sleep at night and I wasn't getting enough oxygen to my brain. This could lead to brain damage, stroke, heart attack and many other things that could kill me, so I was prescribed a machine which blew in air so that my nostrils and throat stayed open at night and I'd be able to breathe normally. They may as well have said we're going to put a Darth Vader mask on your face every night to help you sleep better because that was what the contraption felt like. I looked at the doctor and said, 'Are you freakin' kidding me! I can't sleep with that.' But, after trial and error, now I can't sleep without it. The mask makes me breathe easier and I fall into the deepest, most peaceful sleep. Once that was sorted my health picked up again and I was back into it.

•

Once I started mentoring a few people in the triple R project I realised that there are many people with disabilities who are amazing established artists. I came up with a project which I intended to pitch to SBS called *My Voice*. It was a series of four-minute movies that profiled five artists with disabilities. We had Dan the dancer, a six-foot free-form dancer who had cerebral palsy; Tim, the blind bass player; Jungle, the schizophrenic painter; Kathy, the painter; and a poet who had multiple sclerosis.

My weeks were jam-packed. During the weekdays I was either teaching or mentoring at Arts Access SA, or I was trying to get the new documentary series off the ground. I rang an SBS executive I knew and told him I'd like to book in to pitch the show. We arranged for me to call in June, which gave me two months to perfect my pitch.

On the weekends I spent time with Dad. I would go shopping in north Adelaide, pick up his favourite foods and a fresh batch of DVDs for him to watch. He was becoming more breathless at every visit. He didn't want me to stay too long, because he'd get too tired. His phone calls during the week were becoming less frequent. Then, one day in mid-April he rang me out of the blue. He told me I had to do something for Myles. I replied that Myles was more than capable of looking after himself. Dad told me to listen, and listen well, and despite trouble catching his breath, he launched into a speech.

He said he'd trained me all my life for this moment. He told me that putting me into Regency Park was shit, and he still regretted it, but he did it so I would learn to look after myself. He said it was up to me to take over the family and to look after everyone after he'd gone. I tried to protest that he was going to be around for ages and he told me to shut up and keep listening.

It was hard to hear the pain in his voice as he explained how he'd tried to spare Sia the pain and the responsibility, so that she could do her own thing and find herself on her own terms. And he told me that Myles was a rock, who'd do anything he could for us but he wasn't cut out for moments when emotion takes over. So that meant I was the one who had to step up and take charge.

I told him I would and he said thanks and hung up. I saw him on the next few weekends and he never brought the speech up. In his mind, we'd already settled it all.

On 8 May my phone rang at 4 am. It was someone from the nursing home. I was still asleep and I listened as they told me that they thought my dad had died. *Thought!* No one in authority says, 'Excuse me, but I think your dad has died.' I assumed it was a sick joke so I hung up.

The person called back immediately and said, 'I'm sorry, Mr Kenihan, your father has died.' It hadn't sunk in properly, but I knew immediately what to do. Dad had asked me to lead the family, he'd asked me to take responsibility and make sure that everyone was taken care of. I hung up again, called Myles, and asked him to come over straightaway. When he arrived, I got him to sit me up in my wheelchair and I told him about Dad's death. I then called Sia, who was living in England, and broke the news to her. She was upset, because she had never properly said goodbye to Dad or resolved any issues they had and she never had the chance to tell him how she felt about him.

I then tried my best to get hold of my mum, but she had gone off to the bush somewhere so I couldn't contact her.

I also contacted our brothers, Shawn and Chris, and told them the news. They were both stunned but not shocked. Dad had been ill for years and we all knew it was only a matter of time until the emphysema took him, but losing your father still plays a heavy toll on your heart.

•

When Myles and I arrived at the nursing home, I couldn't go through the door into Dad's room. I didn't want to see him like that. Myles didn't hesitate despite the emotions we were both dealing with so eventually I followed. I didn't say anything, I just sat there and stared at my dad's body with a mixture of love, anger, hate, remorse and guilt. Everything just stopped. I looked at him and said, 'I'll see you later, Dad.' That was it.

Dad had requested that he be buried next to his parents in a plot in an old cemetery in West Terrace, just west of Adelaide, but that burial area had remained untouched for over thirty years and was now difficult to get to, so placing Dad there wasn't possible. I found another cemetery that was quite nice, where we could put a patch of grass over Dad. I actually ended up buying two plots, because I thought I would be the next to go and I could keep Dad company.

A few days later, Mum came back from the bush and started planning the funeral with me, as well as the wake.

There were obituaries about Dad in the *Adelaide Advertiser* and other papers around Australia, and there had been invites placed in the papers to ask mourners to come to the funeral service. We expected Dad's best friend, Eli, his other friends from the Belair Hotel and the RSL, and even a few from the *Adelaide Advertiser* to show up, and it broke my heart when only one of them did. It ended up just being the immediate family and a few other family members and friends. My friends turned up as they knew Dad quite well and wanted to pay their respects and support me. When I realised that there weren't enough pall-bearers because many of Dad's friends had failed to show I was furious. Dave, my cab driver, who was like family anyway, stepped in. Myles gave a wonderful eulogy; he was emotional and even funny at times. It couldn't have been a better send-off for my dad.

After the funeral Sia had to get back to England quickly for work, and Shawn and Chris returned to Melbourne. Mum disappeared again. Life went back to normal, but it seemed empty, different. I would no longer receive a phone call asking me what was on TV that night, or requesting liquorice allsorts, DVDs or cans of mushroom soup. There was no one to talk to for advice. My dad was gone and I just had to get used to it, no matter how much I wished things were different. Dad was right, it was all up to me.

CHAPTER 23
Behind the camera

By June I had the concept for *My Voice* ready and I flew to Sydney to pitch it to SBS. They loved it! I was offered a small amount of funding and told that if I could get the rest from other government sources then I would get the green light. I was ecstatic: my first pitch with SBS and it was a winner.

While I was in Sydney I thought I would pop in to see my old mate JG, who had set up a business called Freehand Television. Another one of my friends, Graham Anderson, was also working there and the business was co-run by Big Brother himself, Peter Abbott. I was only making a social call but they asked me if I wanted to come into a pitch they were doing at Channel Ten. So I rocked in and found out that Channel Ten wanted to go up against *Australia's Funniest Home Videos*, and they needed a concept for the Saturday 6.30 pm time slot. They wanted to take *Funniest Home Videos* out of the picture once and for all. I said, 'Give me a couple of weeks and I'll create something you can't look away from.' Talk about being cocksure!

I don't know where other people's best ideas come from, but I am not ashamed to say mine tend to come when I'm sitting on the toilet. So when I returned home to Adelaide I sat in my bathroom daydreaming about what I'd enjoyed most as a kid and what shows my family enjoyed watching when we were together. And the one that really made my dad laugh was Art Linkletter's *Kids Say the Darndest Things*. Art hosted the first incarnation of the show and Bill Cosby resurrected it years later. It was a show where kids were interviewed in a studio about adult situations and the answers they gave were often priceless. I thought, well, that's never been done in Australia, why not repurpose it, change it from a studio setting to a location setting, and call it *Little People Talking*.

I called JG and pitched the idea to him and he thought it was brilliant. Our next step was to create a series bible, which is a document that determines how the show should be run from the first minute to the last. We wrote out segment ideas, games ideas, who the host should be – it was really detailed. I then went back to Sydney and re-pitched it to Network Ten. They loved it too. I couldn't believe it! I was going to be two for two in the space of four weeks. One show at SBS and another at Ten.

The agreement was that Channel Ten, Freehand and I would all put $15,000 in and that together we would have $45,000 for the pilot. It was all set. We had been given permission to use James Mathison, the host of *Australian Idol,* for a couple of days so we quickly went into pre-production for the pilot. The pilot consisted of James going to a chocolate factory with a bunch of schoolkids and questioning them on how the chocolate was made and what they thought about being in a factory. So we flew James in and had a pre-production meeting with the directors. Peter Abbott flew in for the filming too. We hired twelve kids through a children's casting agency and took them to Haigh's chocolate factory in Adelaide's Parkside. It was hilarious seeing the kids running around trying to put their fingers in everything and James trying to stop them, but at the same time having him mischievously try and steal chocolates himself. In private James is a quiet and softly spoken man, but when the camera is on him the light bulb switches on and he's absolutely magical on a television screen. He follows the Bert Newton model too: no autocue. If you can deliver a piece to camera without autocue you've got my seal of approval. James had the kids sitting in the palm of his hand. They gave him very funny answers and it made for a great piece of television.

Next, we went to a primary school at Rostrevor and we cast another bunch of children and interviewed them about adult subjects. The cameraman wanted to set up some basic lights and have the children move around for him but Peter Abbott didn't like that. He said, 'You're in the kids' space so you move around them.' He wanted the kids to be as comfortable as possible and if that meant the cameraman had to move, then that was his job. The day got longer and longer and the kids started to get tired. We could tell that James was starting to grow tired as well. At six o'clock we knew that we had enough footage so we put everything in the can and took Peter and James, and our director, back to the airport.

When I got into the edit suite I was suddenly horrified: every shot that we had filmed that day was out of focus. I couldn't believe it. I didn't know what had gone wrong and if there'd been a problem with the camera, but all the footage was bad. I didn't know what to do. I was shocked and embarrassed and felt like it was somehow my fault. I had to ring JG and Peter Abbott and admit to them that there had been a stuff-up and the footage was no good. They were completely enraged and asked if I had paid the cameraman and, stupidly, I had done this straightaway. There was no recourse to get my money back and I couldn't just easily reshoot. I had to take the footage that I had and edit it together the best I could.

When you're dealing with footage that is basically worthless, it's like chopping up mud. You can make a good mud pie, but it's still a mud pie. So, as much as I tried putting the pilot together it still looked bad. I couldn't bear showing it so I called Channel Ten and confessed what had happened and begged them to give me another chance to shoot it again. The show meant everything to me; it was my first chance at creating my own format and creating a TV show that I wasn't in. Channel Ten agreed, but it meant that the remaining part of the shoot had to come out of my pocket.

With the little savings I had left, we arranged for another shoot in Sydney. We used a different cameraman, one who was hired by Freehand, hand-picked by John and Peter themselves. We were able to get James for one more day and I auditioned another bunch of children from Newtown Primary School. We filmed in a second-hand store, where there were lots of gadgets and gizmos and clothes for the children to play with and answer questions about.

One of the funniest moments was when one of the boys found a laser disc and didn't know what it was. He thought it was a giant record that spat out silver music until James told him there were things called laser discs (that were like DVDs on steroids) but they were something that never took off. We finished the day at the primary school, asking the kids about George W. Bush's political moments, John Howard, anything that we thought would see them give an answer which was unique, genuine and incredibly funny. What we filmed in that one day helped to create a great fifteen-minute pilot to give to David Mott. He absolutely loved it and immediately commissioned six episodes to start the series off. I'd done it. I created my own format, the first of what I hoped would be many. JG and Peter Abbott were so proud. They knew I'd risked everything to create my own show.

The green light meant I had to move to Sydney for twelve weeks to pull it all together. I couldn't believe it. I was so excited, I raced home to tell everyone.

I had learnt a thing or two from my time in show business though, so I wasn't completely reckless. I knew that in TV everything could turn on a dime, so I decided not to quit my job at Art Access SA just yet. I still had my SBS show to do too and I was just as invested in that.

Even so, I packed up my house and went househunting online to find a wheelchair-accessible place to live in Sydney. I started arranging for my care to be transferred to Sydney and organising new carers there. Then, three weeks before I was due to leave, David Mott rang me and told me that he had changed his mind because James didn't want to do the show, and if James wasn't in then it wasn't going to happen. I asked for a reason and he said that James just changed his mind.

I was livid. I had spent all my money – $25,000 of my own savings – on this one dream, this one shot. I got so angry with David, I said, 'You can't do this to me, you can't fuck with my future like this.'

'Be careful, Quentin,' he said.

I replied, 'I will not be careful, David, you're making the wrong decision and you're being a dick about it too.'

He hung up.

I called Peter and John and told them how David and I had argued. They were sad and a little bit angry as well. They knew that I shouldn't have flown off the handle at David. It wasn't a personal decision, it was strictly business. Even though I'd invested all of my savings, it was still business. I had to face the fact that what I thought was going to be my first real success turned out to be a massive failure. And I was flat broke once again.

•

I didn't have time to wallow too much because I had to get myself out of my financial difficulties. I decided to work my way through it so I took on as many shifts at Arts Access SA as I could. I ended up mentoring disabled artists there three or four times a week and was starting to get a handle on all the different personalities. There were people who had acquired brain injuries, people who had cerebral palsy, people who had spina bifida – they had different journeys, different upbringings and different artistic endeavours that they wanted to pursue. Some wanted to be painters, others photographers and a few wanted to be poets and writers. One even wanted to be a DJ.

Mentoring people was enjoyable but I still wanted to achieve my own dreams. I realised that I needed help. I approached Sarah Wishart, who had been my project officer at the South Australian Film Corporation when I made *The Claw*. She listened to my ideas and she felt that *My Voice* was a project that she could add to, and champion. She helped me with budgeting, and organising the treatment and the script, and basically told me how to write grant and funding applications so we could get the show off the ground with the offer that SBS had given us. To my surprise, we were shortlisted by the Australian Film Commission and the South Australian Film Corporation. We were flown to Sydney to have an interview with a panel of film-makers and were successful in gaining enough funding to get the green light to make the film. Just when I thought I'd blown my chance I was going to end 2005 on a high.

By the summer of 2006 we started shooting a five-part, four-minute documentary series that would appear on SBS in-between television shows and would also be used as an educational resource and be available on the internet.

I couldn't believe it. I had experienced such extreme ups and downs in 2005 and, emotionally, it had pushed me further than ever before. Losing my dad had left me feeling empty, but also in a strange way it made me realise that what happened next was up to me. I had to make things happen. And I did. I'd created a South Australian Film Corporation TV show, had it commissioned, had it taken away from me, then created another TV show and was on my way to start shooting it. It was a year of big emotions. That year also gave me a sense of strength and purpose. I was far more resilient than I'd ever realised. Even though I got knocked down repeatedly, in both my personal life and business, I didn't give up. It was just like getting sick and being in hospital. You take the hit, you dust yourself off, then you get up and you try again. I knew the next year was going to be something special and, as it turned out, I was right.

CHAPTER 24
The drinks are on me

At the beginning of 2006, I had so many things to do, it wasn't funny. I was pushed and pulled from every which way and I loved it. As well as working on *My Voice,* I managed to help Myles and a few mates put an application in to the South Australian Film Corporation so he and his friends could create a computer game called 'Little Green Men'. The game had an alien ship with two little aliens who would fly around, and the object of the game was to shoot cows. That's my brother's imagination for you.

So part of my day would be spent driving my wheelchair to North Adelaide, talking to him and his mates about business strategy and workflow. My afternoons would be spent either in an office off Hindley Street that I hired or on location shooting *My Voice.*

Despite all the work, it was a pleasant time because I felt needed. I also felt like I was accomplishing something. I was working on a project that was going to highlight people with a disability who were doing something. They were contributing to the community and I thought that was going to do more from an advocacy point of view than anything I'd done previously.

I still had my work at Arts Access SA and the mentorees from 'Reins, Rope and Red Tape' were starting to progress well. Many of them had started developing shows for the 2007 Adelaide Fringe Festival. The Fringe Festival used to be held every second year but it is now an annual event and is the biggest arts festival in the Southern Hemisphere.

Then, one week into production on *My Voice*, I got pneumonia again. It was extremely frustrating, as once again it landed me in hospital, which meant that I couldn't go out on location to direct the documentary series. Every time I started to get a run going with my film-maker dreams, my body let me down. It gave me the shits.

We had to delay the production process for two weeks while I sat in hospital frustrated that I couldn't just get up, rise above it and push on with my work. I had been in Blackwood Hospital for a week, and Dr Adams was not completely convinced that I was better, but against his advice I discharged myself. I promised I would take all the necessary medicines and that I would take as many tablets as needed to keep the fluid off my heart. It had only been a year since I had had congestive heart failure, so discharging myself was quite risky. But at the time I thought

I'd rather die doing something I loved than waste away in a hospital bed. Most people would consider it a stupid decision, but when you face death as often as I do, going out with a bang seems like the best option.

I had things to do, places to be, people to see. The shoot got back on track and I hid my pneumonia and pushed on. Everything was starting to go well again. What surprised me the most was how much I identified with each artist who was depicted in *My Voice*. Jungle, a painter who has schizophrenia, spends his life expressing his dreams, his fears and his hopes through his art so people could look at it, identify with it, love it and take it home with them. I found that quite moving. Here was someone who experienced torment every day inside his head, yet he still managed to spill it all out on a canvas, or door, or plates, or wooden objects – in fact Jungle paints anything he can. Jungle's house is a portrait unto itself. He's painted the whole house and you can see it from the street. His artwork is a testament to how hard he's struggled to obtain a sense of peace and an understanding of life. I felt like I was doing the same thing – creating the documentary to say that this is the face of a person who is not letting their disability stop them; this is what inspiration and talent can create. I was proud of it.

Once filming was finished we set up an editing suite at the SAFC and, together with cinematographer and editor Brian Mason, I sat down for the next five weeks and cut the documentary series together. The best way to know that you have a good editor is to just give them the footage for a few days to play with and see what they create. Once I did that, it was good fun sitting down and talking to Brian about the best ways to shape and present the series. What was also brilliant was that there were lots of other film-makers at SAFC preparing or shooting their own films. They would come into our office and check out what we were doing and give feedback. It was a fantastic networking experience and showed me that I was a part of the film community, I wasn't just some corporate television guy who ran over Jennifer Lopez's dress or made TV commercials or sang on *Australian Idol*. I wasn't some wannabe host; I was a film director creating something of value for the community.

They say that behind every great man there is a great woman and during *My Voice* I had just that. Sarah was awesome. Whenever I needed help, she was there; whenever I needed championing, she was by my side. But she was never afraid to tell me when I was out of line or if something wasn't available in the budget or wasn't possible. She was my voice of reason, my shining light, the person who I could go to and have a rant, complain, discuss creative ideas and get good answers back. *My Voice* is as much hers as it is mine.

After five and a half weeks, Sarah, Brian and I delivered *My Voice* to SBS. We were able to get a website built for it that had a section schools could use and which would act as a study resource. We sent out a program for primary schools to get involved with. *My Voice* aired between 2006 and 2008 and from the feedback we got it was a success. Sadly, SBS don't do interstitial programs (short clips or stories between regular programming) anymore as they've been forced to become more commercial and now run ads. I personally miss the days when SBS was a fully subsidised network as it created a lot of freedom and opportunity for film-makers like me who had something important to say.

Around the time I finished work on *My Voice* I got a phone call out of the blue from Remco Marcelis, a start-up capitalist I'd met when I was working at Imagination. Remco's relationship had just broken down and he needed someone to hang out with. I didn't know him personally, but if someone wanted to party, I was just the person to provide that service. During the day I would work at Arts Access SA and by night I would be cruising bars with Remco trying to fit in as many shots of Cowboy Cocksuckers as I could before I threw up. We had a few full-on weeks until we decided that we needed to slow down and gather our heads a little.

Things were getting hectic. I was approached by Logic Films to create a state-based cooking show, one that could actually create a celebrity chef. I don't really know how to cook, but if Logic Films wanted a new cooking show then I was going to give it to them.

After a week of thinking about it, I came up with the concept of *Off the Menu*. Being a state-based show meant that we could approach local restaurants and hotels to be a part of it. The chef would film an episode at a restaurant or pub and find out what was on their menu; he would then create another dish to be placed on the menu of the restaurant for two weeks, so that

244

people who saw the show could sample the food. The chef was a guy by the name of Christian, who owned a few restaurants around Adelaide and was becoming well known for his culinary abilities. He was a big personality and someone we thought could host the show well.

We filmed a pilot at the well-known Kings Head Hotel, reportedly Adelaide's first pub. It took a day and a half to shoot and a day and a half to edit the pilot and we planned to pitch it to Channel Nine and then Channel Seven. Unfortunately our host jumped the gun and announced to the media that he had made a successful pilot, which was going to air on Channel Nine. Television 101 decrees you don't announce you have a hit show until the network commissions it, otherwise they're likely to say no, which Channel Nine did. So *Off the Menu* was exactly that at Channel Nine. We then tried to get Channel Seven to come on board but they thought it was a Channel Nine hand-me-down and declined as well. Christian didn't realise it was best to keep quiet until a deal was done, and I didn't think to emphasise this. He's still a mate of mine. You live and learn.

•

Whenever I had time, I was out partying with my friends. During my early evenings I would hang out with my neighbours, waxing lyrical over coffee. Later in the evening, I would head off with Remco, or another friend, and hit up a bar or club and end up absolutely wasted. That was fine on the weekends, but not so good during the week. I had recently taken on a new support worker, Ian, and he was none too happy about me rocking up home completely drunk every weekend and he didn't mind letting me know it. I'm sure Dr Adams wouldn't have approved either, but I was still keen to go out with a bang. By the end of that year I was in full party mode.

At the time, I didn't realise I was not in a great place emotionally. After I turned thirty in 2005, and after my dad died, I didn't know what was left to come or if it would all end soon. After all, I wasn't meant to live past my first day. It was a weird time for me, and I had never felt so confused. I was so full of emotion but I didn't stand still long enough to think about what I was doing or how it was affecting other people or, worse yet, how it was affecting me.

Remco was still upset about his relationship breakdown, so I thought it was up to me to pick up his spirits and cheer him up. We used to go to a bar on Rundle Street and there we met a guy named Filip, a young stylist who wanted to get into the fashion industry. He was a funny guy, he laughed at my jokes, and we became thick friends, fast. Every Friday night I would rock up to the bar, put $500 on my tab, buy eleven bottles of wine, put them in ice buckets and then invite anyone and everyone to come and have a drink with me. For about nine weeks I was the life of the party. It's amazing how many fair-weather friends you can attract when you pay for a shitload of booze. Filip, Remco and I funded that bar for an entire summer. I'd be entertaining everyone, or making out with some chick who wouldn't have gone near me had it not been for the free booze.

When you're spending that much money at a bar every week, you're going to run out of money pretty quickly. I'd been saving for a house or unit I could finally call my own. But now my money was gone and the party was over. I was broke, compromising my health and not in a great head space, and I finally realised that things had to change.

CHAPTER 25
Unrequited love is quite costly

Looking back, I can see now that after my dad died I was lonely and worried about how my life was going to pan out. I had good friends and family but I wanted more than that. I wanted someone to love, who also loved me. I was wrestling with the idea that, just like Dad had told me when I was fourteen, I may not get it.

I've shared my gratuitous partying and alcoholism with you, you've learned of the drugs, and of my attempted rock and roll lifestyle, but I haven't shared the love and sex part yet. Well, strap yourselves in, dear reader, because here it is: the chapter about love, sex and relationships. Jean-Claude Van Damme will definitely want to read this bit, but I will admit it has been the most painful part to write. I tried to leave it out, but to tell my story honestly I need to reveal the brutal truth.

I hadn't been what you would call very successful in the relationship department, in fact you could say I'd been quite abysmal at it. I'd always had my father's voice in the back of my head with the image of that brothel from the car window and being told that's the only way I'd ever be loved.

When I was twenty I had a relationship with a girl for three months. We'd first met at the Oakbank Scout Camp when we were both ten and we knew each other till the age of thirteen, when she stopped coming to the camps. I met up with her again when I was twenty and we dated, but we were both too scared to do anything really physical, so I remained a virgin.

Losing my virginity didn't happen the way I (or my dad) thought it would. I had just moved into my purpose-built unit in the centre of Adelaide. A friend came over to help move some furniture for me and when we finished she turned to me and asked if I'd christened the place. I said, 'What do you mean, "christen the place"?' She asked if I'd 'broken it in'. 'It's not a ship,' I said. 'You don't break a bottle of champagne on a house.' She rolled her eyes and said, 'You know! Have you had sex in the house?'

I told her I hadn't had sex, full stop. 'Look at me, I'm hardly on the most eligible bachelor list, so come on.' She looked at her watch and said, 'I'm not doing anything for forty-five minutes so let's get this done.'

'Are you serious?'

She was.

Afterwards, we looked at each other and, yep, it got weird. We had broken that barrier; the barrier you don't cross when you're in the friend zone. I got back in my wheelchair, she got dressed, she said goodbye and that was that. I have never seen or heard from her ever again. But I want to take this moment to thank her for her friendship . . . and for my awesome house-warming gift.

After that I wanted more. But the fact was, it wasn't that easy. After I got back from filming *Quentin Crashes Hollywood* I was so stressed out and feeling pressure to please the network that one of my friends suggested I go to a knock shop and spend an hour having a good time. I debated it long and hard in my head. Do I go, don't I go? Am I wrong if I go, am I wrong if I don't go? I felt sick just thinking about it. But something had to give. My father's words rolled through my brain: 'It's the best you're going to do, it's the best you're going to do, it's the best you're going to do.'

I found a place that was wheelchair accessible, I wore sunglasses and a hoodie and I rocked up in the beginning of the afternoon, because I didn't want to be noticed in the busy rush-hour crowd of the evening. I didn't enjoy myself too much because I felt a wad of guilt buried deep within the pit of my stomach. I raced out of the brothel and completely threw my guts up on the pavement. What had I just done? I had paid for someone to have sex with me. I'd paid for someone to give me some human contact because no one in this world wanted to do it. I felt pity for myself. I vowed that I would never do it again.

Eight weeks later, I did. I'd forgotten about throwing up, and the guilt I felt. All I remembered was the hour that I enjoyed. I started going more and more. At first I'd go every three months but as time went on my visits became more frequent. I had met most of the girls at the venue I was visiting and was no longer throwing up with guilt afterwards. I know the issue is complex but for me it was simple: these women were there to perform a service and I was paying for that service. It was a tough job, but it was a job they had willingly agreed to do. Not all the girls would see me. Some couldn't deal with the fact that I was in a wheelchair and wouldn't come near me with a barge pole.

I understand that physical lust is different to love. I have been in love a number of times; I have even asked a girl to marry me. Like most people at one time or another, I was too wrapped up in my own selfishness and my perceptions of what I wanted relationships to be like for it to work out. That girl said no.

I haven't paid for sex in over eighteen months. I'm not going to again. I've decided that I won't have any form of sexual relationship unless it's with someone I have a true connection with; someone who feels the same way about me as I do for them. Until then, I just have to keep my father's advice out of my head.

CHAPTER 26
'You've got twenty-four hours to live.'

After a few years at Arts Access SA I was starting to get a bit restless. I was quite proud of what I was doing – helping out disabled artists – but the small arts organisations in South Australia sometimes felt cliquey and political, two things I don't do well. I had learnt to hold my tongue a bit more but I decided it would be best to try and find a job back in the industry I was most suited for: film-making. It wasn't too long before I got what I wanted.

Around my thirty-third birthday, in 2008, I contracted another lung infection, which put me in hospital yet again. I was barely settled in after my initial examination when a doctor came in quite timidly and said, 'I'm sorry, Mr Kenihan, I think you should get your family here and get your affairs in order. We're not sure if we can keep you alive for the next twenty-four hours.'

I looked at the man and said, 'You know what, mate, you're not the first and you won't be the last person to tell me that I've only got twenty-four hours to live, but if you think you can't save me then I want you to go away and not come back. If you think you can save me, then I want you to go out there, regather yourself then come back in and tell me how you're going to do it.'

The doctor left immediately and was replaced by another. When he came into my room he said, 'You're really sick and, yes, you could drop dead in the next twenty-four hours, but I'm going to pump you so full of antibiotics that you're either going to die of shock or we'll knock this infection on the head.' That's what I wanted to hear, not some timid get-your-shit-together-you're-about-to-die spiel. Death doesn't scare me, but I am not going until I am ready. I wasn't ready that day. I was pumped full of antibiotics and ended up in intensive care for a couple of weeks. Intensive care isn't a place you want to be, although you get the pleasure of only having to deal with one nurse who is constantly looking after you. You don't have to talk to anyone around you, but you're in a pretty sad and sorry state. I kept myself asleep for as long as possible while I was there.

Death was never far from my mind, though, and I made sure to call my family and friends, telling them what they meant to me so that if I was cast off the face of the earth they knew they'd been important. It felt pretty morbid. It always is when you're lying in a hospital bed faced with your mortality. Each time I go to hospital, I never want to leave things unsaid, I never want to leave this world with an unresolved argument or having caused hurt feelings for which I have not apologised. I made a lot of hospital calls from intensive care but luckily for me I survived to live another day.

When I recovered enough to go back to work, things weren't good. A number of other disability arts organisations had grouped together and lobbied Arts SA to remove the funding it had given to Arts Access SA and, before we knew it, the organisation was under the gun. I had made the decision that I was not going to go down with a sinking ship.

I got together with the people who made *Off the Menu* and we made a plan to create five pitch documents for five television shows, then go to Sydney and pitch them to all the networks. I rang my old boss at Freehand, JG, and he was encouraging. He told me to come over to see what we could do together.

I flew to Sydney with Ian, my support worker. We took the cheapest hotel we could find near Channel Ten in Pyrmont as we felt that was a good place to start our pitches. Once again I met up with David Mott (we'd ironed over any bad feelings) but none of the proposals got off the ground. I was bummed, but I was used to the vagaries of the pitching process so as I left the meeting I was already thinking about my next move.

Instead of getting a cab back to the hotel, I decided I'd wend my way back through Pyrmont to Darling Harbour and play tourist for a while, but I came across a flight of steps which I didn't see and I flew down them, nearly falling out of my wheelchair. As I was falling, a nice old man caught my chest and pushed me back into my chair just as I was tipping out, but it was too late and my legs had buckled over. I shattered both of my kneecaps and my left hip.

I didn't know what to do. The guy asked me if I was okay and, in my shock, I said I was fine. I couldn't remember the name of the hotel where I was staying and when I tried to call Ian the phone rang out. I called my friend, radio host and Foxtel presenter Penne Dennison, who lived in Sydney. I told her I thought I'd broken my legs. I was calm and didn't sound injured so I am sure she was puzzled. She told me to call an ambulance straightaway. I hung up but then I didn't know if there was an ambulance that could take my wheelchair and I wasn't about to leave it on the side of the road in the middle of Pyrmont, so I did what I always did when I was in trouble, I called Myles. I told him I was in a really bad way and that I'd broken both my legs and needed him. He told me to get to hospital.

I was going into shock as I reached the Maritime Museum but managed to hail a taxi which took me to the nearest hospital. I rang JG on the way and he met me there. At first, the hospital staff didn't believe that I was able to break both my legs and hip at the same time and still remain calm. But John explained to them that I broke bones for a living and that if I said I had two broken legs and a broken hip then goddamn it they'd better listen. The pain still hadn't really struck me but within an hour of being admitted to emergency the muscles in my legs started contracting and I was in agony.

John was able to reach Ian, whose phone had run out of charge, and he was soon at the hospital by my side. The X-rays showed that I had two shattered kneecaps and there were multiple fractures in each of my knees. I had also fractured my left hip. It was just as I had suspected. I was given a heavy regime of morphine, and everything started to lose focus. The contractions were still coming. I don't think that I had faced such bad pain since I had broken my back in 1996. I was in a bad place, but then all of a sudden Myles walked through the door. I couldn't believe it, my brother was there to take care of me. It turned out that straight after he'd got off the phone to me, he'd left his work and, within an hour, had got a seat on the next flight from Adelaide to Sydney.

Myles took over the situation and arranged for a wheelchair ambulance to take me to a hospital where I was able to get longer term care. The hard part was that the doctors and nurses were afraid to move me. Ian didn't feel comfortable moving me either so Myles said to the hospital staff, 'I'm going to need Quentin to have as much morphine as he's allowed before I move him.' The nurse said if I had too much more it could kill me. Myles told her I'd rather die than feel what he was about to do to me, so she should give me the morphine. He had to sign a waiver saying he was responsible for my wellbeing and that if I died the hospital wouldn't be sued. Myles signed it, they gave me more morphine and, as gently as he could, Myles picked me up and placed me on the bed. I was unconscious soon after. I didn't wake up for two days. I was lost in a sea of morphine and pain.

When I woke up and reality returned, the first thing I did was call David Mott at Channel Ten to tell him what had happened. All he said was, 'You tough bastard.'

I hadn't needed Mum for a medical situation in a long time, but this was different. She would know how to find a good surgeon and so we tracked her down in New Zealand and she came as soon as possible.

At the hospital, I had to share a room with men and women of all ages. There was no central air-conditioning and it was a hot summer so the rooms were sticky and sweaty. The nurses were quite lovely under the circumstances. They gave me as much morphine as possible. Myles had to get back to work in Adelaide. Ian stepped up to the plate. He wrongly felt responsible because he hadn't been there to stop me going down the stairs. Ian is a wonderful bloke, a lot older than me and quite religious, but we get on well. It wasn't his fault. If anyone was to blame it was the Sydney Council as they had not clearly marked the steps and intersection.

•

I can't remember if it was Mum or someone else who got me talking about the obstacles I and other disabled people encountered just travelling around a city but I recognised that what happened to me was an opportunity to highlight the need for proper markings in public areas. I sold the story to *Woman's Day* and *A Current Affair*. The reporters and camera crew came to visit me in my hospital room. I remember being high on morphine, the cameras coming in, chatting to them and them leaving but that was about it. Later, I asked Ian if I had made sense. He said that somehow I'd pulled it together, smiled and talked coherently and passionately. Dad used to say to me, 'Never let them see you cry and never let them see you bleed,' and so whenever I was on camera I would always try to be positive. Not because it was an act, but because I wanted others to see that people with a disability weren't crying with their hands out all the time. I wanted them to see that we weren't any different from anyone else, that we could be positive and give back to the community just like everyone else. People with a disability shouldn't be segregated. We should be part of the community. Making our cities and towns, our transport system and our buildings more accessible and safe was one way our governments could help that happen.

After the *A Current Affair* story went to air my friends became aware of what had happened and there were flowers and chocolates delivered to the hospital. It made me feel loved. I only had enough clothes for three days, as that was how long I was supposed to stay in Sydney, and when Penne Dennison found out she immediately bought a whole bunch of clothes she thought would fit me and brought them to the hospital. Pen's a wonderful person, and I admit I had a crush on her when we first met, but by then she had become one of my best friends. I was so grateful she was looking out for me.

While all this was going on, my mum was doing her best to organise a care flight from Sydney to Adelaide through the Royal Flying Doctor Service so I could get home. It took a couple of weeks but Mum managed to do it. When I was able to travel, I flew back to Adelaide. I was so grateful. Everyone had rallied around me when I had needed them the most – even my mum, and she hadn't done that in a long time. We'd had a bumpy relationship and we hadn't really talked much for a couple of years, but the way she stepped up meant a lot.

Once I was back in Adelaide I was in a private hospital with a private room with, thank goodness, air-conditioning. During the days it was pretty lonely as it was during the Adelaide Fringe Festival and lots of my friends were either performing or working, so I didn't get a lot of visitors. I understood completely but it was depressing being on my own and not being able to get around. Then one sunny afternoon when I was feeling particularly sorry for myself, comedienne Corinne Grant walked into my room. Corinne had seen a tweet that I had sent out that afternoon saying that I was back in Adelaide and she rocked up to the hospital on the off-chance that she would be able to visit me. I was pleasantly shocked. She spent the whole afternoon with me. We laughed, we joked, we talked about everything apart from my predicament. It was like talking to someone I had known for many, many years, but it was only the second time we'd met. From that one visit, and that lovely act of kindness, we've been good friends ever since.

•

Luckily it wasn't too long before I was out of hospital and on the road to recovery. I needed months of physio to get my legs stronger again, but something had happened to my hip and knee. The ligaments were torn and the doctors told me that I would need surgery. Performing surgery on me was risky though due to the scarring on my lungs from so many infections. The problem with my ligaments meant I could no longer transfer myself in and out of my bed on my own and I would need carers to help me all the time. It was a crushing blow. I'd always been fiercely independent and I had built up my upper body strength so that I could still transfer myself from my chair to bed if need be, even if it took me a while. I didn't want to have to rely on a support worker to do something as basic as getting me in and out of bed in the morning for the rest of my life, but there was nothing I could do. I just had to adapt and move on. It sucked, though.

After I got out of hospital, Mum came to check on me. We started talking about all the things that had happened in the past and the choices she had made. It made me understand that she had been battling her own demons and had her own struggles. She'd never expected to have a son born with a disability and she'd tried to cope as best she could until she couldn't cope any longer, especially during and after her marriage breakdown. It didn't excuse a lot of her actions but it made me understand them a whole lot more. And then it made me think about the choices that every mother makes at a moment's notice, and what choices have they made throughout history. From that I came up with the idea to create a documentary that would chronicle the last one hundred years of motherhood, looking at how the role of women had changed in Australian society. Sarah Wishart came on board again and we also attached another producer, Rebecca Somerton. We hired a female director by the name of Rebecca Barry and we went back to SBS with a proposal to get some funding. We were successful, and my strike rate at SBS was now two from two. We also obtained some funding from the SAFC. We had eight weeks to present SBS with a script and we entrusted Rebecca Barry to write it.

Around this time, I got a new job as a project officer with SAFC.

The first couple of weeks in the job were pretty hard; the other staff were all upstairs and I was downstairs in an office by myself because of the poor wheelchair access.

After a little while, I settled in and loved what I was doing.

My job was basically to read scripts, assess them and recommend them for funding. I worked on some amazing projects, like a film called *Necessary Games* that was made by a company called Closer Productions. It was about people with a disability and how they saw themselves in life. It was full of dance, a little bit abstract, but people loved it. It was a pretty good job, but one that required a lot of paperwork and I was starting to realise that typing was becoming quite strenuous for me. It sounds crazy but it took a lot out of me and I was beginning to get breathless. As the months went on it got worse. Even taking myself to the toilet was starting to get me out of breath. I wanted to keep it a secret from everyone for as long as possible, because I didn't really know what it meant. Finally,

I went back to my lung specialist and was told to keep taking antibiotics, steroids and lasix when I needed them and to make sure that I stayed active, which I did. But I couldn't shake the feeling that something was wrong.

CHAPTER 27
Patched up

My new work was fulfilling and gave me a feeling of hope. With that hope came a different sense of myself. I am not sure whether it was that conversation with Mum or just the perspective that comes with age, but I realised that it might be time to look back and perhaps look inward. So much had happened to me during my life and some of it had been pretty bad. I remembered how much the hypnotherapist had helped me when I lived with the McLeans so I decided to try some psychoanalysis.

At my first appointment I was surprised how comfortable I was with the process. It was like a floodgate opening and years and years of pent-up sadness, angst and aggression flew out. I discussed everything from broken bones to Regency Park Centre.

Around the time I first started seeing the psychologist, things were a bit stressful for me personally. Work was good but my mum was at home one day and felt dizzy. She managed to call triple zero but passed out during the call. An ambulance was dispatched. Mum was taken to the hospital and placed in intensive care. It was a heart attack. Myles had moved to Sydney where he was working as a computer programmer, and Sia was living and working as a fashion designer in Melbourne. I was the only one on deck. I got the phone call at work and immediately rushed to be by her side.

It was so weird sitting beside Mum's bed. The shoe was on the other foot. Mum was in a coma. She looked so fragile, frail and quiet. I called her brother, Paul, as Mum had put him down as the person who would make medical decisions for her if she was unable to make them for herself. I told Paul what was going on and asked him to fly over to Adelaide, but he said that he had faith in the doctors and nurses and was being informed of my mum's situation every day so he was going to wait. Unfortunately, that brought about the end of our relationship. I told him and the doctors and nurses I would make any decisions, should that be required. I asked Myles and Sia to fly over. It was a tense time. There was so much uncertainty about whether Mum would live or not. I decided that if she lived I had to work at re-establishing a proper relationship with her before it was too late.

When Mum woke up, it was clear that she was not the same. She was foggy and unsure of herself. She'd forget words, certain sentences or what had been spoken ten minutes before. It was hard seeing her so vulnerable. I wasn't used to it.

Things with my friends were also changing. Several of my friends, like Penny and Michelle, had married, and so had Remco, so I didn't have my late-night drinking buddy anymore. Gradually people moved away or their lives filled up with other commitments and there were fewer friends around who had the time to hang out.

I started spending more time with Filip with an F. We realised that we had a lot in common. We both loved superhero movies and *Star Trek* and he taught me a lot about the fashion industry. Filip has a unique gift for making you feel good as soon as you're in the room with him. He has been to visit me every time I've been in hospital, except once when he was ill himself. I think that shows a loyalty and trust that few friends I've had have shown.

I still loved the work I was doing at the SAFC but I was finding the physical aspects, like typing, harder and harder.

I knew I wasn't going to stay at the SAFC forever. The only question was, when would I get restless again?

·

The year 2010 started as most other recent years had, with a trip to the hospital to treat my pneumonia. It was becoming like a broken record. Every year around January and February, when the seasons started to change, I would be in hospital feeling like I was on death's door. But, more worryingly, I was starting to develop scar tissue around my lungs and it was becoming harder for me to do things without getting breathless. For example, cooking food or putting things away – general household duties that enabled me to stay independent – were getting tough to do. For the most part, I was able to hide what was happening from my friends and family because I didn't want them thinking I couldn't look after myself. It was bad enough having to rely on carers to put me to bed and then get me up in the morning. I wasn't going to give up on anything else if I could help it.

Around this time, I'd been watching news reports of the Queensland floods and my friends and I decided to band together and create a fundraising gala to raise as much money as we could for the flood victims. Former Adelaide contestants from *My Kitchen Rules* and radio announcer Mel Greig were involved and we decided to have a celebrity pantomime. I put my hand up to write and direct it and that was that. So I got together with Ryder Grindle, who was good at comedy, and hashed out a 45-minute pantomime based on mashed together fairytales. I also asked the makers of *Top Gear* to offer a hot lap with the Stig to be auctioned off at a silent auction. There was so much work to do and I was loving every minute. All the crew donated their time at no charge and we pulled together every South Australian celebrity we could think of – footballers, radio personalities, TV celebrities, politicians – to perform at the Adelaide Town Hall.

On the day of the gala we were so nervous. We had a letter in from the prime minister, we had a message from Kevin Rudd, whose own electorate had been affected, and Queensland Premier

Anna Bligh sent a video message wishing us all the best for a successful night. We had been rehearsing all day for days. I was directing everyone and I don't think I've ever been so nervous, but luckily I had Filip there to calm me down. I couldn't believe we had only thought about this project two weeks before and now suddenly it was a reality. Every media outlet was there to record the event and, to my surprise and delight, it went off without a hitch and at the end of the night we had raised over $100,000 for the Queensland Floods Appeal. Just nine of us, banding together for one cause, had achieved that result. It was remarkable to be a part of it.

I was feeling pretty good about myself after the gala, but that didn't last more than a few days because I was told I would have to reapply for my position at the SAFC and, in the end, someone more qualified got the position over me.

I was devastated but, once I settled down and got over my hurt, I realised it was a good thing because I was becoming more breathless each day. I also had an idea of how I could work with the SAFC in a much better way. A couple of years earlier they had hatched an idea to create a scheme called Film Lab, where they would run development workshops and then fund four or five low-budget feature films into production. I thought it would be a good idea to run a similar program for television shows.

Together with Shane McNeil from the Media Resource Centre, we pitched the idea of a TV Mini Lab to SAFC and they liked it. I couldn't believe it. Suddenly I had to start being an adult again, running my own company and teaching people how to develop TV shows.

We spent a couple of months developing the workshop program and approaching some of the best TV executives, actors and producers in Australia to come and run classes. I was even able to get myself an assistant. Shane knew a young girl named Eleanor who was studying film-making and eager to help us get the ball rolling. She was a breath of fresh air.

A couple of my friends thought that I might be interested in Eleanor as she was a young, attractive film-maker. But actually I felt rather paternal towards her. She was so eager to learn and to be a part of the industry, I thought of her more like a little sister.

The workshop series was going well and the next step was taking our first batch of film-makers to France to learn about distribution and selling at MIPCOM, an annual trade show held in Cannes where studios from around the world buy and sell new programs and formats for international distribution.

I hadn't been to France in seven years, when I stopped over for a few hours on my way to Monaco to film *Quentin Crashes the World Music Awards*. But I had a secret that was going to make travelling overseas tough.

•

The last few times I had travelled interstate I'd needed oxygen to maintain my breathing on the plane. Without it my oxygen levels would get too low and I would start feeling light-headed and end up passing out. I had to use oxygen provided by the airline and because I travelled with QANTAS so often they didn't mind giving it to me. But Ian and I travelled to France with Malaysian Airlines and I had no idea the dramas it would cause.

On the first leg of the flight, I couldn't breathe at all. We were at a higher altitude than on domestic flights, so it was as if I was choking on sand. I asked the stewards if they could provide oxygen for me and they reluctantly did. When we arrived in Kuala Lumpur, we were escorted straight to security. Apparently if you needed oxygen you were supposed to buy it ahead of time and, despite supplying all of my medical details when I booked, the airline said the paperwork hadn't gone through and that I wouldn't be able to leave KL until it was cleared. So I was stuck there while everyone else was already arriving in France. I was so pissed off I made a video blog about the discrimination. Finally, the airline received the paperwork and I boarded a flight to France but I was told I wouldn't be able to return home unless I was able to provide a new doctor's certificate stating I was well enough.

That was a problem for another day and I got off the plane and went straight into helping the film-makers pitch their projects. I was also able to get into a symposium where Gene Simmons from KISS was giving a talk about TV marketing. At the end, he asked the audience if there were any questions and some guy asked for his autograph. Gene got angry that that was the only question someone could think to ask. I raised my hand and said my question was 'Can I have five minutes with you outside this forum, alone, so I can pick your brain?' He thought that was hilarious so he said yes. I ended up being a part of the sixth season of his TV show as we sat there talking about marketing. Gene was knowledgeable and it was a lot of fun chatting to him.

As I was leaving the symposium I ran into Greg Quail, who had directed *Quentin Crashes Australian Idol*. He had started his own company called Quail Television and he was there pitching projects. We had a drink and he said, 'Mate, you're in the wrong game. You should come and work for me.'

At first it was just a joke but then we looked at each other and we thought, hang on, that actually isn't such a bad idea. I'm good at developing shows and he was good at making them. And so there on the strip at Cannes, I was headhunted to go and work as a development executive for Quail Television.

But first I had to get back to Australia, and that was a bigger task than I imagined. I had to get a doctor to examine me and sign a certificate saying that I was well enough to travel and I soon found out that getting a French doctor to do that on a moment's notice is a) not easy and b) not cheap. It was a case of 'I'll sign it for you depending on how many euros you put in my hand'. It ended up being 600 euros, a bribe basically.

Once I gave Malaysian Airlines the certificate they were still apprehensive, so once again I got on YouTube and started ranting and raving about my predicament. What I found out quickly though was that Russell Crowe had seen my tweets and was re-tweeting them to everyone else. He then started tweeting

Malaysian Airlines himself saying, 'Why can't Quentin come home?' The situation was featured on the *Today* show with Karl Stefanovic and it ended up being a big social media let-down for Malaysian Airlines, which they didn't need. Suddenly they welcomed me with open arms. I couldn't believe it. I had exchanged tweets with Russell Crowe a few times, but here was old Rusty standing up for me when I needed it. I was so grateful and so flabbergasted I immediately started tweeting him and thanking him. I was whisked into the Malaysian Airlines first-class lounge, which was pretty sweet treatment considering only days before I'd been told that I wasn't allowed to go home.

While I was in the lounge I met *American Idol* winner, Adam Lambert, and we had a drink and a chat about our different experiences on *American* and *Australian Idol*. It's crazy how the world works. One minute you're not wanted and the next minute the doors are wide open.

•

Upon getting home I was so jet-lagged but I didn't even have time to have a shower because I had to get straight from the airport back to the TV Mini Lab to teach. After that it was the weekend and I think I slept for thirty hours straight.

Once TV Mini Lab was done and dusted I was ready to move on to start a new career at Quail Television as the head of factual development. I was going to head straight to Sydney but a family drama stopped that.

My mum was still unwell from her recent health ordeal and had agreed to let Sia and her partner live with her for a while to help out. However, when Sia arrived with a truck full of furniture, Mum stopped her at the door and said no. Sia was completely flabbergasted. She'd spent thousands of dollars packing up her life and quitting her job so that she could come and help my mum get her life back together. Mum had had a change of heart at the last minute and didn't want her moving in. Sia was distraught and the removalists were there waiting, so she rang me. I raced to Mum's place and walked into the biggest argument I have ever seen between my mum and my sister.

I didn't know whose side to take at first because I didn't think I had the whole story, but it quickly became obvious that Mum had made a snap decision that had thrown my sister's life into turmoil. So I came to Sia's defence, giving both barrels to Mum. Things were said, there was swearing and yelling, but finally a truce was agreed. That didn't last long, and within a couple of weeks Sia and Mum were no longer speaking to each other. Sia and her partner ended up moving in with me.

I was working from home by then and Sia noticed I was talking to myself. I hadn't noticed. She told me I needed a dog so I could talk to it. It just so happened that my next-door neighbour had two chihuahuas and one had just had puppies. I took one look at a little runt of a chihuahua with a white patch on her chest and fell completely in love. I decided to call her Patchy.

Today, Patchy is my best friend and goes everywhere with me. She travels on my wheelchair into town, she sleeps under the covers with me, she wakes me up with a cute face and a lick, and she knows when I'm feeling sad or ill. She's adorable and I'm so grateful to have her.

I had a new job, a new dog and things were on the up . . . or so I thought.

CHAPTER 28
Catching my breath

I was travelling to Sydney once a month for my work with Quail Television but things weren't as good as they seemed. Greg wanted me to pitch reality shows, which I didn't care for, and I wasn't having much success. Greg was busy trying to develop other shows overseas so he didn't have time to give me any guidance.

The work situation was starting to get me down. I felt like I was always just sitting in my house, working by myself, while everyone else I knew had more social jobs.

I started to become depressed and that depression began to filter out. I found myself emailing Greg a lot, demanding his time. My health was suffering too. I was becoming more tired and breathless. It was increasingly difficult to go through a day without sleeping for a few hours in the middle of it. I didn't know what to do as I was becoming unsure of myself – which was confusing in itself as I'd been so confident for years – so at times I would just stay home.

Days at home would turn into weeks where I wouldn't see anyone apart from a few friends. It was all too hard, work wasn't fulfilling me and I was becoming more and more fearful in social situations.

To give myself a lift, I began creating a blog on YouTube, which helped give me a creative outlet and also get rid of some of my angst.

The year 2012 did not start well. Greg told me that the focus of his business had changed and he was moving to America. This meant he was letting me go. The timing was bad.

After that, things spiralled down even further and I developed pneumonia again. I was not breathing very well on my own and the doctors told me that I would need to have oxygen full-time, not just on planes, but twenty-four hours a day, seven days a week. I was devastated. It felt like a slow death sentence. I'd have to be connected to an oxygen tank to stay alive. I fell into a depression, a deep depression that I hadn't ever experienced before, not even when I was first in the Regency Park Centre. The last time I had felt bad I had turned to drugs to try to quell the pain in my heart, but this time I knew that was a bad idea and that it would only make things worse. Talking didn't seem to help either. The depression grew. The idea of having to carry an oxygen bottle around everywhere, and the restrictions that would bring, was too much. It was hard enough for people to see a person with a disability as able and equal, but a person with a disability who had the look of a terminal patient, with oxygen specks on his face . . . well, that was just too much for me. After I was discharged from hospital I went home and I stayed there. The oxygen was cumbersome. When I went out, I would be hooked up to an oxygen tank on the back of my wheelchair, but at home I would have to drag a long oxygen cord connected to an oxygen concentrator around the house with me. It would get tangled in my wheels and a few times the cord snapped and I had to quickly try and find the back-up oxygen in order to breathe while I rang for help. When I did go out, the oxygen tank would only allow me to stay outside a certain number of hours per day. It was so frustrating, I would often sit at home and cry at my predicament.

I had no job to go to and I didn't want to go out. I didn't like people seeing me with oxygen specks. I suddenly looked different; I was different. People didn't understand and I lost some friends.

I stopped talking to my family. I sent an email to all of them – my mother, my sister, my brothers – telling them how angry I was and that I no longer wished to have anything to do with them and that they should just leave me alone. I started pushing my friends away as well. I just wanted to be left by myself in my own pool of self-pity.

I stayed home, trying to come to terms with how my life could move forward. My support worker, Ian, was my rock. He made sure that I was never without oxygen or food. I had zero care factor about whether I lived or died, so cooking for myself was not a priority. He also took all the slings and arrows that I threw at him on the chin. He knew that I didn't mean any of it and that it was a depressive phase I was going through. My psychologist visited three times a week to try to help me come to terms with how my life had changed in such a short space of time. Just two years earlier I was rocking around Cannes on the French Riviera and now I needed an oxygen tank to just get out the front door. I couldn't take it.

I started voicing depressing diatribes on Twitter and Facebook about how I thought my life was over and how I wished death would come swiftly. My depression was affecting my ability to see reason. I didn't see a future for myself. The only image I could picture was me slowly starting to rot in a wheelchair.

If it hadn't been for people like Penny, Michelle, Filip and Remco, I think I would've killed myself and been done with it, but no matter how many times I tried to push them away they just wouldn't go. Filip would come over and get me to watch stupid TV shows. When I argued he made me leave the house. At first it was hard. I didn't want people looking at me. Filip said it was natural that people were going to stare, but I just had to rise above it and show people that I was active and still able to get on with life. He told me to think of it as acting and sooner or later I would start to believe it myself.

I didn't believe it, but I was sick of being in the house so I would agree to go out. I was surprised that it felt good to be outside. What was really surprising was that most people didn't say anything about my oxygen tank. If anyone asked, Filip would answer, 'It's his new fashion accessory.'

•

Filip suggested that I start filming and vlogging more as it was a good way for me to stay active as a film-maker. I was ready to try anything.

I started off small at first, just doing quick little vlogs here and there, but later that year I began interviewing internet celebrities. I got in contact with one of my favourite YouTube bloggers, iJustine, and managed to create a video that received over 13,000 views. I was really surprised! I didn't know that I could get that type of traction so quickly.

I started making more elaborate videos. I created vlogs for the Adelaide Fashion Festival, I interviewed the models, the fashion designers, anyone who Filip suggested would be an interesting person in front of the camera. People knew that I was having trouble with my self-image and self-worth and they opened their arms to me and welcomed me in. Those vlogs gave me a bit more self-esteem and started me thinking that maybe I still had something to offer the world after all. I was also learning what was stylish and decided to up my fashion game. I bought shoes as my signature item as I don't walk, so they'll never get ruined.

But shoes weren't enough to save me from my darkness. And they were more a symptom than a cure. I figured that if I was going to die there was no point saving anything or worrying about any debts because I didn't think I'd live long enough to pay them. I decided to blow my money and have fun while I could. With that mindset it wasn't hard for me to spend up big. If I wanted anything I just bought it and put it on the credit card. I went to the restaurants I wanted to go to, ate out at the best cafés, and went to concerts. I thought that as long as my rent, electricity and phone bills were paid, everything else could take a flying leap.

My focus was making entertaining vlogs and that was it. I didn't really care about myself at that point. I grew my hair; I grew my beard. I was starting to become a stinking lout.

Ian would insist that I go under the shower every few days as the BO was becoming noticeable. Towards the end of the year, my mum was so worried she insisted that I talk to her. We had a good heart-to-heart and she made me realise that I should make peace with my family. When I died I didn't want them to feel bad that we hadn't spoken, so I swallowed my pride and apologised to all of them.

My health was deteriorating rapidly. My lungs weren't able to absorb enough oxygen and my blood oxygen levels remained low, even with added oxygen, so finding the amount of litres I needed in order to stay healthy was trial and error. I also couldn't eat as much as I used to because every time I ate, my stomach would push up my lungs and I would become exhausted. It wasn't uncommon for me to have a two-hour power nap during the middle of the day with my dog Patchy resting on my lap.

By the end of the year I was no better. I was still seeing my psychologist but I had no plan about how to move forward with my life; I was just happy to see the back of 2012. My plan was to start afresh. I wanted to have a goal, but I didn't know where to start. The year was a write-off – personally, professionally, medically and financially. I just had to hope that 2013 would be different.

•

It wasn't. In January I found the courage to tell my psychologist that I was suicidal. My online posts were getting darker. People would ring me and I would ignore their calls. In March, I ended up in hospital with pneumonia and I didn't want any visitors. I wanted to die alone. Every day, I tweeted out how much I hated life and how there was nothing worth living for. I sat in my hospital bed for hours in complete silence with the curtain closed around me, just staring at the ceiling trying to count the number of squares in the ceiling panels. I wanted death to claim me quickly.

One morning, after a particularly pitiful rant on social media, I got a random phone call. A deep, soothing voice said, 'Hello, g'day mate, it's Russell Crowe.'

I said, 'Yeah mate, good on you,' and hung up.

The phone rang again and I picked it up.

'Mate, it's me, it's really Russell Crowe.'

'Prove it.'

'My name is Gladiator,' he replied.

Holy shit, I thought, the Gladiator's ringing me.

Russell told me he was calling because he was worried about me. I said a) that's very nice and b) how did you get my number? He laughed and said, 'I'm Russell Crowe. I can do anything.' I thought – that's fair.

He then talked about the dark stuff I was putting out on social media and I told him it was hard to be cheery when I was lying in hospital dying. He wasn't having any of it. He told me I wasn't dead yet, that I was talking to him and typing all this stuff on Twitter, and it seemed to him my mind was pretty active for a dying person.

I argued (it's what I do) and told him he didn't understand. I was on oxygen permanently, I didn't have a job, my friends weren't around and everything was shit.

He wouldn't let me off the hook and said, 'Well, if you're going to die, have some dignity about it, shut the fuck up and do it already.'

I was really pissed off and told him he didn't know me and he didn't know how hard my life had been. He agreed and said, 'I don't know how hard it's been, but I do know that you have never given up on yourself until now. You have always put yourself out there to inspire others but now it seems as though you're pathetic – you have given up on yourself and everyone else – and that's not the Quentin I know and not the Quentin you grew up to be, so either start dying already or shut the fuck up.'

I was stunned. I was lying in a hospital bed and the Gladiator was ringing me up and kicking my arse. I was lost for words and all I could manage was, 'Fair enough.'

Russell said, 'Don't brush me off with a fair enough. If you need help, ask for it. You fail to realise that there are hundreds of people around the world who love and care about you, mate, and I'm one of them. If you need help ask for it, if you need money I'll lend it to you. You just need to get back on your feet and realise that your life is not over. You still have so much more that you could be accomplishing, not just for yourself but for others. It's time you start realising that and stop feeling sorry for yourself.' He went on to say he couldn't support my behaviour right now, I either had to give up or start moving forward. Then he said, 'I'll wait for your phone call' and he hung up.

I sat there with my head spinning. Three minutes later my friend JG called and said basically the same things as Russell. After I got off the phone from him I stared up at the ceiling, but I wasn't counting the tiles this time. I was thinking about what Russell and JG had said. I thought about my life and what I had accomplished. Then I started thinking about the future and what else there was for me to do.

When I got out of hospital, I wasn't sure what to do first as there were so many options. I could try and get a TV show up and running, but that meant my fate was in the hands of others. I could try and do something I had always been successful at – making people laugh with a short film. *The Claw* was gaining some traction on YouTube and over 40,000 views had accumulated over a few years. Many people had asked me if there was ever going to be a sequel. After about three weeks, I had a working script for *The Claw 2*. I tweeted the idea to

Russell and asked if he would donate some money towards the script. He made a deal that if I displayed a sticker for his rugby league club, the Rabbitohs, on the back of my wheelchair for a term of three years he would donate a few thousand dollars to a crowdfunding campaign which I had set up. Russell ended up donating $5000, which was a brilliant start, and he re-tweeted my tweets about my crowdfunding project. iJustine and her sister Jenna donated money and tweeted out as well, which led to their fans donating too. With other donations from friends and family, and from Facebook friends, I accumulated $11,000, which was higher than the $10,000 target I had originally set.

I was on my way again.

I realised that we needed some star power in the film so I sought about casting comedian Bruno Lucia, my friend Penne Dennison and, in an exclusive cameo, the newsreader from Channel Ten, Sandra Sully, who I always had a secret crush on (not so secret now!).

I called the original director of photography, David Belperio, and he agreed to donate his time as well. My friend Eleanor, who used to be my assistant at SAFC, came on board as the production coordinator and put together a great crew for me. I also ended up taking on a co-producer, a woman by the name of Katie Powell. Katie was working at the Media Resource Centre in Adelaide and she was able to work brilliantly with logistics and the crew.

Just like that, my zest for life had suddenly returned. It was like I'd never stopped. I was ready to get back into film-making,

I was ready to get back into life. I was ready to get back to embracing love and friendship. But before I did I had to apologise to all the people I had pushed away. I made a lot of phone calls and it felt good to make amends. It felt good to be alive.

•

It was so good to be doing something that I loved, and having Bruno as part of the cast was a wonderful thing, because he made sure that the jokes were as funny as they could be.

Just before production I got sick again, but not with pneumonia. I had tubes coming in and out of me and the doctors didn't know what was wrong. Eventually it turned out I was suffering from gastric reflux disease caused by stress and certain foods, and my body was shutting down. It was a wake-up call and, rather than spiral down into depression again, I realised I had to learn to let go and trust in the people I had around me on the film. I didn't have to do everything.

We made the decision not to shy away from the fact that I was now wearing oxygen. The character who I played in *The Claw* would have aged thirteen years, just as I had, and even though he was a superhero he had had bad times, which meant he needed assistance just like I did. It turned out to be a great character and plot point for my movie.

The movie was a lot of fun to make and, as far as I was concerned, the end result was pure comedy gold. There were a few stuff-ups along the way, but I got to make out with a gorgeous girl and had my face slapped by three other gorgeous girls. Instead of faking the slaps, I got the girls to really whack me. One hit me so hard she nearly knocked me out, but it was all for a good cause.

I was on such an emotional high after we wrapped the film that I steeled myself and sat down with my mother and resolved things. I told her that I was no longer angry at her for all the things that had happened between us and that I was just sad that it had stopped us from having a good relationship for so many years. We decided to wipe the slate clean and start again. Since then our relationship has been nothing but wonderful and I can't say enough good things about her. She's such a talented person, she's taught me a lot and I'm glad that I've finally managed to make up with her and only focus on the present and the future.

The high didn't last though. The editing of *The Claw 2* was not as successful as I had hoped. We were rushing to make the deadline for Tropfest because we were hoping to be shortlisted like the original film had been. I got a friend and editor, Stephen Deeble, to edit the film for me but I couldn't give him much time. It was rushed and we both knew it didn't feel as good as it could be, but with only seventy-two hours we were pushing the deadline. I asked a great composer by the name of Sean Timms to do the post-production of the audio and to also compose a couple of small tracks for the film. When it was finished it was shipped off to Tropfest but not before I tried to get a seal of approval from Russell Crowe, who was the majority stakeholder.

He had a look at it and then rang me and said he wasn't happy. I was crushed. 'What's wrong with it?' I asked. He told me he could see I rushed the edit. I had to admit he was right. He gave me some tips on how it could be made better but it had already been entered into the festival.

I felt bad because I looked up to Russell and he'd basically become a mentor and a friend. But I took all he said on board and learned from it.

Around that time, ABC radio asked me to do some movie reviews for them. Initially it was a one-month trial with one movie a week, because the person who they originally used had been taken ill. The segment was on the morning show with Matt and Dave, who at the time presented the number two radio show in their time slot. It was a great experience and I quickly built up a good rapport with the two hosts.

It's funny how when you're successful and you're thinking positively things can start to steamroll. Two weeks after *The Claw 2* I got a phone call from my old agent, Abby Edwards, who worked for Onya Soapbox. She said that George Miller, the director of *Mad Max: Fury Road,* wanted to talk to me. I wondered why. I had auditioned for his film three years earlier and never heard anything back. A few days later, George rang me. I was absolutely petrified. I didn't know what he wanted. He told me that someone had shown him a copy of *The Claw 2* and it had prompted him to think about how I had auditioned for *Mad Max: Fury Road* but, at the time, he couldn't think of a way to put me in the script.

He asked me what was going on in my life. We chatted for about forty minutes without him saying a word about *Mad Max.*

At about the forty-one minute mark, I got anxious and blurted out, 'George, are you ringing me up to offer me a role in the film? Or is this just a general chitchat?' He said, 'Oh, my dear Quentin, I decided on putting you in the film before this conversation took place. I just wanted to know what sort of man you are so I could work out what kind of character to write for you.'

I couldn't believe it! The dream I'd had when I was fifteen, and what Scott McLean and I had talked about all those years before at the Susan River Homestead, was finally coming true. I was going to be in a big budget Hollywood action film. I got off the phone and screamed for joy.

A week later I was in Sydney getting ready to act in the film. The production designer, Colin Gibson, had created a seat and harness for me to sit in while I was filming. It was a kind of throne for my character, whose name was Corpus Colossus. The seat was about eight feet off the ground and hung off a bungy cable. It was actually quite comfortable as it was made out of a leather couch and a Harley-Davidson seat, but it took quite a bit of effort for Ian to get me in and out of the harness. It was modified so that it could be placed on a stand to make it easier for him.

George insisted on being part of every decision about costume and makeup, so I had to try on a few different outfits until he chose one he liked. The makeup artist then spent hours and hours working on a look for George to choose. We also considered various ways to create scars and boils on my body with prosthetics makeup. I had failed to tell the makeup artists that I had a few tattoos, which made them a bit upset as they had to create tones and shades to cover them up. After one layer of makeup, photos were taken and emailed to George. He would then create notes for the makeup artist, and the makeup would be washed off and applied again with the changes he suggested. After about six hours in the makeup chair I was a sickly, albino-looking person who had a large, enhanced chest scar, which meant that I would just be wearing shorts and a large iconic necklace. We then had to sort out what they wanted to do with my hair. George wanted to approve this personally so the next day I had to drive out to the old Sydney reservoir where they were filming green screen scenes with the cast and some big trucks. I'd missed out on meeting Charlize Theron by one day but I got to say hi to Rosie Huntington-Whiteley, Zoë Kravitz and Courtney Eaton, who were playing the wives of my father in the film.

It was interesting seeing George work as he would basically take each cast member aside and talk to them quietly and then go and tell the crew what would happen next. I was taken into the makeup and hair tent and my hair was cut very short. We showed George and he suggested we try a mohawk. My hair was then shaved on both sides, leaving a cool-looking mohawk that was gelled and spiked like a spear. George didn't like that either and eventually decided that he would like my head shaved like my brother's in the film, Rictus Erectus, played by former professional wrestler Nathan Jones. I was able to see a few shots of what George was filming before I was sent away. So with my head shaved and the makeup and harness finalised, it was just a matter of waiting a day till the production was ready for my shots. I was nervous as I didn't know what to expect.

On my day off I sneaked over to Russell Crowe's sound stage where he was shooting *The Water Diviner* and hung out with him while he directed some of the scenes. I also got to catch up with my old mate Steve Bastoni, whom I'd met when he was starring in *Police Rescue*. And I met actress Olga Kurylenko, who had been a James Bond girl and was also well known for her other action films. She was so lovely and everyone was welcoming.

The next day it was my turn to shoot some scenes. I got into the studio at about 6 am and spent three hours in makeup. I had a break to have some breakfast and then waited until George was ready to shoot our scene. When I went to the huge set I saw it had been built for that one scene with me, which kind of blew my mind. There were lots of beautiful women who were stuck up in milking harnesses – milking mothers as they were called in the script. I met Nathan and also Hugh Keays-Byrne who was playing my father, Immortan Joe. George sat us all down and asked us to read through the scene a few times without any acting or inflection, so we were able to time the scene between each actor. Then they put me in the harness and hoisted me up next to an old telescope, where, for the next nine hours, George directed me. It was so much fun and I was so in awe of him. I was able to add little nuances, like slapping Nathan in the face after I said my line to make my point that I was the smarter one and therefore the more dominant, even though I was so much smaller than he was. We finished shooting at about 9 pm and I was absolutely exhausted but elated. I was finally doing it – I was in a big budget action film and working with a director who I had admired for more than twenty years. I was also grateful that I was being treated as an actor creating a character and not just someone coming in for a cameo. I went back to the hotel and slept like a log.

During the next day's shooting, I was on another big set that was made to be a giant winch for cars to be wound down to ground level. I was surrounded by the war boys, young kids who were painted up as little warriors. My character was in charge of them. I got in early, went through makeup and then was put in the harness around 10 am.

Children can only work for forty minutes of every hour on set and they have to be given a twenty-minute break after that. So after every forty minutes the kids would leave the set and I would be left there hanging by myself with Ian to keep me entertained. He was really great; he always stuck by me and made sure that my oxygen was all right, that I was breathing okay and not getting too stressed out. It was really hot under the lights and I would have to drink little sips of water, but not too much as it was too hard to get me down for a toilet break. The scene was supposed to finish with me getting my throat slit by one of the milking mothers, but because there were children around we couldn't actually do it for real (or pretend real), so we simulated it and the blood was added digitally later. After about eight hours of shooting my death scene, George came out from behind his monitor station and said everything was wrong. 'I can't kill Quentin.'

He apologised to the woman who played my wife and who had been scripted to slit my throat and said that he would place her in another part of the film a few days later. He then told the whole crew that we'd be coming back the next day and shooting an entirely new ending to the scene.

George leaned over to me and said, 'Quentin, tomorrow you are going to be crying. You are going to be crying a lot.'

I didn't know what he meant, but I was willing to give it a go and I was really happy that I was not being killed off. It meant that if there was a sequel I might be up for it. The next day I got in especially early. I think I got there about 5.30 am and I went straight into makeup. I didn't even bother with breakfast because I just wanted to get in there and start acting. George showed me footage of my character's father being killed and discussed how he wanted me to cry in various ways. He then told me to use an acting technique called repressed memory, where I think of really horrible things that had happened in my life and use them to start crying.

I started thinking of my own father's death and how I hadn't really cried about it. I recalled the moment I learnt of my father dying and when George yelled action, the tears started to flow. George would shout out different emotions for me to show and different ways of crying he'd like to see. He'd say, 'Sob to me, sob to me, now wail, wail, now tiny sobs, now calm it down a little as if no one can hear you crying.' We went through all these different emotions for about an hour and then I yelled 'Cut'. I was exhausted and needed a break. I told George I didn't think I had any more tears to give. He said, 'That's okay. We can always fix that,' and he told the makeup team to put eucalyptus vapour in my eyes. It stung so much. After each take, they would have to reapply it as my eyes dried out quickly. On top of all that, we had to stop every forty minutes for the children to have a break.

To get the right takes at the right moment took fifteen hours. At the end of the day I was absolutely spent, my eyes stung and I was emotionally drained, but we got what George wanted. I was stoked.

The next day was pretty easy. I had to do some reaction shots to Charlize Theron and Tom Hardy, who was playing Max. I spent an hour with him. We spoke about his time working as Bane in *The Dark Knight Rises* and he told me he was heading to England to play the role of two brothers, Ronnie and Reggie Kray, who were gangsters in London in the sixties. He also gave me some acting tips and techniques on how to create a character. He was such a genuine, down-to-earth man, but a huge star, all at the same time.

I went back to work and got the shots George needed and then I was done. My time on *Mad Max: Fury Road* had finished. Everyone gave me a round of applause for my hard work and performance but I was sad because it was over way too soon. I wanted to stay on set and continue to be a part of the action.

Before I left I raced over to Russell's studio and said my goodbyes to him. He gave me a hug and then, out of the corner of his eye, he noticed someone. He yelled out, 'Hey Angie, it's Russ.' He then motioned me to follow him. I didn't know who he was talking to, but as we moved closer I realised he was greeting Angelina Jolie, who was filming *Unbroken*, her directorial debut at Fox Studios as well. Russell gave her a hug and then introduced me to her. I reminded Angelina about how I had interviewed her in 2001 for *Quentin Crashes* and how it was such an influential moment in my life as she was the first celebrity to be so generous, and that made it okay for other celebrities to follow her lead. She stayed and talked to me for a good half-hour after Russell left. We talked about her health and her work with the UN and her family. She was so lovely and sweet. Even without makeup, she is as beautiful as she looks on screen. I asked if I could take a selfie with her just to make sure that the moment was real. I felt a bit of a goose asking, but she was happy to oblige. I even got a kiss on the forehead from her and Ian got a hug, which made his day too.

I left Fox Studios feeling as though I had finally fulfilled my destiny and ticked off the biggest goal on my bucket list, something that seemed unreachable back when I was fifteen years old. Dreams do come true if you wish hard enough and work hard enough to achieve them and hang in there when the times are tough. I thought back to the day before Russell called me in that hospital room and how I was thinking that I wanted to die. It was a big lesson. No matter how bad things seem, there is always a chance that the next day, or the day after, or two years later, something wonderful could happen. As long as you don't give up. I had a selfie with Angelina and a role in *Mad Max* as proof.

CHAPTER 29
I'm forty, now what?

My high from filming *Mad Max: Fury Road* lasted months. I wasn't sure what my next goal was or what my next adventure would be. I kept thinking back to what George Miller had said before I left the set: 'Well, Quentin, you've done it! You've conquered television, you've conquered film, so what's next?' I told him I didn't know, and he asked if I had thought about doing theatre. I brushed it off. But I started thinking about it, and, after a while, concluded it wasn't a bad idea.

I decided to come up with a theatre show that I could perform myself. But what could I write about? I couldn't just write about my life, could I? There had already been two documentaries and Mum's book about my life, but the real story hadn't been told: the good, the bad and the ugly sides that were hard to tell but that showed a more complete Quentin Kenihan. What if I revealed the stories that people hadn't heard before, the deeper stories, like what went on behind the scenes of TV interviews and my drug addiction? But it needed to be done in such a way that it didn't make people feel absolutely woeful. And was I brave enough to expose myself like that? Was I ready for any criticism? I decided I was.

I talked to a few friends and one suggested that since I was turning forty the next year, I could do it on my fortieth birthday about my fortieth birthday. Perfect! *Quentin Turns Forty.* Then I thought that wasn't enough as the story hadn't ended yet, there were still adventures to be had, so I decided it should be called *Quentin: I'm 40 . . . Now What*? Gold!

The next question was how to raise the money to put on the show. I remembered that Arts SA had a fund for disabled artists called the Richard Llewellyn Arts and Disability Trust. I checked on the website and learned that I could apply for $10,000 to develop my work. But I'd need help to pull the project together and write the script.

I started thinking about the comedians I knew and the name that kept popping into my head was Tim Ferguson. Tim is an actor and comedian who was (and is) one-third of the brilliant and widely successful trio The Doug Anthony All Stars. I rang Tim and said, 'Tim, I want to create a show, a one-man show, for next year's Fringe Festival. I have the stories but I don't have the jokes, so I need someone funny to turn part of my tragedy into humour.' Tim thought about it for a second before he said, 'I'm in.'

I contacted an old friend, John L. Simpson, who I'd met while acting in *Thunderstruck*. He was a distributor and former theatre producer and I pitched the idea to him; again it only took a second for him to agree to be a part of the show. Things were starting to fall into place like the perfect jigsaw puzzle and I started feverishly writing the grant application.

Eight weeks later I got the answer I'd been hoping for. Yeehah! The first $10,000 for the show was in and I was ready to start developing the concept and pulling all the pieces together.

Suddenly momentum changed. And, as usual, it was my body that let me down. I was fast asleep when I must have twisted peculiarly. I woke as I felt something click and then I heard a crack. I knew something was wrong. My back was in agony, as if I had broken it again. I started screaming in pain. My screams were muffled by the sleep mask I was wearing, so Myles, who was staying with me at the time, couldn't hear me. My dog, Patchy, immediately shot out of bed, opened the door herself and started scratching and barking at my brother's door until Myles woke up. He heard me screaming in pain and came running. I told him I must have put my back out and I needed some painkillers. He gave me two Panadeine Extra and soon I was fast asleep again.

The next day when Ian came to get me up, it took me a long while to be able to relax my body enough to allow him to put me in my wheelchair.

Sitting up was actually really painful, but I thought I had just put my back out so I didn't panic. I told myself that all I had to do was sit in a comfortable position and let my muscles relax so everything would slip back into place. I put up with the pain for two days but on the third day I woke up and couldn't move. I was frozen with pain. I got Ian to ring the ambulance to take me to hospital. The doctors took X-rays and CAT scans and couldn't find a fracture. They thought I had torn a muscle or ligament and time would heal it. I knew it was worse than that so I insisted they transfer me to a private hospital. I asked around and found a doctor who was good with people with osteogenesis imperfecta, Dr Maria Dellamulva. I was whisked off to the Memorial Hospital in North Adelaide. The next day Maria ordered an MRI, which is a lot more detailed than a CAT scan, and sure enough, my L3 vertebrae had a fracture.

The first thing I did was ring my friends and tell them what had happened. This time I asked for support and as many visitors as possible. I also called Russell as I knew he'd want to know. He said, 'You poor bastard, you will do this to yourself, won't you?' We talked for a good while and I could feel myself getting negative. I told him how it had taken ten weeks to get out of hospital the last time I had broken my back, and he asked how committed I was back then to getting better quickly. He was right. I needed to focus on healing and make a plan for my recovery, so that's what I did. I asked the physio to come in the next day and we started working on my leg muscles so that I would have the strength to get back into the wheelchair as soon as possible. The trade-off was that I needed endone, a form of morphine. I spoke to the doctor because I was worried about getting addicted again and she said I was going to have to take it and be mindful and honest about how I was feeling. I mustered all of my strength every day and did leg exercises to try and keep my back muscles moving and to strengthen them. When I wasn't doing that I would sleep, because sleep is a natural healing process.

To cheer me up every week, Ian would sneak Patchy in through a back door and I would have a cuddle with my little fur baby. She'd stay for about twenty minutes and then she'd inevitably bark and that was her exit cue.

The nursing staff were excellent. Sometimes you'll get nurses who want you to be awake at 7, showered and shaved at 9.30, ready for morning tea at 10.30, lunch at 12 and a nap at 1 and then woken at 5 to have your dinner. There was none of that there, I was allowed to go at my own pace, which was wonderful.

Sometimes I would stay awake all night and sleep all day and do little leg exercises by myself. But after two and a half weeks I realised that I had to go harder if I wanted to get better faster. My physio said we had to do it, and even though it hurt like hell, I made it back into my wheelchair after three weeks. I was sitting upright again, and could move around. The first thing I did was go outside and smell the fresh air. My greatest fear is spending the rest of my life staring at the four small walls of a hospital room. I was only out for an hour, as my back started to become too sore, but I had proven to myself that I could do it. I went back to my room beaming with pride and more determined than ever not to let my disability stop me again.

I started to increase my sitting-up ratio to fifteen minutes every day for the next two weeks until my physio and doctor both agreed that it was time for me to go home. I couldn't believe it; after a major fracture in my spine, I was going home in under five weeks. I was going to stay positive. I spent a week at home resting before I decided that it was time to get my butt moving and literally get my show on the road.

The doctors said that it would take twelve weeks for my back to heal properly and that I should avoid any major bumps or jolts, which meant only small trips in a taxi and no big wheelies or burnouts around the city. Doctors want to ruin all my fun, but I did as I was told.

Filip organised a photoshoot to create a poster for the show, which went really well, and the script was coming together so I booked The Bakehouse, one of Adelaide's most popular independent theatres for a two-week run. That's when I hit a snag. The theatre required a deposit of a couple of thousand dollars, which I didn't have.

I was racking my brain about how to sort that one out when my phone rang. It was David Mott, my mentor and old boss from Channel Ten. He called out of the blue to tell me he was in Adelaide for a few days and wanted to catch up.

It was so good to see him. We chatted about old times, TV shows and what we were doing. I told him about the show. While I was talking, my phone kept ringing as The Bakehouse was still chasing the deposit and they couldn't hold the date without it. I tried not to let on to David that I was stressed but he could read me and asked what the problem was. I told him. He asked how much I needed and I said $2500. I was hoping he might have some ideas to help me raise the money but I never dreamed he'd offer to pay. He did just that. I couldn't believe it. He told me I'd been great to work with for all those years, and that he wanted to do something together again. I was nearly in tears at such generosity. It proved to me that David wasn't just my boss but a good and dear friend, someone who cared about me. Thanks to him, the theatre was booked.

By the end of October, the script was finished, which meant I had to memorise my lines for rehearsals. I called Russell again because he was always a good source of advice and he said, 'There's no secret to learning dialogue. You just have to do the work. You have to sit there and repeat it over and over again until it's in your head.' He suggested finding someone I could trust to help me work on my voice and personality on the stage. It was good advice and I knew just the person: Angie Christophel. Angie had helped me get the audition for *Thunderstruck* and was my former agent and acting coach. I sent her the script and we met to discuss it. She told me she thought it was a tough-ask for me because I'd never had so much dialogue and had to carry the focus on my own. She said she would have to push me and I had to accept that and not argue. I told her I trusted her completely and was in her hands. I had to go away and lock everything in place because we would start rehearsing together on 8 January 2015.

•

The new year came and I had to hit the ground running (figuratively speaking). Every day I rehearsed my lines with Angie. She would get me to put the script down and try and recite what I had just read. Every time I got a word wrong, she would pull me up. I had to read it verbatim, with no acting and no inflection whatsoever, so I locked every word into memory. Once that was done, it was a case of getting the stagecraft right, getting the inflection right. Just sitting in a wheelchair and reading text from a script is one thing, but I had to move around the stage with as much physicality as I was able to provide. It wasn't just about telling my story, but creating a performance that people were going to understand and enjoy. It all took time and wasn't easy to process. Angie was encouraging though, and she gave me tough love. She knew when I needed to be pushed and when I was too tired to go on. It was exhausting and I was also nervous, but eventually I had the show down pat.

When I wasn't acting I was working with my friend Markus Hamence, a well-known set designer, to create the set. Markus is also the makeup artist to a lot of the acts that come to Adelaide during festivals. With his input, we created a party atmosphere with boxes of presents, champagne bottles, streamers and balloons. He had a giant happy birthday sign made up and a huge graphic that would be projected behind me. Filip and I created all the photos and video inserts which needed to go into the show and then we got together with our lighting and sound director Stephen Dean to block it all out.

The play was going to premiere on 23 February and, if all went well, would run for a week in February and a week in March. We split the weeks so it wasn't too physically demanding. That meant I would be performing on my actual birthday, 27 February. I wanted to combine that performance with a birthday party. I was hitting forty years of age, a milestone most doctors, and most of my family, hadn't actually believed I would achieve (and in dark days I didn't think I would either). I rang Shawn and Chris in Melbourne and asked them to come to that performance. They both agreed. Sia tried to be there but she was working as a flight attendant and couldn't rearrange her schedule for that day, which was a bummer. We found a great venue for a party afterwards and everything was set, so I invited nearly all of my friends to the birthday show.

I was really nervous about my mum hearing some of the things I was going to reveal in the performance, like why I went into Regency Park Centre and the behind-the-scenes stories about my drug addiction. There were also stories about how I felt I was pushed into stardom by my parents. I wasn't sure how she'd react. Then I started getting worried what everyone else would think. Would they even come?

I called George Miller and he said, 'Just take it easy, pace yourself and realise that it's just a show. Things go well and things fail, but the ultimate part of the story is that you had the courage to go and do it.' That was George, always there with brilliant pieces of advice when I needed it the most. I think he was proud of the fact that I'd done what he had suggested. He even invested $1000 into my crowdfunding campaign, which helped me get enough money to put the show on.

I felt elated. Once again people around Australia and the world had rallied around me. I was so grateful and I didn't want that to go unnoticed, so I rang up my old friend Brian Mason, who had done the camera work for the SBS show *My Voice*, and asked him if he and his production company would come and film my performance so we could put out a DVD, and also put it on YouTube for the rest of the world to see. He agreed to do so at a much reduced price and also became another one of the sponsors for the show, for which I was very grateful. Things were coming together.

•

John L. Simpson, the show's producer, took a week off work before the show started so that I could focus on the performance and he and Angie could sit down together and watch my final dress rehearsal. We worked out that it would be stronger with a finale, a bit of a singsong, so I asked a friend of mine, Stuart Wright, who is an amazing guitarist and in one of South Australia's most successful rock bands, King Krill. He agreed to help, so we started rehearsing the song that I'd sung in public throughout my life, 'The Rainbow Connection', made famous by Kermit the Frog.

Soon enough, opening night arrived. I was petrified that no one would show up. We had bookings for the first night that filled about three-quarters of the theatre so we needed a lot of walk-ins. I found out the *Adelaide Advertiser* were sending a reviewer to the show, so I couldn't stuff it up.

•

Markus sprayed my hair with some blond hairspray and brushed my face with bronzer to make sure that I didn't look pale and white. I think he put a little too much on because in the photos it looks as though I've been sitting out in the sun on a Miami beach for too long. But I didn't care, I was just excited to get out on the stage and perform. Stuart and I did one final rehearsal of the song and then it was twenty minutes to show time.

I froze. I couldn't go out there. I was so nervous. I wasn't sure what to do, but then I thought I'd better do something, so I took deep breaths and told myself to pull it together. It worked. By the time curtain call rang I was calm, focused and ready to go. The lights went down and there was a hush. The only lights I could see were those on my wheelchair. The only sounds I could hear were the ones from my oxygen canister, and then my name was called and I thrust myself out on the stage.

It was like a dream come true. I was still for a second just to take in the moment, to see eighty-five people seated, all waiting to hear me speak. They were applauding, and as the applause died down I realised I had to say something, I had to perform. Everything started to come naturally but then, about a third of the way through, I forgot my lines. Rather than just stop and pause and forget everything, I actually said, 'Hang on, guys, I've forgotten a line, wait for it, and wait for it,' quickly racking my brain to work out what I actually had to say. 'Oh yeah, there it goes,' and that became part of the show. I started interacting with the audience, saying hello to various people in-between telling stories, because I wanted them to feel as though they were a part of the performance as well.

•

After I forgot my first couple of lines, everything else went well. People laughed, people cried and people applauded at the right moments, and then it was over. Everyone clapped and I went out and had a meet and greet with people who had stayed and we sold some DVDs. And then it was finished. I couldn't believe it, first show down and it was a success. We all hugged and celebrated. I got home and slept for what felt like an eternity. I woke up and decided to conserve my energy for the night's performance and then Ian showed me *The Advertiser*'s review. They had given me four stars out of five. Holy heck, it was a brilliant review which said that the show was emotional, funny and a look into the life of someone that we thought we already knew. I couldn't have been more elated. It spurred me on to make the next show even better.

That night I couldn't wait to get to the theatre, I couldn't wait to get on stage. But when I went out on stage there were only twelve people in the crowd. I decided that didn't matter. I gave the same energy and the same performance, but afterwards I went out and sat down with the audience and thanked them for coming to the show and for being a part of my little world for a short amount of time.

The crowds grew each night. And then it was my actual birthday show, the one that I was so excited to perform. I looked out in the crowd that night and almost all my friends and family were there. I was nearly in tears from the start. A lot of people who I loved and cared for had paid money to come and see me. Mum was there, so that freaked me out a bit. But I put everything into my performance and didn't hold back. I put extra jokes in because a lot of the original jokes were about people who were already in the room. After the show I received a standing ovation and we decided to do an encore. Stuart came back out and we decided to sing *The Rocky Horror Picture Show* song, 'Time Warp'. The theatre owner wasn't impressed and tried to shut us down because we were well over time, but the crowd drowned her out and we just started singing. I didn't care if I was going to get chastised after it. Sometimes it's easier to say sorry than ask for permission. We got the audience involved and I asked them to jump to the left and step to the right, we got them to put their hands on their hips and bend their knees . . . You know the rest. It was a huge success!

After the show we went to a bar and partied the night away. I had made a vow that I wasn't going to drink, but as soon as I arrived, someone put a glass of vodka lemonade in my hand

and, unbeknownst to me, it was a double. I quickly washed it down. My friends then bought me another one, and another one after that. After six drinks I was quite sloshed, but I didn't care, I was with all my friends. My mum pulled me aside to tell me there were certain parts of the show she didn't like and certain things she thought were a bit unfair. I was waiting for her to go into detail but she didn't. She just told me she was very proud of me and that she loved me.

I gave her a huge hug and thanked her. I hope she will be just as proud of me when she reads this book. I know she might think I've bagged her in parts, but I had to tell it like it was. None of it takes away from the fact that I do love my mum. I understand much better now that everyone makes mistakes and bad choices. She and Dad were just trying to live their lives and deal with their struggles the best way they could.

•

As usual, when I push too hard my body lets me know I should slow down and, during the last few shows, I started getting a few welts on the back of my shoulder. I went to the doctor and he told me that I had shingles. Apparently the chicken pox virus can lay dormant in your system and physical or emotional stress can bring it out. Great! Instead of cancelling the shows I had cream and dressings put over me and continued. The show must go on!

When the final curtain call came it was to a packed house. I was incredibly proud of how it all turned out. Afterwards, I had a wrap party but I didn't drink. I stayed completely sober.

I wanted to be able to thank the crew and my friends for being part of this crazy eight-month journey.

After it was all over, I slept for three days. I was completely exhausted. The doctors said that it would take four to six weeks for me to get my energy back because of the shingles; it had now spread to half my body and I was covered in hives. But I couldn't rest for too long as I was going to the premiere of *Mad Max: Fury Road* and had publicity to do for it. It was time to get excited about another adventure.

George Miller and a lot of the major stars weren't going to be at the Sydney premiere as they were in Cannes for the film festival, but it was still pretty exciting. The actor John Howard, Megan Gale, Nathan Jones (my brother in the film) and I were asked to be on the red carpet to answer questions. The whole of Sydney's George Street was packed and there were over 300 people wanting to get in to see the film. Most of the red-carpet crowd was crew, but there were stars there as well, lined up to get their picture taken.

I thought I'd get lost but someone from Village Roadshow Films grabbed me and whisked me on to the red carpet. I finally had my red carpet moment! It was 'Quentin, look this way', 'Quentin, smile that way', 'Quentin, look fierce'. Then I did media interviews. It was probably one of the coolest things I've ever done in my life. We were then whisked upstairs to a VIP room, where there were drinks on hand for guests. There weren't many disabled spots in the theatre and I discovered that Hugh Keays-Byrne, who played my father in the film, needed a wheelchair that night, so he sat next to me. As the lights went down and the curtain went up, Hugh and I held hands and the movie started to roll. I have to say that when I first saw myself on screen, I did scream out a loud 'Hey, that's me,' and everyone in the crowd laughed.

The movie was monumental and I was so proud that audiences were reacting positively to my performance on screen. It was my ultimate dream-come-true moment and I was soaking it up for everything it was worth.

When the movie was over I got to hug costume designer Colin Gibson and cinematographer John Seale and they told me that there was a secret afterparty at the exclusive Ivy nightclub. When we got there it was absolutely packed and it was hard for me to get the wheelchair around. I did a quick hot lap around the room, hugged a few people, chatted to others and then decided to call it a night. I must have grown up because I thought, why end up ruining a great moment when I could end the night on a complete high? I went back to my hotel and fell into a blissful sleep. The next morning I caught up with Nathan Jones and his partner Fawn for breakfast, and then it was time to head home and wait for the movie to be released in cinemas.

When the film was released everyone was talking about it. It shot to number two in the box office in America and number one in Australia. It would end up making $358 million dollars worldwide, was nominated for ten academy awards and won six of them. I was so pleased for everyone involved, especially for George.

The rest of 2015 was slower, but I was still working as a movie reviewer for the ABC and I wanted to do more. My producer Eliza said that if I could come up with an idea, she'd help me pitch it to the station.

I came up with a concept called 'Big' – the smallest man on radio interviews the biggest stars in the world. The idea was that the stars would tell their stories in the hope of inspiring others. The ABC gave me a month to test it out; four shows which would be played on the ABC's digital network.

I couldn't believe it, I was getting a show on radio. My first guest was Darren Hayes from Savage Garden, and it went really well. My second guest was iJustine. Then the ABC gave me a big opportunity – they said I could interview former prime minister Julia Gillard. I was elated. I was going to interview our first female prime minister, who had also brought in the National Disability Insurance Scheme. There were stipulations on what I could and couldn't ask, but I prepared as many questions as I could. The people in her office asked to see what the questions were, but I refused to hand them over. I said that I wanted it to feel spontaneous, so if Julia Gillard couldn't roll with it, then we were going to have to cancel the interview. They agreed and soon enough, the former prime minister was in my studio.

We talked for a good solid hour, even though the show would be edited down to half an hour. That day I well and truly met my match. Julia was a brilliant communicator, she listened intently and thought about every word and every response. She asked me tough questions as well, which completely surprised me but I welcomed them. The interview was over too soon.

The show became a big success and the ABC offered me a monthly spot called BIG on local ABC radio in each state, a show that I've been doing ever since. I love it.

CHAPTER 30

Taking the elevator back down

So here we are. We've reached the final chapter. Have you enjoyed the stories I've told? Have you learnt more about me? Have you gotten an insight into the man I've become? If not, let me summarise for you. I was born into a life of pain and suffering with a debilitating disability which never goes away or takes a day off. I've fractured every bone in my body at least once. I gave up counting at 560 fractures. My mother told me she stopped counting when I turned twenty-one. Up until then she'd recorded one thousand broken bones. I go to sleep at night and have nightmares about those fractures. I wake up and live with the arthritis, scar tissue and mental trauma that they have burned into my memory. I have depression and regularly seek counselling for my mental health. I struggled with addiction and overcame it and I will freely admit that sometimes my words get me into big trouble.

Since turning forty I have decided it is all about perspective. So, every day when I wake up I try to bring positivity, hope and something inspirational to myself and to others. If that sounds cheesy, I don't care.

Let's talk about inspiration for a second. Some people in the disabled community have labelled me the 'Inspiration Porn Star', the poster child for everything wrong with how the disabled community is viewed by society. It is their belief that my early fame and my grandiose image of myself makes me comical and that I do not represent the goals of equality and inclusion they think I should be trumpeting. I think that is crap. In my opinion, the opposite is true.

Have I gained personally from putting myself out there? Absolutely! Have I sometimes been outspoken to achieve my goals? Again, absolutely! Do I feel I owe anyone an apology? Absolutely not! (Well, actually, maybe a few people, but I will do that privately.)

I started with nothing and yet I never backed down until I achieved what I wanted in life. I chased my dreams with both hands and got them. If that's not flat-out inspirational then I don't know what is. I also believe I've begun my journey, as Kevin Spacey would put it, 'to take the elevator back down', to teach others what I have learnt and assist them on their own journeys. If that makes me an inspirational porn star then I can happily live with that title.

I hope I have inspired you to live your life on your own terms. Any dream is possible if you're willing to work hard, sacrifice your patience and, at times, your sanity. I want people to realise that it doesn't really matter if you reach your big dream straightaway because, once you've reached it, you're just going to want more. As the man I met in hospital told me all those years ago, the journey to get there is the best part.

I have been fortunate to have a few special mentors in my life, like my father Geoff, my old bosses at Imagination, Shane Yeend and John Gregory, and most recently Russell Crowe and George Miller. They helped me understand my place in the world and my role in it. They taught me the rules of life that I now hold dear and hope to pass on to others one day.

At times, telling my story has been harrowing and I haven't shown myself or my family in the best light. But it was a spotlight of truth. Nowadays I am closer to my family than I have ever been because I've learnt to accept who we all are and to forgive. I can't judge anyone for the decisions and actions of the past. Without those experiences, and without the love of my mum, dad, brothers and sister, I would not be the man I am today. I probably wouldn't even be here.

I've reconciled myself to the fact that my father was correct. I am loved by many, I love many in return but I know it isn't likely I will ever find love and an ongoing intimate relationship. I doubt I'll ever have that shared life with someone I can call my own. It's hard to see past the steel, tubes and society's views on what is attractive, and I no longer expect anyone to try. I can live with that.

My doctors have told me that my dependence on oxygen is growing stronger and that I am probably in my last decade of life. I have always ignored doctors' opinions about my longevity but the truth is my body is letting me down. Until it does completely, I am going to live every moment fiercely but if there comes a time when my quality of life is compromised and things turn bleak, I won't hesitate to take matters into my own hands and end my life on my terms. I don't intend to go through what my father went through.

But until that time comes I'm going to start on my new bucket list and see how far I get. Once again I'm dreaming big and expecting a lot. But if you aim high, who knows what you can do. Here's my new list:

1. To live to see the National Disability Insurance Scheme fully implemented around Australia. (Get your act together, politicians!)
2. To love my family and friends more and hold tighter to them than ever before.
3. To go to LA, Las Vegas and New York.
4. While in LA I'd like to have dinner with actress Jennifer Lawrence (my future wife?) and producer Jerry Bruckheimer. I'd love to meet singer Wayne Newton. Finally, I want to go to New York to see a Broadway show, be in the audience of

The Tonight Show with Jimmy Fallon and to see the New York Yankees play.

5. I'd love to meet and see singer Jewel perform one more time. Her words and music are a constant source of inspiration.

6. I'd love to be a series regular in a TV show. I've never seen an actor with a disability actually represented correctly on television and I'd love to be the one to open that door.

7. Okay, this one is a big one. I'd love to act in a Marvel or DC Comics movie or television show. It links back to everything I hold dear and would prove once and for all that you can be your own superhero if you want.

8. I'd love to make one feature film. In fact, I want to direct the perfect Australian romantic comedy. I don't think we've had that yet.

9. I want to continue my community citizenship and raise awareness and funds for charities.

It's a pretty good list. I am going to try my damnedest to tick them all off. Wish me luck!

And so I guess that's it. I hope you chase your own goals and dreams and remember when you achieve them to smile and think about all the doubters you had to pass along the way and how good success feels. A superhero doesn't need a cape, just the right attitude.

Acknowledgements

I have so many people I want to thank and writing this book gives me the perfect opportunity to do just that.

First and foremost, to Mum and Dad, for the good times and the bad; and for teaching me the lessons I needed to learn, whether I was ready for them or not.

To the rock of my life, my brother Myles, who carried the burden of me whilst still becoming the smartest and most likeable man I know.

To my sister, Sia, for constantly making me 'get over myself' and my own ego.

To my brothers Christopher and Shawn (and their partners Roz and Andrea), who are wise, endearingly dysfunctional and who can magically turn tofu into anything.

To my home crew: Penny Finch, Michelle Moore, Paul Utry and Sarah Larsen, Rob Torok, Jodie Gaffney, Nicole Dumbleton, Sebastien Thoraz and Andrew Paterson.

To my brothers from another mother: Dave Hope, Filip Odzak, Stuart Wright, Ian Kissock, Osher Gunsberg, Benjamin Van Eyk, Philip Elms and Kanesan Nathan.

To the loves of my life: Penne Dennison and Imogen Bailey.

To the journalists I love and adore: Sandra Sully, Tracey Spicer, Chris Bath, Jessica Rowe, Angela Bishop and the two most important, Ray Martin and Mike Willesee.

To my mentors in life: John Gregory, Shane Yeend, Peter Abbott, Dick Smith, George Miller and Russell Crowe.

To the people who believed in me when no one else would: Michael Hirsh, David Mott, Stephen Tate, Mark Morrissey, Grant Anderson, Angie Christophel, Abby Edwards, Tim Clucas and Tim Ferguson, and my cousin Karen Smith.

To the haters and adversaries who doubted me along the way: success is the greatest revenge and this book means I kicked your arse!

To the people who have helped with this book: Elisa Black, Fiona Gurd, Vanessa Radnidge and everyone at Hachette, especially the teams in editorial, sales and publicity.

To all the fans and friends who have supported me along the way – THANK YOU! There are too many of you to acknowledge individually but I must highlight Ron and Pauline Bromley and the Vermont Lions Club, who were there as soon as they were needed, without having to be asked.

Acknowledgements

To the people who inspire me: Jewel, George Lucas, Casey Neistat, Justine and Jenna Ezarik, Robin Rhys, Houssam Abiad and Delta Goodrem.

If I've forgotten anyone I'm truly sorry! Finally, to my dog Patchy, for keeping me sane.

hachette
AUSTRALIA

If you would like to find out more about Hachette Australia, our authors, upcoming events and new releases you can visit our website, Facebook or follow us on Twitter:

hachette.com.au
facebook.com/HachetteAustralia
twitter.com/HachetteAus

And you can find Quentin on these social media channels:
facebook.com/QuentinKenihan
instagram.com/qkenihan
twitter.com/qkenihan
YouTube.com/users/qkenihan
Snapchat: qkenihan
Vine: qkenihan
Beme: qkenihan